THE RAMBO REPORT
FIVE FILMS, THREE BOOKS, ONE LEGEND

"Finally! The definitive work on the global phenomenon that is Rambo has arrived! From his inception in the mind of the great David Morrell to his introduction in 1972's novel, *First Blood*, through two subsequent novelizations and five Sylvester Stallone films, Nat Segaloff explores a character who reflected the changing mores of a nation and became a cultural icon. *The Rambo Report* is more than a book that celebrates one of the most significant and compelling characters of the past century—it is a time machine that takes the reader on Rambo's journey from 'some nothing kid for all anybody knew' (the novel's first sentence) through a metamorphosis and ascension to the status of legend. *The Rambo Report* far exceeded my highest expectations!"

—Jack Carr, #1 *New York Times* bestselling author of
The Terminal List series

"As he did in *The Exorcist Legacy: 50 Years of Fear* and *Say Hello to My Little Friend: A Century of Scarface*, Nat Segaloff both recounts and celebrates the Rambo films, novels, and the people who created them. He shows that they were more than action movies—they were a phenomenon that provides us with a sharp-eyed, highly readable record of the times in which they were made."

—Lawrence Grobel, author of *The Hustons, Conversations with Capote, Al Pacino: In Conversation,* and *Conversations with Brando*

"As both a film writer and a lifelong fan of all things Rambo, I'm happy to say that *The Rambo Report* is, and will forever be, the definitive work on the subject. Nat Segaloff covers every aspect of Rambo's history, significance, and enduring impact on American culture."

—Andy Rausch, author of *The Films of Martin Scorsese and Robert De Niro* and *The Taking of New York City: Crime on the Screen and in the Streets of the Big Apple in the 1970s*

SAY HELLO TO MY LITTLE FRIEND
A CENTURY OF SCARFACE

"Nat Segaloff, noted film historian, author, and veteran show business insider, has struck gold with *Say Hello to My Little Friend: A Century of Scarface*. There is nothing in this fascinating tome that is not addressed in this in-depth study of both the 1932 version and the 1983 remake. Whether discussing the social aspects surrounding the films and the circumstances of their creation, or the people and production involved, Nat Segaloff delves deep to unearth it all in startling detail. It's surprising it hasn't been before, but thankfully it took an entire century to get it right. A must-have for any and all fans of great reportage."

> —**Dwayne Epstein**, *New York Times* **bestselling author of** *Lee Marvin: Point Blank* **and** *Killin' Generals: The Making of* **The Dirty Dozen,** **the Most Iconic WWII Movie of All Time**

"Not content with tracing the origins, production, reception, and legacy of Howard Hawks's film and Brian De Palma's remake with an incredible wealth of detail, Nat Segaloff takes digressions into the history of the main players, Prohibition, the cocaine trade, and many other subjects, always in a concise and entertaining manner. For all these reasons, *Say Hello to My Little Friend* is the ultimate all-in-one guide on *Scarface* that will teach you everything and more."

> —**Laurent Vachaud, co-author of** *De Palma on De Palma*

"Al Pacino fans will devour this book. It identifies *Scarface* as the driving force behind Pacino's evolution as a star. The analysis of his Tony and Paul Muni's Tony in the first *Scarface* is fascinating, as are all of Segaloff's stories about the Mob and how it infiltrated Hollywood during the film industry's golden age."

> —**Robert Hofler, author of** *The Way They Were* **and** *The Man Who Invented Rock Hudson*

"A decade after establishing himself as an intensely low-key version of the American gangster as Michael Corleone in *The Godfather*, Al Pacino created a legendary role of a different sort in Brian De Palma's high-octane 1983 remake of the 1932 gangster drama *Scarface*. Veteran film writer Nat Segaloff's *Say Hello to My Little Friend* marinates in the merging of massive egos in a high-stakes context but also offers digressions into the history of the Cuban drug trade and the evolution of the American dream by way of the criminal underground. Mr. De Palma's *Scarface* was a box office bomb upon its release, but as a brute-force commentary on unhinged avarice, it has taken on mythic dimensions in the 40 years since its release. Mr. Segaloff rhapsodically captures the manic appeal of a once-reviled and now fetishized gangland odyssey."

—*The Wall Street Journal*

THE EXORCIST LEGACY
50 YEARS OF FEAR

"I highly recommend *The Exorcist Legacy: 50 Years of Fear* to all aficionados of my father's book and film. I have read all of the books about *The Exorcist* out there and to my mind it is the best of the lot: interesting, entertaining, accurate, and comprehensive. Segaloff reveals details about the making of the original film that I didn't know in spite of the fact that I was present during much of the making of it. Above all, this book honors my father's legacy and for that I am grateful to its author."

—**Michael Blatty, son of William Peter Blatty (author of *The Exorcist*)**

"You'd think that at this late date there wouldn't be a lot left to say about *The Exorcist,* one of the most skillfully manipulative movies ever made. But you'd be wrong! Veteran journalist Nat Segaloff engrossingly charts the making, marketing, and enduring reception of the spiritual horror blockbuster that has haunted the nightmares of two generations of filmgoers, as well as spawned a cottage industry of theories about the 'curses' that allegedly bedeviled the production. Plus you get background info on the various sequels and offshoots that continue to this day. It's a great read even if you're not a lapsed Catholic!"

—**Joe Dante, director of *Gremlins, Innerspace, The Howling,* and *Matinee***

"*The Exorcist* is not just a classic, but a living, breathing presence in our culture. Nat Segaloff has followed it from the very beginning and is uniquely qualified to chart its history and impact."

—**Leonard Maltin, film critic and historian**

"Nat Segaloff's deep dive into *all* things *Exorcist* will spin your head around with exhaustive details, smart reporting, intriguing insights from cast and crew members, philosophical and religious explorations, and more. Segaloff tells his tale with intelligence, warmth, and lively occasional doses of skepticism and snark."

—Stephen Rebello, author of *Alfred Hitchcock and the Making of Psycho* and *Dolls! Dolls! Dolls!: Deep Inside Valley of the Dolls, the Most Beloved Bad Book and Movie of All Time*

"*The Exorcist Legacy* conjures new scares while telling a great story about a landmark horror film. Insightful, surprising, and damn fun!"

—Jonathan Maberry, *New York Times* bestselling author of *Kagen the Damned* and editor of *Weird Tales Magazine*

"This is it: the definitive look at the power and impact of *The Exorcist,* from Blatty's conception of the original novel, its criminally underrated successor (*Legion*), and the terrifying films that erupted from those seminal works into mainstream movie houses. Segaloff chronicles this legacy not as a fly-on-the-wall, but as a battlefield medic with his finger pressed firmly on the pulse. If there's a more comprehensive and exhaustive history of *The Exorcist,* I have not read it."

—Ronald Malfi, bestselling author of *Come with Me* and *Black Mouth*

"This encyclopedic overview of the Exorcist franchise by film historian Segaloff (*More Fire!*) will satisfy even the most obsessive fans. A publicist on the original 1973 film directed by William Friedkin, Segaloff devotes the bulk of the book to that movie, describing the difficulties of designing believable demonic makeup for actor Linda Blair's possessed character and Max von Sydow's struggle as a nonbeliever to get into character as a Jesuit priest. Segaloff also delves into the numerous spin-offs, sequels, and prequels; the 1971 William Peter Blatty novel that Friedkin's film was based on; and the 1949 alleged exorcism in Cottage City, Md., that inspired Blatty, which Segaloff suggests may have just been a case of a troubled 14-year-old boy acting out to avoid school. . . . The author's love for the original film buoys this, and his insights into how Blatty's ruminations on faith and the existence of God animate his book and screenplay shed new light on the story. The result is a competent celebration of a horror classic."

—*Publishers Weekly*

"The power of Nat Segaloff's research should compel fans to pick up a copy of the behind-the-scenes book."

—*Entertainment Weekly*

"In his dutiful, soup-to-nuts book about the movie and its legacy, Segaloff, who was publicity director for a Boston theater chain where the movie showed during its original run, addresses the question of what made so many 'Exorcist' viewers throw up."

—*The Los Angeles Times*

THE
RAMBO
REPORT

FIVE FILMS, THREE BOOKS, ONE LEGEND

NAT SEGALOFF

CITADEL PRESS
Kensington Publishing Corp.
kensingtonbooks.com

CITADEL PRESS BOOKS are published by

Kensington Publishing Corp.
900 Third Avenue
New York, NY 10022

All Kensington titles, imprints, and distributed lines are available at special quantity discounts for bulk purchases for sales promotions, premiums, fund-raising, educational, or institutional use. Special book excerpts or customized printings can also be created to fit specific needs. For details, write or phone the office of the Kensington sales manager: Kensington Publishing Corp., 900 Third Avenue, New York, NY 10022, attn Sales Department; phone 1-800-221-2647.

10 9 8 7 6 5 4 3 2 1

First Citadel hardcover printing: May 2025

Printed in the United States of America

ISBN: 978-0-8065-4357-4

ISBN: 978-0-8065-4359-8 (e-book)

Library of Congress Control Number: 2024951808

The authorized representative in the EU for product safety and compliance is eucomply OU, Parnu mnt 139b-14, Apt 123, Tallinn, Berlin 11317; hello@eucompliancepartner.com

To those who fought the wars,
and to those who fought to bring them home

And especially to
David Morrell
Creator, Advisor, Friend

"He was a vagrant, you said. What the hell else could he have been? He gave up three years to enlist in a war that was supposed to help his country, and the only trade he came out with was how to kill. Where was he supposed to get a job that needed experience like that?"

—Colonel Sam Trautman, *First Blood*, novel[1]

"Civilian life is bullshit—genuine bullshit. In the field we had a code of honor! You watch my back, I watch yours. Back here there's nothin'. Man, I can fly tanks, I can drive gunships, I was in charge of million-dollar equipment . . . and I can't even keep a job parking cars! Every time somebody looks at me wrong, I want to wipe the ground with their face! There's just no honor on the street . . . nothing! Listen, man, I dream this shit almost every night—sometimes I wake up and don't know where the fuck I am. I don't talk to anybody for hours . . . days sometimes. I try to block it out of my mind, but I can't."

—John Rambo, *First Blood*, screenplay[2]

"When I'm playing Rambo, I look in the mirror and I see that my eyes have lost a certain zest for life . . . because Rambo doesn't revel in his adventures. And even when he wins, he doesn't win."

—Sylvester Stallone[3]

A Note on Titles

The chronology of the *Rambo* films and their discontinuous titles may cause confusion. For example, *Rambo: First Blood Part II* (1985) was called *Rambo* outside the United States. When the movie actually titled *Rambo* in 2008 was released internationally, it was called *John Rambo*.

This key may help the reader keep them separate as referenced throughout:

1. *First Blood* (1982) (set in America)

2. *Rambo: First Blood Part II* (1985) (set in Vietnam; sometimes called *Rambo II*)

3. *Rambo III* (1988) (set in Afghanistan)

4. *Rambo* (2008) (set in Burma; sometimes called *Rambo IV*)

5. *Rambo: Last Blood* (2019) (set in Mexico; sometimes called *Last Blood* or *Rambo V*)

Additionally, "Rambo" appears in this book as both a character's name and in film titles. When used as a character name, it is shown as Rambo; where used in a film title, it is shown as *Rambo*. It is also used as shorthand for any and all of the Rambo films not named specifically, much in the way "Hollywood" is used to represent a particular American filmmaking sensibility, not the town where movies are shot.

Contents

Foreword

by David Morrell

On April 16, 1986, I was at a London television studio, waiting to be interviewed on the UK's most popular morning show. I was there to publicize the British release of one of my non-Rambo novels, *The Fraternity of the Stone*, but a few moments before the interview, someone on the program's staff showed me that morning's front page of a London newspaper and its headline: U.S. RAMBO JETS BOMB LIBYA. A day earlier, the article explained, US jets had attacked Libya in retaliation for a Libyan-directed terrorist bombing of a West Berlin discotheque, where two Americans had been killed and seventy-nine wounded. As you might expect, my interview was no longer about *The Fraternity of the Stone*.

That wasn't the first time (and wouldn't be the last) when Rambo's name was used in a political context. In June of the previous year, then-President Ronald Reagan had joked that he'd seen a Rambo movie the night before and knew how to respond to the next terrorist hostage crisis. Later that summer, the president again referred to "a recent, very popular movie" and vowed to reporters that he would attack America's tax code "in the spirit of Rambo." The movie he kept referring to was 1985's *Rambo: First Blood Part II*, the sequel to 1982's *First Blood*, the first movie in which Rambo appeared, based on my 1972 novel.

Rambo: First Blood Part II couldn't avoid attracting political attention, given its premise that Rambo (a Vietnam veteran suffering from PTSD) accepted a mission to return to Vietnam—to the prisoner-of-war camp from which he'd escaped—and search for evidence that American POWs were still captives there. Delivering a frequently quoted line in the movie, Rambo asks Colonel Trautman, his former Special Forces commanding officer, "Sir, do we get to win this time?" In theaters, some Vietnam veterans cheered, believing that the US military could have been victorious if only politicians hadn't interfered.

Adding to the political context, the movie's release year, 1985, marked the tenth anniversary of the fall of South Vietnam's capital, Saigon, to North Vietnamese forces and the urgent evacuation of the few remaining Americans (mostly diplomats) who'd remained there. The film's debut on Memorial Day weekend evoked that military history and made history of its own. It was the first movie to appear simultaneously on more than 2,000 screens (2,074). Its opening week box-office receipts ($32,548,262) were the largest opening for any movie that year and the largest ever for an R-rated movie. Its year-end domestic total was $150,415,432, the second largest for 1985, and its domestic-international total, $300,400,000, was the year's second largest in that category, also.

That summer of Rambo, people woke up and went to bed with him. NBC's the *Today* show featured several making-of features about the movie. On *The Tonight Show*, Johnny Carson (the king of late-night television) impersonated Rambo in an eight-minute comedy routine that assumed everyone had seen the movie and transformed the popular children's program *Mister Rogers' Neighborhood* into *Mister Rambo's Neighborhood*. Carson wore an exaggerated muscle suit, carried numerous weapons, and blew up his postman for singing songs that had the word "red" in them, such as "Red Sails in the Sunset." Back then, the color "red" was associated with Communist Russia, not with the Republican Party, and

Carson mistakenly assumed that Rambo was a crusading anti-Communist, one of many times the character has been misinterpreted. Meanwhile, major newspapers such as the *New York Post* and the *Boston Herald* serialized my novelization, which was a *New York Times* bestseller.

The originating movie, *First Blood*, had political implications of its own, dramatizing PTSD and the long-term psychological damage that many Vietnam veterans suffered. My novel had its own political origins. In 1966, I emigrated from Canada to study American literature in graduate school at Pennsylvania State University. That year, the Vietnam War was intensifying, but in my hometown—Kitchener in southern Ontario—I'd barely heard about it. When I arrived at Penn State, I didn't understand the frequent references to Vietnam in newspapers, on television newscasts, and especially from other male graduate students, who worried about an increased military draft that would send them to fight in the jungles of southeast Asia.

Jump forward to 1968. I'd finished my master's degree and was working toward a doctorate (my dissertation was about the postmodern American novelist John Barth), but I had difficulty concentrating on my courses during one of America's most chaotic years. In January, in what was called the Tet Offensive (named after the Vietnamese new year), North Vietnamese forces attacked more than one hundred South Vietnamese targets, many of them US military bases. The United States responded by sending two hundred thousand more combat troops to the region. Antiwar protests escalated, continuing into March when a company of US soldiers massacred as many as five hundred unarmed civilians in the South Vietnamese hamlet of My Lai. In April, Martin Luther King Jr. was assassinated. In June, Robert F. Kennedy was assassinated. In August, an estimated fifteen thousand antiwar demonstrators arrived in Chicago to pressure Democratic convention delegates as they chose their presidential candidate. When National Guardsmen and Chicago police officers confronted the protestors, the many nights of violence appeared minute-by-minute on network television.

There weren't twenty riots. There weren't fifty riots. There were several *hundred*, some condemning the war, others demanding civil rights, still others combining them because, as *Time* magazine reported, in Vietnam the ratio of Black combat troops to white ones was double the ratio of Blacks to whites in the overall population. The Black combat death rate compared to white casualties was higher also. Every day, across the nation, another major city resembled a war zone: Cincinnati, Detroit, Louisville, Los Angeles, Miami, Philadelphia, Pittsburg, Trenton, Washington, D.C. (blocks from the White House), on and on.

I watched in dismay as the Vietnam War seemed to come home. Although I was in academia, my ambition was to become a novelist. I wondered what would happen if a decorated Vietnam veteran returned to the United States, hating what he'd learned about himself. What would happen if he wandered through the country to see what he'd been fighting for? What if he grew long hair and a beard and looked like a war protestor? What if his appearance triggered a hostile response from a small-town police chief, who was a 1950s conservative old enough to be the veteran's father and himself a veteran from Korea, a quite different war? The two would represent America's political divide and the then much-discussed generation gap (older Americans tended to support the war; the younger generation believed they couldn't trust anyone over thirty). A third character, Colonel Sam Trautman, Rambo's former commanding officer, would represent Uncle Sam, the system that created Rambo and would destroy him.

I devoted three years to writing the novel, some of them at Penn State and some at the University of Iowa, where I went to teach American literature in the English department. *First Blood* was published in 1972 and received reviews in almost every major newspaper and magazine. Columbia Pictures purchased the movie rights. The novel was taught in high schools and universities, including by Stephen King, who used it as a text when he taught creative writing at the University of Maine. It was translated into thirty languages. It's never been out of print.

But controversy alone (much of it outdated) can't explain why, almost daily, the name occurs in movies, television series, talk shows, social media, newspapers, conversations, etc. It's in dictionaries. It's used as a verb and an adjective as well as a noun. Several times, it's been a question on the TV game show *Jeopardy!,* referring to both the movie and my novel. The name is so pervasive that when I heard it last night in an episode of an espionage series on television, I needed a moment to remember my relationship to it.

So, when Nat Segaloff told me about his plan to write a book about the Rambo phenomenon, I was delighted. He and I first intersected when he interviewed me for his book *Stirling Silliphant: The Fingers of God.* As you'll learn, Stirling's scripts for the 1960–64 television series *Route 66* (about two young men in a Corvette convertible traveling across the United States in search of America and in search of themselves) motivated me to become a writer. Eventually, Stirling and I became close friends and worked together on the 1989 NBC miniseries of my novel *The Brotherhood of the Rose.* Nat in turn had worked with Stirling as a publicist for 1974's enormously successful disaster movie *The Towering*

Inferno, for which Stirling wrote the screenplay. Over the years, Nat interviewed him and wrote the definitive book, *Stirling Silliphant: The Fingers of God*. We shared many stories about him.

Nat has also written about movies for the *Boston Herald* and taught at Boston University and Boston College. His other books include studies of film icons such as Arthur Penn, William Friedkin, and John Milius, along with histories of movies such as *Scarface* (both versions), *The Exorcist* (all the versions), and *The Towering Inferno*. Nat has a talent for in-depth research and discovered information about the Rambo movies that surprised me. Although I didn't write the scripts for any of them, I had a close relationship with Carolco Pictures, the company that produced the first three Rambo films. Over the years, Sylvester Stallone and I had many lengthy conversations about the character and the movies. I had substantive conversations with Sly's costar Richard Crenna, also, and with Andy Vajna, one of the two cofounders of Carolco. Whenever I was in Los Angeles, Andy always welcomed me to his office. Sometimes, we chatted for as long as a half hour, an eternity for a mega-producer. He even drove me to his Beverly Hills home and introduced me to his family. Thus, I could provide Nat with information for this book that otherwise wouldn't have been available.

Rambo fans will find a wealth of information here—the unusual source of Rambo's name, for example, and the real-life model I used for the character—but students of popular culture and film history will find plenty to interest them, also. The ten-year evolution of my novel into the first Rambo film was one of the most prolonged, complicated processes in Hollywood history—a drama in itself. The complications continued. As America changed, so did Rambo. There are at least four versions of him. The Rambo in my novel is different from the Rambo in the first film. The second and third films interpret the character differently again. In the fourth film, the character returns to the Rambo in my novel. In the fifth movie, once more he's someone else.

To echo the song in the first movie, it's been a long road—over half a century since the traumatic events of 1968 prompted me to write the following sentence: *His name was Rambo, and he was just some nothing kid for all anybody knew.* From a novel to numerous screen incarnations to a cartoon television series to video games to lunch boxes to toys to collectibles to an off-Broadway play to dictionaries to presidential invocations and more, Nat Segaloff provides a detailed record of that journey.

Introduction and Acknowledgments

Rambo may be a fictitious character, but he has his roots in the reality of war. As created by David Morrell, he is an intelligent, highly trained human killing machine designed to elude or, if necessary, eliminate the enemy. He was not designed for peace, and although he was discharged from Special Forces after America left Vietnam, Vietnam never left Rambo.

He is also not alone. As many people observed when the novel *First Blood* was published in 1972 and when the film *First Blood* was released in 1982, there could be lots of Rambos among us, who never recovered from their combat experience.

As you'll read, Morrell was inspired to write *First Blood* after meeting Vietnam veterans in the classes he was teaching at Penn State University in the late 1960s. Similarly, long before I ever contemplated writing this book, I met a nascent Rambo for a documentary I was making in the late 1990s. He was a wiry, bespectacled kid of about thirty, and he was wearing, not a headband or bandoleros, but an orange jumpsuit provided by the Massachusetts Department of Correction. My producing partner Gayle Kirschenbaum and I had created a show for HBO about the American parole system. Nobody else at the time was doing this kind of program, and we were fascinated by the way states grant guilty people their freedom. Massachusetts was confident and gracious enough to let our crew tape several of their Boston hearings.

The young man in question had been given a life sentence for killing a Vietnamese immigrant. The inmate, who was white and had been a soldier, willingly admitted his guilt. This is the first step in applying for clemency. Under questioning from the parole board, all of whom were political appointees, he explained his actions by saying that he had snapped during a street altercation and ended the man's life.

Regardless of how many times the young man insisted that he was explaining his actions but wasn't justifying them, the board members could not parse the distinction. They kept asking, "Are you saying that the United States military made you kill this victim?"

"No," the young man repeated with growing frustration. "I killed him, but the military taught me how."

Predictably, he was not granted clemency. Moreover, his segment never aired; HBO chose to go for a crime of passion where the moral issues were less controversial. But the young man's situation stuck with me, not only for the drama of the hearing itself but also for the implication that the American military was, by definition, creating generations of potential killers. This is one of the themes that drive Morrell's three Rambo books and the five films that have been made from them to date. It is also one of the reasons I wrote this book. I also wrote it to celebrate one of the most compelling and original literary creations of the twentieth century. Rambo stands with Sherlock Holmes, Tarzan, and James Bond as an icon of popular culture, who began in novels, was translated into films, and had global impact. In fact, I would argue that Rambo is the most powerful in that his name is in dictionaries and has entered the lexicon as a symbol as well as a character.

The Rambo Report would not exist—indeed, Rambo himself would not exist—without David Morrell. As you'll read, he created Rambo as a means of articulating the discoveries he was making as a man, a teacher, and a writer. He and I met through someone who mentored us both at different times and shared those concerns: Stirling Silliphant. My story starts with theirs.

When he was a seventeen-year-old living in Canada in the early 1960s, David wrote a fan letter to Silliphant, a prolific television and screenplay writer who was cocreator and chief writer of the immensely popular TV series *Route 66*. Where anyone else might have thrown such a letter onto the slush pile, Stirling was intrigued by the young man's request for career advice, and he wrote back. A correspondence was born, then a relationship. David blossomed as a writer and, in 1972, published his first novel, *First Blood*.

In 1984, David, by then a bestselling author, wrote *The Brotherhood of the Rose*, the first book in his trilogy about two orphans, raised to be assassins, who begin to doubt their calling. It so fascinated Stirling, not only with its craft but also with its potential as a television miniseries, that he brokered a deal to produce it for NBC, then worked closely with David to bring that project to fruition.

I similarly fell under Stirling's mentorship when, as a regional publicist on the 1974 movie *The Towering Inferno*, which he had scripted, I booked a promotional press tour for Stirling and his new wife, Tiana, when they visited my home base of Boston. Years later, when I was asked by editor Patrick McGilligan to profile Stirling for the University of California Press's *Backstory* series, I got back in touch with him. By then he had relocated to Thailand, but we picked up by fax (no Zoom or WhatsApp in those days) where we had left off in person twenty years earlier.

Stirling died in 1996. When I learned from Tiana that he had wanted me to celebrate in print their life together, I took the opportunity to write his biography, which became *Stirling Silliphant: The Fingers of God* (BearManor Media, 2014).

One of the people I interviewed for that book was David, and thus we began our friendship. If Stirling's handprints are on both our backs, I like to think we have a couple of Stirling's generous pats there as well.

As Rambo's creator, David was both a fountain of information and a source of comfort throughout the writing of this book. My appreciation and affection for him cannot be quantified. I owe the book's accuracy to him, and if there happen to be inaccuracies, I accept their blame myself.

I owe enormous thanks to my friend, documentary filmmaker Jeffrey Schwarz, who jump-started this book's contents.

I extend deep thanks to my agent, Lee Sobel, and to our colleagues at Kensington/Citadel with whom I have enjoyed producing two previous books, especially Steven Zacharius, James Abbate, Ann Pryor, Rick Willett, Joe Gannon, Stephen Smith, and Rebecca Cremonese.

The tireless archivists at the Margaret Herrick Library of the Academy of Motion Picture Arts and Sciences are a singular resource: Matt Severson, director; Howard Prouty, acquisitions archivist; and Caroline Jorgensen, Elizabeth Youle, and Genevieve Maxwell of the National Film Information Service, as well as their colleagues who preserve Hollywood's past. Others who have been there for me along the way are Susan and Robert Feiles, Gary Fleder, Craig Gering, GoTranscript.com, Lesley Harker, Barry Krost, Gary J. Kunich, the Lahmani family (Ivanna, Ami, Adam, and Joseph Benjamin), Matt Martin, Anthony Mattero, Timea Palacsik, Kyle Petrulio, Herbie J. Pilato, Hartley Pleshaw, Daniel Schweiger, Sarabeth Shadeen, Tiana Silliphant, Devin Snell, and Kelly Winn, and a friend who was there when the pages almost went blank, Christopher Darling. Gratitude as well to Gerald "Gerry" Herman, whose helping hand was the hand of friendship and grace. I extend special gratitude to journalist Pat H. Broeske, who covered Sylvester Stallone on countless occasions for various publications and came away with stories and insight, both of which she shared.

Thanks as well to the people who agreed to be interviewed or offered counsel for this book as well as those whose names do not appear for reasons of modesty, protocol, or paranoia. I know who you are, and I cherish your help.

CHAPTER 1

Why Vietnam vs. Why Vietnam?

Some movies are more than movies—they become barometers of their times. *Casablanca* (1942), for example, came to symbolize America's reticence to enter World War II until the war became personal. *Easy Rider* (1969) spoke to a young audience that had grown apart from its parents and told Hollywood that the youth audience had arrived. *Star Wars* (1977) marked the end of the sliding moral scale of the Me Decade and reset the gauge to the old days of unsullied good guys and unredeemable bad guys. As rising production costs perched every studio production on the precipice of a financial abyss, however, it became risky for a film to stand for anything braver than escapism.

But the *Rambo* films broke the mold. The first two, in particular—more than *The Deer Hunter* (1978) or *Apocalypse Now* (1979), as good as they were—reopened a discussion that had long been festering about the Vietnam War. The debate continues despite America's entry into subsequent conflicts all over the world.

At this publishing, the Rambo saga has lasted forty-three years from the first film and fifty-three from the book that inspired it. During this time, the American public's sensibilities changed from hawk to dove and back to hawk. Similarly, the character of Rambo changed from a man whose pain led him to attack his own country to a man who learned to channel his violent skills against foreign enemies. Within, he remained a troubled soul; the only things that kept him from being a mercenary were the purity of his motives, the fact that he worked for free, and the pain he felt while killing.

Know Rambo and you know America. $819 million at the box office says so.[1]

The Rambo phenomenon offers a psychological and political portrait of the United States from 1972, when Morrell's novel *First Blood* appeared, to 2019, when *Last Blood*, the final film (so far) in the series, was released.[2] Both Rambo and his country endured profound changes across those tumultuous years. Rambo began as one person and ended as another; similarly, the America of 1972 would become something far different by 2019. This book charts that journey in terms of the five Rambo movies and the three Rambo novels that spanned it.

"John Rambo"[3] may be an invented character, and *First Blood* may be a fictitious story, but the truth they tell is undeniable, and that truth begins with the ongoing controversies behind the Vietnam War. Rambo is the human ghost of the war come home, and like the fog of the war itself, it is impossible to see it all from one perspective. As a character, his history is clear. In the book, he was a teenage kid from Colorado who left an abusive home in which his father beat his mother, and escaped by joining the army. In the movies, he left his family's horse farm in Bowie, Arizona, to fight in a war that he believed was in support of a country, which, it turned out, didn't support him.[4] Everything in the Rambo universe—the sequels, the novelizations, the television cartoon series, the merchandise, the spin-offs, the ancillaries, and the internet worship sites—plays with that irony, sometimes honestly, sometimes disingenuously. It is imperative, therefore, to look at the war first, and then at Rambo, to see how one affected the other.

Each generation in the twentieth century has faced

a point at which its past and future divide with such force that nothing that follows can be the same. For people who reached their majority during the Jazz Age, for example, the slaughter of World War I and the Great Depression forever colored their social, moral, and especially their economic sensibilities. World War II and the Holocaust were the events that stunned and redirected what has been called the Greatest Generation. And for the Baby Boomers born in the late 1940s, the world turned upside down in the 1960s and '70s with the war in Southeast Asia.

To be sure, there were other traumas for those who came of age in the second half of the twentieth century. The Communist witch hunts; the blacklist; the civil rights struggle; the assassinations of John F. Kennedy, Martin Luther King, Jr., Malcolm X, and Robert Kennedy; Watergate; television; the women's movement; gay liberation; rock 'n' roll;, comic books; drugs; the Pill; the space program; and other social and technological changes were far from trivial. But it was the war in Vietnam that tore the nation apart and made the generation most in jeopardy of being called up to fight it— young men in particular—reassess their notion of America's place in the world and their obligation to preserve it. Suddenly the patriotic slogan "my country, right or wrong" was being broadly and soundly challenged. Whose country was it? And was it right or was it, in fact, wrong?

These themes inform the events of *First Blood* and Morrell's conception of the man named Rambo, a highly decorated US Special Forces Vietnam veteran who walks into a small town wanting only to get a hamburger. It introduced audiences to a figure who would embody the anguish that many of them had been feeling about the war regardless of where they stood. Those who saw the 1982 film adaptation as an antiwar statement pointed to Rambo as the symbol of the exploitation and victimization of their generation. Rambo's rampage against a small American town demonstrated that, if we do not come to terms with what we have created, we as a nation will turn against ourselves. Not until the 1985 sequel would Rambo become a wish-fulfillment engine whereby the soldier would exact revenge on the North Vietnamese, symbolizing the belief, still held by many Americans, that the military could have won the war if only the damn politicians had allowed them. How Rambo went from victim to victor is a significant journey that this book discusses.[5]

That journey began with a dialogue that Morrell (then a graduate student teaching in Penn State's English department from 1966 to 1970) had been having with returning veterans who were his students and sought to articulate their anguish. To understand that yearning and how Rambo became their voice, it is necessary to explain the Vietnam War in terms of the men who, in many cases, were destroyed by it.

"Why Vietnam?" In the early 1960s, that question was just beginning to be discussed in school seminars, workshops, and teach-ins across America, but not until July 29, 1965, was it posed in a speech by President Lyndon B. Johnson. LBJ had been overwhelmingly reelected[6] the previous year, and he used his deceptively folksy Texas manner to make his first public acknowledgment of the war in a speech during which he announced he was escalating it.

"My fellow Americans," he began, "not long ago I received a letter from a woman in the Midwest. She wrote, 'Dear Mr. President: In my humble way I am writing to you about the crisis in Vietnam. I have a son who is now in Vietnam. My husband served in World War II. Our country was at war, but now, this time, it is just something that I don't understand. Why? Why Vietnam?"[7]

The letter may or may not have been genuine, but the

moment certainly was. Before the end of that year some ten thousand prints of a government propaganda film titled *Why Vietnam* with footage of that press conference would flood the nation's schools, libraries, military bases, and television stations.[8] But the documentary had one important distinction, as historian Tom Engelhardt[9] has noted: the lack of a question mark. This positioned the title *Why Vietnam* as an answer, not an inquiry. Indeed, the narration—after criticizing Neville Chamberlain, Hitler, Mussolini, and the Anschluss as examples of ominous diplomatic compromises—goes on to justify US presence in Southeast Asia with striking simplicity. "South Vietnam has asked for greater support to resist that pressure and has received it," the narrator states before flashing back to 1954 when "French troops are fighting the last battle of a long war over what had been called French Indochina."

The film never asks what the French were doing in someone else's country in the first place but instead goes on to muse, "It's a strange, three-cornered struggle: non-Communist Vietnamese fighting Communist Vietnamese and some of both fighting the French." The documentary then explains that, with the evacuation of French troops, a peace treaty signed in Vienna divided the country into the Communist North and non-Communist South. Subsequently, more than one million refugees fled from north to south. "From then to now," the narrator says, "the basic story of United States help to Vietnam is simple: The Communists have steadily increased their pressure on South Vietnam.[10] Left unsaid is that the South Vietnamese government, which had asked for greater support, was the one that had been installed by the US. It was a government that proved increasingly corrupt, as Neil Sheehan established in his 1988 book, *A Bright Shining Lie*. In short, the US invited itself in, replacing (at their request) the French.[11]

But by the time of LBJ's speech, the die was already cast that would divide Americans. A year earlier, on August 4, 1964, there had been an incident between a pair of North Vietnamese torpedo boats and the US destroyers *Maddox* and *Turner Joy* in the Gulf of Tonkin off the coast of Vietnam. The next day, the Johnson administration, insisting that shots had been fired on an American vessel, persuaded Congress to vote a resolution to assist any Southeast Asian country whose government was considered to be jeopardized by aggression.[12] This was called the Gulf of Tonkin Resolution and for a decade was used to justify the Vietnam War. Not until 2005 were documents declassified showing that nothing had happened on August 4 except bad naval intelligence and poorly translated intercepted North Vietnamese messages.[13]

The war was waged, but it was never declared, a constitutional violation that Congress took a long time to address. Secretary of Defense Robert S. McNamara, in charge of implementing Johnson's edicts through 1968, thought that an air war would have the double advantage of demoralizing the North Vietnamese people and limiting the number of US ground troops that were needed. This turned out to be a mistake, as McNamara later admitted, because Vietnam was not just a ground war but a guerilla war.[14] Not until President Richard Nixon invaded Cambodia in April 1970 and, more distressingly for the Viet Cong, aligned the US with China, did the Hanoi government in North Vietnam decide to come to the peace table. In the meantime, thousands of people died or were wounded, not so much to stop Communism (as many later historians theorized) but to prove American credibility to its allies.[15]

While LBJ's 1965 rhetorical question was the first official public justification for United States presence in Southeast Asia, unofficial US presence had begun twenty years earlier, in the ashes of World War II, with a devastated Russia, an impoverished France, and an America who stood "at the summit of the world" as Winston Churchill pronounced.[16] Once the Japanese—who had occupied Vietnam, displacing the French during World War II—departed in 1945, Ho Chi Minh, the Communist leader in Hanoi, issued a Declaration of Independence that borrowed from the American Declaration of Independence and the French Rights of Man and the Citizen. Where President Roosevelt, during the war, had opposed French occupation but kept silent so as not to upset a wartime ally,[17] FDR's successor, Harry S. Truman, had to face the peace. As revealed by Daniel Ellsberg and Anthony Russo in the *Pentagon Papers*, Ho wrote to then-President Truman asking for recognition. Truman never responded.[18] After Ho's People's Army of Vietnam, commanded by General Võ Nguyên Giáp, drove out the French at Dien Bien Phu in 1954,[19] a peace agreement at Geneva confined the French to the South while the Viet Minh held the North.

Archimedes Patti, who was then an officer in the OSS (Office of Strategic Services), explained the misguided foray for the WGBH-TV documentary series *Vietnam: A Television History*: "Ho Chi Minh was on a silver platter in 1945. We had him. He was willing to be a democratic republic if nothing else. Socialist yes, but a democratic republic. He was leaning not towards the Soviet Union, which at the time . . . were in no position to help anyone. So really, we had Ho Chi Minh, we had the Viet Minh, we had the Indochina question in our hand, but for reasons which defy good logic we find today that we supported the French for a war which they themselves dubbed *la sale guerre*, the dirty war, and we paid to the tune of 80 percent of the cost of that French war and then we picked up 100 percent of the American-Vietnam War."[20]

In 1955, then-President Dwight D. Eisenhower sent seven

hundred military "advisors" to shore up the weakening South Vietnamese puppet government. In May 1961, newly inaugurated US president John F. Kennedy committed an additional five hundred US Special Forces troops and military advisors, and by the end of 1962 he had ordered eleven thousand more. A year later—after his November assassination—there were sixteen thousand.[21] This number was contrary to the Geneva Accords, which limited the United States to seven hundred.[22]

Nowhere in the half-hour documentary *Why Vietnam* (nor in much of the mainstream media at the time) was it noted that the United States was insinuating itself into a civil war. In fact, the US was not eager for Vietnam to be reunited. To effect this, the US installed Ngo Dinh Diem in Saigon and worked against holding reunification elections. Diem's regime was so corrupt that, by 1958, a guerilla movement arose in the North to topple him. When Diem and his brother Ngo Dinh Nhu were assassinated in a CIA-backed coup on November 2, 1963, there were celebrations in the street, which the US portrayed in the States as protests. Two years later the National Liberation Front was formed in the South for the same purpose of protesting.[23] According to the *Pentagon Papers*, in all of Vietnam, only the Viet Cong—that is, the Communist-led army—held any credibility.[24]

All told, some 550,000 US troops were sent to Vietnam between 1954 and 1975, of whom 58,000 were killed and even more wounded physically, emotionally, or both. The rift that the war created at home was also devastating, dividing families, communities, and the government itself.

Several explanations were offered at the time for US involvement in a country that posed no military threat to America:

1. The Domino Theory held that one nation falling to Communism would lead to others doing so;

2. The South Vietnamese government needed support;

3. Desire to spread democracy;

4. Support for Vietnamese independence;

5. Credibility to US allies that America would protect them if needed.

Less noble reasons (some of which have been borne out by time) were speculated:

1. Giving immense, unchallenged money to weapons manufacturers;

2. Trying to capture vast offshore petroleum reserves at the Bạch Hổ (White Tiger) oil field in the Cuu Long basin of the East Sea east of the Mekong Delta for US oil companies;

3. Control of the fertile Southeast Asian agricultural "rice basket" (largely destroyed by Agent Orange) that would allow the US to starve Communist China into submission;[25]

4. Continuing the French exploitation of Southeast Asia's mineral resources.

The toll affected America, which is where *Rambo* fits in. Stateside, the Vietnam conflict inspired the largest antiwar movement in American history. Although small at first, it gained momentum throughout the sixties among students and people who were outraged by reports of atrocities being committed by soldiers, such as the March 16, 1968, massacre of civilians, including children, at My Lai in Quang Ngai province. That operation, led by Lieutenant William Calley, was reported by Seymour Hersh on November 13, 1969.[26] This and other revelations led to troops being labeled "baby killers" by protestors on their return from tours of duty (Rambo rails against this in the emotional climax to the first movie).

By then, countless rallies, marches, sit-ins, teach-ins, and less benign forms of protest such as building occupations and bombings were rupturing American society, dividing families, and setting, for example, blue collar workers ("hardhats") against protestors ("hippies") despite condescending claims by the liberal/radical Left that they represented the working class. Cynics would claim that young people who were protesting the war were motivated in part by their reluctance to be drafted into the military. This was augmented by the ability of college students, who were overwhelmingly white, to get 2-S educational draft deferments while less advantaged young men of color were shipped off to fight and die. The resulting schism between the political Left and the Civil Rights Movement was exploited by prowar factions.

The antiwar movement was further divided by the December 1, 1969, draft lottery in which the Selective Service System, which managed conscription, held a drawing that paired calendar birth dates with numbers from 1 to 366. Men of draft age receiving numbers 1–122 were certain to be drafted; 123–246 would possibly be drafted; and 247–366 (counting leap year) were more than likely to escape service. In one swift, cynical move, the Nixon administration effectively turned the antiwar movement upon itself when many of those who were "safe" lost interest in opposing the war. Then, on May 4, 1970, National Guard troops fired on protesting students (and many others who weren't protesting) at

Kent State University in Ohio, killing four young people and wounding nine. Antiwar demonstrations shut down universities coast-to-coast. The outrage of alienated young people was reignited. The war had come home.

Those injuries have not healed; among the most severe is the invisible wound of PTSD (post-traumatic stress disorder) affecting combatants. As will be explained in more detail, PTSD is a mental and behavioral ailment that results from being exposed to great stress. It has been recognized as a reaction to a wide array of experiences such as sexual assault, witnessing a horrible event, child abuse, traffic accidents, or a disaster. For numerous Vietnam veterans, however, the cause of PTSD was the war itself. All the basic training in the world cannot insulate military personnel from what it is designed to do: help them kill the enemy. The Veterans Administration says that an average of seven out of each one hundred combat veterans will develop PTSD.[27]

One of those statistics is John Rambo. His PTSD returns him emotionally to the mindset of full-out battle, the one form of behavior with which, because of his training, he feels comfortable and in control. Everything he does in *First Blood* can be traced to this: the sullenness, the defensiveness, the flashbacks, the stealth, the anger, and (in the book) the death toll. How it affects his behavior in the sequel films is part of his struggle to survive. As he tells his adoptive daughter, Gabrielle, in the final Rambo film, *Last Blood*, trying to dissuade her from finding her wayward birth father:

> **RAMBO:** Men like that don't change. It only gets worse.
>
> **GABRIELLE:** You changed.

> **RAMBO:** I haven't changed. I'm just trying to
> keep a lid on it every day.

For the generation that fought the Vietnam War and the generation that tried to bring them home, the wounds still exist. Some never will be healed. The antiwar generation remains distrustful of government—not the calculated extremism of today's MAGA and Q-Anon members, but a skepticism born of example after example in which American lives were sacrificed. While there have been some apologies, both genuine and facile, by the men who ordered armies into battle,[28] time and subsequent wars have driven the Vietnam experience unhealed into the shadows of history. Resentments, anger, and misconceptions linger. New scholarship emerges as old documents are declassified and as the people responsible hear death approaching and yearn to clear their consciences.

There remains a segment of the public that believes America was right in being in Vietnam, and they disparage the nation's sloppy, tragic March 29, 1973, withdrawal that abandoned South Vietnamese citizens, many of whom had helped the US, struggling to board the last helicopter out of Saigon. Many Americans persist in the belief that POWs and MIAs remain in-country despite latter-day cooperation between the US and Vietnamese governments searching for them.[29]

This is the background of *First Blood*: a divided nation, an alienated and damaged veteran, a resentful lawman, and a war whose peace treaty settled nothing in the hearts and minds of those who fought its battles. As shall be shown, the theme of *First Blood*, both the book and the film, reflects these conflicting emotions. What happened in subsequent films reversed this and turned Rambo into an avenging force who, in trying to make peace with himself, made war on others. Despite sequels that were set in Afghanistan, Burma, and Mexico, the Vietnam experience is imprinted on all of them. In each, through excitement, action, and death, Rambo is portrayed as a victor. Yet he knows otherwise. Not until the last film is the audience obliged to know it, too.

With Rambo locked and loaded, the saga begins.

CHAPTER 2

David Morrell: The Man Who Created Rambo

Before Rambo was Sylvester Stallone, and even before he was "just some nothing kid for all anybody knew," he was the synthesis of what the then-twenty-five-year-old David Morrell had been hearing from a handful of students he was teaching at Pennsylvania State University in 1968. Usually, students learn from their teacher, but in this case, their teacher learned from them. This is how Rambo became Rambo and David Morrell became an author.

The American war in Vietnam was growing in intensity throughout the 1960s, and Walter Cronkite was reporting it on the nightly television news. There were nationwide demonstrations against the war, and Cronkite was covering those, too. Students at Penn State and other schools across the nation were determined to stop the killing.

The Canadian-born Morrell, however, kept his silence. He had to.

"I think it's important to emphasize what the immigration officer said when my wife, my infant daughter, and I crossed the Canadian border into Detroit in 1966, preparing to go down to Penn State. He told us to remember that we were guests, that we were not citizens, that we did not have a right to a political opinion, that, as good guests, we should keep quiet about whatever thoughts we might have about what was happening in the United States. Those thoughts landed on the pages of *First Blood* rather than in conversation."[1]

Morrell came to Penn State because of his admiration for

Ernest Hemingway scholar Philip Young, who was a professor there. Morrell had been accepted at the school after finishing his bachelor's degree at St. Jerome's College in Waterloo,
Ontario. But he had also finished another kind of degree at
the University of Silliphant: a course in writing and human
drama courtesy of the TV series *Route 66*, and a growing
friendship with its primary scenarist. At Penn State, in addition to his graduate studies, Morrell taught essay writing to
first-year students.

"At one point, I had a group of Vietnam veterans, not
many, it might have been five, out of a class of perhaps thirty,
who resisted taking instruction from me because we were
the same age. They'd been through terrible experiences in
Vietnam and [wondered] what gave me the right to give
them direction when I should have been over there fighting.
I explained to them that I was Canadian, that I was married,
and that I had a young daughter (the last two of which, even if
I'd been an American, would have made me ineligible for the
draft at that time). Once they realized that their perceptions
were different from the reality, we were able to talk. They
became my teachers about what it had felt like to come back
from Vietnam."

People who have known battle seldom discuss it with
those who have not. These students, however, in the comfort
of a classroom with a sympathetic listener, opened up. "They
told me about jumping for cover from loud noises and having
trouble in relationships," Morrell remembers, "having trouble
sleeping, relying on alcohol—maybe drugs also, but in those
days people didn't talk about drugs except marijuana. Generally, they gave me a sense of how disoriented they were emotionally in a civilian context. They were experiencing what
we now call symptoms of PTSD, but at the time, there wasn't
any expression for it except *shell shock*, *battle fatigue*, or other

terms that were left over from World War II and Korea. Those conversations (and Walter Cronkite's TV reports about the war in Vietnam and the riots at home) were what made me decide to write *First Blood*."

He got the name *Rambo* indirectly through his wife, Donna (see the sidebar about the Rambo apple), and fashioned him, in part, on the multi-decorated World War II hero Audie Murphy (see the sidebar about Murphy). Morrell's hero would be "as confused as those young men in the class that I was teaching and [he] would be trying to figure out what he'd been fighting for. I wondered what Audie Murphy would have been like, knowing how disturbed he was in real life—if he'd grown long hair and a beard and the police were going to shave it all off, and he had a flashback to Vietnam. How would Murphy have reacted?"

Morrell hadn't written a novel before. He sought advice from Philip Klass, who wrote science fiction under the name William Tenn and was a fiction-writing teacher at Penn State. Klass assigned him the task of writing a short story every week. "It was tough," Morrell says. "In addition to my graduate-school classes, I wrote maybe a dozen stories for him. One day he called me into his office, and I thought, 'Here it is. I've been discovered.' But what he said was 'These are terrible. You need to stop.' But instead of sending me away, he then started to teach me. He said, 'Every writer has a dominant emotion, and if you can access that dominant emotion, then you become unique because nobody else is like you. You need to be yourself.' Then he looked at me and said, 'I think your dominant emotion is fear. I'll give you one more chance. Write a story about fear, but I don't mean fear of drowning or heights or fire, because they're all symptoms. I mean fear that's deep in you in a way that you don't understand.'"

By this time, Morrell was a graduate assistant to Philip

Young, whose book about Hemingway² had prompted Morrell to go to Penn State. While Young spent a summer at a family cottage in the Finger Lakes district of New York, he allowed Morrell to use his home as a writing retreat. One afternoon, after repeated efforts to write the story about fear that Klass wanted from him, Morrell gave up.

"Then a strange thing happened. Although I was sitting in front of my portable typewriter at Philip Young's kitchen table, I suddenly imagined that I was walking in a forest." Years later, in his writing book *The Successful Novelist: A Lifetime of Lessons about Writing and Publishing*, Morrell described the experience.

> Bushes crowded me. Sweat rolled down my face. I heard noises behind me. At first, I assumed that a squirrel was rooting for something in the underbrush. But as the crunch of leaves came closer, the sound seemed more and more like cautious footsteps. Someone was in the forest with me. Someone was creeping up on me. I can't express how vividly I felt that I was actually in that forest—and how fearfully certain I was that someone intended to kill me. As abruptly as it came, the illusion ended. I suddenly found myself staring not at a forest but at my desk and the typewriter on it, a blank sheet of paper taunting me. I'd never experienced any other daydream as powerfully. I didn't understand what had happened, but one thing I was sure of: I wanted to know what happened next. Thus, I began my first real short story.

It was called "The Plinker," a term that describes someone who likes to target shoot, the target in this case being the story's main character. Nervous, Morrell gave the story to

Klass and went away, expecting another rejection. Instead, a few days later, Klass summoned him and asked, "What happened to you? This is a good story." Klass spent several hours with Morrell, discussing ways in which the story might have been improved. A few weeks later, Morrell brought Klass some early pages of *First Blood*, which includes harrowing forest scenes similar to the one in "The Plinker." Klass liked them even more than he'd liked "The Plinker." Then the hard work began.

Morrell originally began *First Blood* with an action sequence of Rambo running through the forest with the helicopter chasing him. (This sequence is included in a 2015 limited edition of the novel published by Borderland Press/Gauntlet Press.) "My assumption was that people would be excited, asking 'Why is this man running, and who wants to kill him?'" Klass and crime writer Donald E. Westlake (a friend of Klass) told him that this was wrong. "No one knew more about storytelling than Donald E. Westlake," Morrell says. "He told me that starting in the middle of a story and then going back to the beginning in a flashback is wrong. It interrupts the plot's forward motion. It's clumsy. And it's usually confusing because the reader doesn't know who any of the characters are. 'Straighten it out,' Klass and Westlake told me. 'Start with the first time Rambo and Teasle meet.' It sounds obvious now, but that's the sort of practical lesson that apprentice writers need to learn. The next thing I knew, this sentence came into my head. *His name was Rambo, and he was just some nothing kid for all anybody knew, standing by the pump of a gas station on the outskirts of Madison, Kentucky.*

"The next problem was that I went in too many directions; I had scenes about how one of the deputies lived, I had scenes about the justice of the peace who sentenced Rambo for vagrancy and how *he* lived. It was just a whole lot of things that didn't belong. I cut that stuff out, and abruptly I saw the structure. It was Rambo-Teasle, Rambo-Teasle, Rambo-Teasle. I realized that if I gave readers only two perspectives and I kept alternating from one to the other, readers wouldn't know who to cheer for. They might say, '*This* guy is right.' But when they move into the other character's point of view, they'll say, 'No, I was wrong. *This* guy is right.' I wanted readers to be absolutely conflicted about whether they sympathized with Rambo or Teasle in the climax. To me, their differences were generational—a disapproving father against a disapproving son (most older Americans seemed to support the Vietnam War while many younger Americans didn't). In the middle of what can be considered an allegory was Colonel Trautman, whose first name is Sam, as in 'Uncle Sam.' He's the system that created Rambo and, in the end, destroys him."

Another factor that made the novel different was Morrell's interest in trying to find a new way to write action novels. "They're often filled with clichés, such as 'A shot rang out.' I wondered if there was a fresher way to do it, to eliminate all the familiar expressions and try to make the incidents seem as vivid and real as possible."

Philip Klass introduced Morrell to his (and Westlake's agent) Henry Morrison. Morrison was impressed by the novel but told Morrell that he thought its strong action made it a more likely choice for a paperback publisher rather than one that specializes in hardbacks. Instead, within six weeks, Morrison sold *First Blood* to the hardback house M. Evans and Company, which until 1972 had mostly published well-known nonfiction titles such as *Body Language*, *Open Marriage*, and *The New Aerobics*. The novel was reviewed, as Morrell recalls, "everywhere. For a first novel, this never happens. I mean, *everywhere*. *Life Magazine, Time, Newsweek, Saturday Review, New York Times, Washington Post,* San Francisco, LA, hundreds of reviews. Every one of them was positive except for *Time* magazine, which called it carnography, the meat novel. The reviewer said, 'If you like Lieutenant Calley massacring those villagers at My Lai in Vietnam, you will like this book.' Of the amazing number of reviews, this was the only bad one, and of course, it bothered me, but the reviewer at least understood, even if he disapproved, that *First Blood* was something new. I was trying to do for action novels what Sam Peckinpah had done for Westerns in *The Wild Bunch*, which was released in 1969 when I was in the middle of writing the novel. I never got over seeing *The Wild Bunch*."

First Blood was just the beginning. In the years since its publication in 1972, Morrell has become known as "the master of the high-action thriller." He has written twenty-seven additional novels, many of them *New York Times* bestsellers. His work has been translated into thirty languages. He received Lifetime Achievement awards from the International Thriller Writers organization and from Bouchercon, the world's largest conference for authors and readers of crime fiction.[3] In 1986, he gave up his American literature professorship at the University of Iowa but often serves as an advisor to young writers. From Philip Young, Philip Klass, and Stirling Silliphant, Morrell says, he learned not to chase the market, and to be yourself. "You might not be a success," he says, "but at least you didn't set yourself up for failure by trying to be a second-rate version of somebody else."

As for Silliphant, his first mentor, Morrell kept in touch with him not only when they worked together on the 1989 NBC television miniseries of his novel *The Brotherhood of the Rose* (q.v.) but as close friends for the rest of Silliphant's life (he died in 1996). "I sent him a copy of *First Blood* in '72 when it was published, and he phoned me to say how much he liked it," Morrell says. "I was thrilled. I worshiped him. I could never have written *First Blood* if not for his *Route 66* Vietnam veteran's episode and also his 1967 Oscar-winning script for *In the Heat of the Night*, because in a way, Sidney Poitier, the stranger who comes to town and tangles with Rod Steiger's police chief, is another version of Rambo."[4]

Just how pervasive Rambo has become was brought to Morrell's attention in Poland. He was on a publicity tour there in 2001 and was surprised by how many journalists wanted to interview him. He was even accorded the Presidential Suite in his Warsaw hotel at a time when former President Bill Clinton was visiting and was assigned a lesser suite. As Morrell explained in his essay, "Rambo and Me: The Story Behind the Story":

> So many journalists asked for interviews that I met with them for twelve hours in a row. They all spoke English. A woman in her mid-30s noted that I seemed surprised by all the attention. She said that I needed to understand how Rambo was viewed in Poland. During the Solidarity years when Polish youth protested against the Soviets, the Rambo movies were forbidden. But in the late 1980s, illegal videotapes were smuggled in. She said that protestors watched the movies to fire up their emotions. Then they put on forehead sweat bands resembling the one that Rambo wore and went out to demonstrate. In a way, she told me, Rambo helped bring down the Soviet Union.

"They must have been talking about the second and third films, not *First Blood*," Morrell clarifies. "Because the

Rambo of my novel and the film would never have been a demonstrator. The political discussions about *Rambo* came later. I remember watching newsreels when the Berlin Wall came down and somebody had written *Rambo* on one of the pieces of concrete."

Rambo continues to inspire in ways that adapt to those who look to him for guidance, inspiration, justification, and approbation. He is at once mythological and real. Nobody appreciates this more than his creator. "I can't control the way various people view the character in different ways," Morrell says, "so the professor side of me observes it as a phenomenon. When I sign copies of *First Blood,* I write, 'Best wishes from Rambo's father,' because the character is a creation—a son, if you like, who grew up and did things that were out of my control, but that are fascinating to me in the way that would fascinate a parent when watching what an offspring does."

SIDEBAR

Audie Murphy

Like John Rambo, a real-life soldier named Audie Murphy went through hell and returned after the war with greater scars on the inside than on the outside.

Audie Murphy was only fifteen when his sister helped him fake his way into the army following the Japanese attack on Pearl Harbor in December 1941 (the exact date and circumstances of his enlistment are vague). One of twelve kids in a Texas sharecropping family whose father abandoned them and whose mother died, Murphy enlisted as much to get out of what he considered to be a stultifying farm life as to serve his country. And serve it he did, eventually earning every combat award the military had, plus Belgian and

French awards for heroism. Among his most celebrated acts of heroism was single-handedly holding off a company of German soldiers at the Colmar Pocket in France in January 1945, then leading a counterattack on the Nazis despite being almost out of ammunition and wounded. All of this occurred after taking part in the 1943 Allied invasion of Sicily, the Battle of Anzio, the invasion of southern France, the liberation of Rome, and other historic battles. Like Forrest Gump, Murphy seemed to be everywhere, except, for him, life was no box of chocolates.

Peace in 1945 brought him home, where he was offered a commission to West Point, but he balked at attending because of the academic rigors for which he felt he was unprepared. Rather than allowing him to leave the service, the army sent the attractive and charismatic young hero across the country where he was celebrated with parades and public appearances as America's most decorated soldier. He left the army in the fall of 1945 and entered service in the National Guard.

It was James Cagney who brought Murphy to Hollywood in 1948 under the aegis of the production company James and his brother Bill had started, but policy disagreements among the three men kept the young actor from appearing in a film for them. Instead, he was first put into a minor role in a programmer titled *Texas, Brooklyn, and Heaven*. In 1951, director John Huston starred Murphy as Henry Fleming in his film of Stephen Crane's classic novel *The Red Badge of Courage*. Casting America's bravest soldier as a Civil War soldier who runs from battle was a cheeky move on Huston's part, and the film was a notorious flop. Five years later, however, Murphy starred in the film version of his 1949 memoir, *To Hell and Back*, which was a box office gold mine, and thereafter he embarked on a screen career, mostly in Westerns, for which he was eminently qualified, given his expertise with guns. In 1958, esteemed filmmaker Joseph L. Mankiewicz starred Murphy in his film of Graham Greene's novel *The Quiet American*, after which the actor returned to his Western roles. In one of his best, *No Name on the Bullet* (1959), he portrays a notorious gunman whose mere presence drives a Western town into a panic. In action scenes in another of his Westerns, *Posse from Hell* (1961), Murphy's eyes display an intensity that suggests he was reliving combat in World War II.

Movie stardom proved no cure for Murphy's inner turmoil. He was known to sleep with a loaded pistol, was subject to insomnia, depression, headaches, and vomiting—the textbook symptoms of post-traumatic stress disorder. For a time, he was addicted to a sedative, but broke his dependency by sequestering himself in a hotel until he had withdrawn. By the time of the Korean War, Murphy was still in the public eye, and he used his fame to speak publicly about the stress that soldiers suffer in combat. He contemplated writing a second book about how the military had trained him for combat but failed to do the reverse and de-train him for peacetime and continued to make Westerns and television appearances through 1969. Married twice, with two sons, he was killed in a plane crash on May 28, 1971, and buried with full honors in Arlington National Cemetery.

His death occurred as Morrell was finishing his novel.

SIDEBAR

Synopsis of the Novel *First Blood*

Part One

A bearded, scraggly-looking young man tries to thumb a ride through the small town of Madison, Kentucky. The kid's name is Rambo.[5] He's confronted by chief of police[6] Wilfred "Will" Teasle, who makes him get in his squad car, then drives him to the other end of town, where he lets him off with a warning to keep moving. After Teasle leaves, Rambo, who has heard this all before, heads back into Madison. There, Teasle intercepts him again at a diner and tells the cook to make the kid's burgers to go. Rambo spots an American Legion pin on Teasle's uniform and sees he's a Korean War vet. Rambo tries to be cordial, but Teasle turns everything he says into insubordination and again drives him to the far end of town. There, Rambo finishes his food and ponders what the Vietnam War has done to him. He decides to go back to Madison. En route, thinking about how he has been treated like this in fifteen previous towns, he vows not to let it happen again.

Rambo waits for Teasle to find him. Teasle checks with radioman Deputy Shingleton at the police station for a message from his estranged wife. Then Teasle easily locates Rambo and tells him to get in the car again. Rambo challenges him at every stage as they drive to the station. With neither man backing down, Teasle gets the justice of the peace, Dobzyn, to book Rambo for vagrancy and resisting arrest. At the jail, the deputies make Rambo strip and shower; when he takes off his shirt, they see scars all over his torso. Deputies Shingleton and Galt attempt to shave him and cut his hair. Rambo flashes back to his confinement and torture as a POW in Vietnam and reacts instinctively by slashing Galt's guts open with the shaving razor. He then grabs Shingleton's gun, shoots Deputy Preston, and rushes from the jail naked, commandeering a motorcycle to escape. Although deputies give chase, Rambo eludes them, vowing to give "a fight Teasle would wish to God he had never started."

Part Two

Teasle and Shingleton race recklessly after Rambo. Teasle strives to catch him before the state police arrive. Deputies Ward and Lester, already in pursuit, get stuck in a stream. Orval Kellerman and his dogs arrive with a policeman. Teasle gives orders to Orval, his old mentor, but then backs off out of respect. As night falls, Orval resists sending his dogs into the woods. Seeing Teasle's determination, he asks, "What did this kid do to you?"[7]

Rambo follows a stream. As he runs, his naked body is lacerated by tree branches. He freezes when a father and son aim a flashlight at him. They have a rifle. When they don't immediately shoot him, Rambo guesses that they are moonshiners protecting their illegal still. He says that he's running from the police and offers to lead the posse away from them if they give him clothes and the rifle, a .30-30 lever-action. They share some corn liquor, the deal is struck, and they go their separate police-evading ways.

By morning, Teasle and Orval are awake. Teasle remembers the equally cold mornings when he served in Korea in 1950. Orval wants to talk about Teasle's wife leaving him, but Teasle does not. Ward, Lester, and a third deputy hear one of Orval's dogs barking in the distance. Shingleton and Mitch, another deputy, arrive from town with hot food. Shingleton reports that he persuaded the state police to block the roads but insisted that they leave Rambo to Teasle.

A helicopter scouts the terrain with its passenger, Deputy Lang, firing shots at the ground while the pilot keeps the machine steady.

Teasle cannot see Rambo, but he still calls out to him to surrender. In the chase, Orval's dogs start yapping and pull him ahead of Teasle.

Rambo is chased to the edge of a cliff. He secures his rifle and tries finding handholds and footholds so he can work his way down the steep façade. The copter sees him and descends. Lang commences firing, coming close as Rambo clings to the rock wall. Steadying himself on a tree branch, Rambo takes aim at the copter gunman and shoots him in the head. Then he shoots at the pilot; the copter becomes so unstable that it crashes to the rocks below and explodes. Rambo makes his way to the ground and hides under cover. He sees Teasle but decides against killing him. He does, however, shoot two of Orval's six dogs, panicking the others, three of whom jump off the cliff and drag a deputy with them. The deputies fire wildly at where they think Rambo is, and Teasle has a tough time getting them to stop wasting ammunition. One of the deputies is so frightened that he soils himself. Rambo shoots Orval, wounding him. Teasle contacts the state police, who advise him that they cannot send anyone to fetch the wounded Orval because a storm is coming in. They also tell Teasle that Rambo is a Green Beret and Medal of Honor recipient.

At the bottom of the gorge, Rambo finds the body of the deputy and the dogs that fell off. He takes the deputy's gun and clothes and renews his vow to get even with Teasle for the fifteen times other cops hassled him because of his appearance. Vowing revenge, rather than try to escape, he stays to fight.

By now, Orval has died. As the posse continues, they hear four rifle shots and realize that Rambo has shot four more men. Teasle, Shingleton, Ward, and Mitch head toward the sound. Ward is shot dead. Teasle goes off to track Rambo. On the way back, he finds Mitch with his throat cut and then hears Shingleton get shot. With all Teasle's deputies now dead, it's one-on-one between Teasle and Rambo. Teasle runs through the woods to escape. Rambo holds off killing him because he wants to be able to see Teasle's face when he does it. Teasle reaches a road and collapses. A state trooper, driving along the road, sees him and radios for help.

Part Three

Teasle commiserates with Captain Dave Kern of the state police as the Kentucky National Guard assembles to join the manhunt. Teasle and Kern lament the lack of professionalism among the guardsmen and Kern offers him absolution for his dead deputies, reminding Teasle that it's the kid who killed them. Teasle takes a pill for his heart. They face the problem that this terrain has never been properly mapped.

Amid the activity, a man arrives looking for Teasle. This is Colonel Samuel Trautman, who claims responsibility for Rambo, explaining that he trained him for Special Forces and adding that Rambo was the best student he ever had. He offers to help. Teasle accepts.

Rambo awakens in a cave; he must have stumbled there and passed out. Working his way up to the entrance, he finds that night has fallen and sees flickering lights below him from a search party. He has a fever. He lights a fire and discovers that he's in an old mine. As he wonders about how he'll survive, he hears shooting outside.

Teasle[8] tries to seem confident while Kern is there, but the carnage around him is oppressive. Trautman reveals that he researched Teasle's Korean War record—he was at the fierce Chosin Reservoir battle—and wonders if Teasle is acting out a personal blood feud as a Korean vet against a Vietnam vet. Teasle realizes that Rambo must have seen his military honors citation on his office wall and respects him. Trautman reveals that Rambo "gave up three years to enlist in a war that was supposed to help his country, and the only trade he came out with was how to kill." He explains that he wants to help

Teasle because he understands Rambo and can go through his pain with him.[9] There is no discussion of the men Rambo has killed.

Rambo kills, cooks, and eats an owl. His chest is swollen and painful from the forest thrashing.

Teasle surveys the cadres of state police and guardsmen who assemble and wait for sunup. With Orval, Shingleton, and the others gone, he ponders why he himself didn't kill anyone when he returned from Korea, but this kid did when he returned from Vietnam. Why? He doesn't understand. He gives the order to go.

Rambo hears the men coming. He follows them, unseen, waiting for—what? Something. He hears dogs and hides in a stream. He considers surrender, but what then? The men are close. There are a lot of them. Kern and Teasle differ on Rambo's strategy, and Trautman begins to lose patience with them.

Back inside his cave, Rambo hears guardsmen outside. He yells to them that he wants to surrender to Teasle, but then he feels a breeze from the far end of the tunnel and realizes there's another way out. Holding a quickly fashioned torch, he feels his way through the cave and is suddenly in an enclosure of bats, stepping in a pile of their guano and the accompanying guano-eating beetles.

Teasle is faring no better than Rambo. Injured from the trek, sick from his heart condition, he rejects going to a hospital and is brought back to his office. He is surprised when his estranged wife, Anna, calls from California to tell him she's not coming back to him.

That night, Rambo steals a police cruiser and a supply of dynamite and begins setting the town afire. Trautman calls to him on a bullhorn to surrender. Teasle tries using a police car to block Rambo, but Rambo rams it and keeps going, setting off explosions throughout the town. Then he gets out and stalks Teasle, first blowing up his office and all his mementos, and finally shooting him. Waiting for a doctor, Teasle brags to Kern and Trautman how he outfoxed Rambo. Trautman loads his shotgun and heads off to get Rambo. Teasle demands to do it himself; he even summons the strength to follow Trautman although he is mortally wounded.

Shot in the chest, in agony, Rambo plans to commit suicide by blowing himself up with his last stick of dynamite. Instead, Trautman shoots him in the head with a shotgun. Teasle reluctantly respects Rambo, even admires him. Then he dies as well.

SIDEBAR

Stirling Silliphant

March 22, 1963, was an important date for Stirling Silliphant, just as it was for American television. That was when "Fifty Miles from Home" aired on *Route 66*, the TV series Silliphant had created with producer Herbert (Bert) Leonard three years earlier.

Silliphant wrote the episode, which introduced a new character, Lincoln Case, played by Glenn Corbett. Corbett replaced George Maharis, who had begun the series starring opposite Martin Milner when it debuted on CBS on October 7, 1960, but was having health problems and had missed a number of episodes.

Corbett was not only new to *Route 66*, but Linc Case was also new to American network series television: He was a Vietnam veteran. He was short-tempered, bellicose, and seething with inner turmoil. In his introductory episode, Case severely beats a young basketball player whom Tod Stiles (Milner) is coaching. In short order, Tod also has a fight with

Case, after which the two men reach an understanding and take off together on their pilgrims' progress. They traveled until the series ended on March 20, 1964, and both the actors, their characters, and their Corvette went their separate ways.

By that time, the Vietnam War was in full swing. In May 1962, President Kennedy had sent five hundred troops to the Southeast Asian country, increasing the seven hundred that former President Eisenhower had deployed when the US took over from the French at Dien Bien Phu in 1954. By the time *Route 66* went off the air ten years later, an additional eleven thousand military "advisors" had been seconded to the South Vietnamese Army.

The war was not something most Americans were following at all, let alone closely, before 1963, when horrific newsreels were broadcast of Buddhist monks setting themselves on fire in protest. Heavily censored by the Pentagon, early combat news film (there were no video or satellite hookups) showed US troops seeking a hidden enemy.

Silliphant, who had begun moving away from his Protestant upbringing and toward Buddhist precepts through his martial arts studies with Bruce Lee (whom he introduced to American television), took notice of what was happening in all of Southeast Asia, not just Vietnam. He was moved to write about it, but no network was interested in producing anything to do with the war, especially a controversial one. Even six years after it ended, nobody wanted to touch another script he'd written that dared to show both sides. It was titled *Fly Away Home* (1981).

"*Fly Away Home* was designed to be a one-year, twenty-two-hour novel for television about the Vietnam War from the Tet Offensive in 1968 until the fall of Saigon in 1975 when the last of the invaders butted out," Silliphant said.[10] "ABC let us make the two-hour pilot, but whatever flicker of courage had caused the network to authorize me to develop such a bold and daring show suddenly was extinguished. I suspect that New York [ABC's headquarters] shot it down. The salespeople probably said to the West Coast, 'You fucking idiots, what are you guys doing? What corporation is going to sponsor *this* thing?'

"I can't even begin to tell you what a crushing blow it was to have this miniseries aborted in the way it was. It sent me into weeks of destructive behavior. I went public. I announced—imagine, I, a lone writer without resources or power—that never again would I work for ABC until certain executives were fired. And I named them. Well, three years later I was back at ABC; all the guilty had been expunged. Vengeance would have been sweet had their dismissals come as a result of my pissing in the wind. But, no, simple attrition did them in. They're gone—and I'm still producing[11]—so possibly there, and there only, can one isolate the triumph, meaningless as it may be. But the bitter bottom line is that what might have been a major contribution to the American psyche—airing the issues of the US involvement in Indochina—never came to being.

"I think the thing that haunted me the most was the fact that for once in all my years of writing I had actually written the last line of dialogue for a script which would have run 1,320 pages and covered a period of seven tumultuous years, cross-cut between Vietnam and the States—and never got to use it. The line was to be spoken by the news cameraman, the part played by Bruce Boxleitner, as, remaining behind after the Americans abandoned Saigon, he is photographing the first NVA tank breaking through the fence at the Presidential Palace. He looks at the faces of South Vietnamese— faces without expression—a series of cameos which tell you nothing—and everything. And he says, more to himself than to anybody, 'Won't anybody say—we're sorry?'

"Over and out. I never got to use the line. And to this moment nobody—no American I have ever heard, certainly nobody in either our government or in our military hierarchy—has ever spoken those absolving words: WE'RE SORRY!"

To the day of his death on April 26, 1996, Silliphant bore scars from the network's sabotage of *Fly Away Home*.

SIDEBAR

How About Them Apples?

Some things get their names from people; these are called eponyms. There doesn't seem to be a word for people who get their names from things, although from time to time it happens. Actress Swoozie Kurtz, for example, is named after a Flying Fortress called "the Swooze" piloted in World War II by her father, Frank Kurtz. Playwright Thomas Lanier Williams III, born in Mississippi, was given the nickname Tennessee by University of Iowa classmates to make fun of his Southern accent.[12] George Lucas's archaeologist adventurer Henry Walton Jones, Jr., got his nickname "Indiana" from a malamute that Lucas owned in the 1970s.

And John J. Rambo, the central figure of *First Blood*, is named after an apple.

As David Morrell has explained in various interviews, he hit upon the name Rambo while writing *First Blood* in Pennsylvania, where he was a student at Penn State, after his wife, Donna, came home from shopping at a roadside fruit stand with a bag of Rambo apples. As a literature major, Morrell was familiar with the French poet Arthur Rimbaud, whose name is pronounced similarly, but "Rambo" had punch. It was short, forceful, and active enough to fit the coiled, disaffected former soldier in the story he was working on. The first name *John* is not in the novel. Used only in the movies, it conjures the Civil War era song "When Johnny Comes Marching Home" by Patrick Sarsfield Gilmore.[13]

The origin of the Rambo apple, however, is more obscure. The name is said to be traceable to Peter Gunnarsson Rambo, a Swedish immigrant to America, who hailed from Ramberget on the island of Hisingen, Sweden, and planted apple trees on his farm after he arrived in the yet-to-be-formed United States in 1640.[14] For a long time, there were rumors that the apples derived from a cutting of one of the trees that had been planted by John "Johnny Appleseed" Chapman in the 1800s, but this seems to have been a folk legend.

The Rambos are described as having greenish-yellow skin spotted with dull red, covered overall with a "grayish bloom." They ripen midway through the autumn and are good for eating, cooking, and making applesauce. Of the hundred or so varieties of eating apples grown in America, the Rambo has two distinct strains: the regular Rambo and the more common heirloom summer Rambo. The latter type generally appears in stores toward the end of August. The French name for apple is *pomme*, but for the Rambo it is *Rambour*.

Because of the success of the films, Rambo has come to mean the Sylvester Stallone movie character first and the gentle *Malus pumila* second.[15]

CHAPTER 3

Sylvester Stallone:
The Man Who Became Rambo

It has become a part of Hollywood lore how Sylvester Stallone, then a twenty-nine-year-old actor, was tired of playing walk-ons as thugs in Neil Simon and Woody Allen films[1] and began writing screenplays for himself geared toward a more positive image. When his friends told him how unsympathetic his characters came off in those scripts, he decided to turn one of them, about a fighter, into a love story. He rewrote it in a marathon three-and-a-half-day session, then held on to it through poverty and depression until he got it produced.[2] The script, of course, was *Rocky*, and it was not only *about* an underdog, but it was *by* an underdog. Although Stallone quickly became an overdog in the Hollywood kennel, he never lost sight of his audience, so that when he was offered *First Blood* in 1981 after a dozen others had turned it down, he saw it both as a challenge to himself as an actor and as something important he could say to veterans.

Stallone was passionate about the message he wanted the film to convey to those who had served their country: that they did their job, they did what was asked of them, that Vietnam was not a war that they themselves had declared, and that they had no choice in its outcome. Nevertheless, they had to suffer the national backlash. This is what motivated Rambo's breakdown speech when confronted by Trautman at the end of the first film: how he was really America's child and fought for America, yet now he cannot even get a job parking cars. Is this the reward for patriotism and service to the country? Said the star, "I started reading up on vets and their actual words, situations, traumas. And I said, 'Wow, if I could put a couple of beats from about twenty different guys' lives, jumble them up, because Rambo hasn't spoken in years, so he's not coming out fluid, there's just this rush, this purging . . . It took me a while to really absorb all these stories and put it in this kind of crazy monologue that was not in the screenplay."[3]

The meaning of patriotism itself became a battleground during the antiwar era. Stallone was caught in the middle. He confessed to having had mixed feelings about the Vietnam War. At first, he said, he was very much behind it, but as it became clear that the United States had no chance of winning, he realized that the men who fought it had become pawns. Complicating his enlightenment was the negative way in which returning soldiers were being treated by the antiwar movement. Not only had they had to fight the enemy abroad, they now had to endure the enmity of those at home. It was a loss of innocence, he reasoned, for men to learn that their country would not back them up.

This is the quandary faced by Rambo in *First Blood* that culminates with his breakdown at the end of the film. Even more taxing was returning to that same frightening emotional place when he later made *Rambo: First Blood Part II.* The contrast between Rambo and Rocky for him could not have been more stark.

"Where Rambo wants to die, Rocky is looking forward to life," he said. "Rambo's more difficult to play because the outcome of the Rocky films is a foregone conclusion; you know he's going to fight again, that he's going to win.[4] When I made [*First Blood*], I was Rambo. I was withdrawn, brooding, hard to live with. When I came back to this luxury [referring to his home, where he was interviewed], I couldn't talk for two weeks. That's when my marriage fell apart."[5] And yet, "the day I start thinking of [Rambo] as an action star only, the day I start thinking about a part, I know that I'm in the wrong movie. The last thing I need in a film role is a lot of analyzing. For me, it's got to be emotional. It's all got to come from [the heart]."[6]

This metamorphosis from angry loner to avenging angel drew Stallone and the films away from Morrell's original concept of a warrior designed for battle who was also damaged by it. In subsequent films, the character was not just settling his own score, but also those of others. His entire persona is driven by emotion. If Stallone appears to have vacillated over the years between attacking a role intellectually versus approaching it emotionally, this shows his development as a performer and as the man who plays Rambo. He admits that Rambo brought out his darker side, quoting a line he wrote for *Rambo II*:[7] "To win a war you have to become war." At some point, he said, Rambo just had to shelve his conscience and do whatever he had to do in order to win. The actor was not unaware that this led to the character of Rambo and the Rambo films being wildly interpreted and misinterpreted over the years, particularly in the sequels, where he has seemingly overcome his PTSD enough to instill it in others. The man who internalized war now wages it. As he describes the toll, Stallone blurs the line between himself and the fictional man he personified for thirty-seven years. The risk was that, as Rambo became bigger than life, he became a caricature rather than a character, and his films became fantasies rather than dramas despite the increasing political consciousness behind them.

"The character of Rambo does win a major moral battle in that he finally comes to terms with what he is," Stallone told interviewer John C. Tibbetts when *Rambo III* was released. "That, to him, is a search he has had since the end of Vietnam. Rambo finally understands his character. He has been denying his birthright. He is born to be a warrior. He is born to be involved in a cause. [But he has] discovered his peaceful side; he lives in a Buddhist temple, and he is at peace there, he really is. But there's also a side to him that needs fulfillment. He goes back and forth, meandering, and my philosophy is don't deny another aspect of your life just because you want to be considered peaceful. There's a side that is just as valid because it's a survival side."[8]

In *First Blood*, Rambo is largely wordless. In his subsequent adventures, he also withdraws into silence at times, always being the observer until he is drawn to action just when the film needs it. His mind does not drift; it just looks inward. It's important to remember that the character is not unintelligent—he is, after all, a highly trained Special Forces operative—but he has become relatively inarticulate. This, Stallone admitted, was Rambo's weakness—the inability to express himself and then to analyze and pursue it without debate. This loss of the ability to communicate led him to believe that he was expendable, a man who remains outside, waiting to be called into action. Having reached that point, what could possibly stop him? Joked Stallone in an interview, "Well, if he gets into a fight with Rocky, that could put an end to both."[9]

This characterization is in contrast with Stallone himself, who is articulate to the point of being garrulous and charmingly funny. It was a trait he had to redirect in his rewrites, burying his natural desire to talk by giving the burden of exposition to other actors. This worked in *First Blood* because he sublimated his words into body language. With *Rambo: First Blood Part II*, he honed his physique to the point where all he had to do was get dressed according to ritual and then just stand there. Other characters set the terms and the conflict.

Stallone constructed his portrayal of Rambo by combining what was in the book with what was in himself. He added to Morrell's creation by making Rambo German and a Native American, a man of the land more than of people, and decided that he found the military uniform physically confining, so he chucked it. He said he added a romanticism to Rambo, making him present in this century but actually out of his time, a throwback to an earlier Americana, or perhaps even to a Shogun warrior or medieval knight-errant. But the most important aspect of Rambo was that he had what Stallone called a total death wish: He may have been lucky to escape but was not afraid to die.

Throughout his career, Stallone has sought to mix his macho roles with lighter ones, usually with success, even though he more than holds his own in interviews despite his frequently minimalist dramatic performances. He claims to have turned down the chance to play Han Solo in *Star Wars* because he couldn't bring himself to "go around in leotards spraying people with a ray gun." He said he lost out on *Superman* because director Richard Donner said he wasn't tall enough. He also reported that he passed on, or withdrew from, *Beverly Hills Cop* and *The Cotton Club*.[10] And his decades-long desire to play writer Edgar Allan Poe has long since been consigned to memory, if only because he feared his Rocky image would inspire the public to mockingly refer to it as *Yo, Poe!*[11]

Richard Crenna, his costar in the first three Rambo films, praises Stallone. "I've worked with so many people through the years who've had a tendency to forget their pasts, forget their beginnings," he said. "I find that most unattractive because, as actors, we're the sum total of all our experiences. And where we began is as important as where we are now. Well, Sly has never forgotten where he came from and what he went through to get where he is. He's always talking about the little bit he did in this film or that film. I find it so healthy that he manages to keep all of that in focus. He's the first to poke fun at his screen image."[12]

Nevertheless, there are contradictions roiling within the seventy-seven-year-old (at this writing) actor. He has a belief in spiritualism instilled by his mother, who favored astrology, and says that he and his then-wife Sasha conceived one of their sons so that he would be born under the sign of Taurus. Although his Rambo is a gifted Special Forces fighter, Stallone himself says he was rejected from the army because of a bizarre rock concert injury. "I had been drinking too much at a Canned Heat concert," he confessed to *Los Angeles Magazine*, "and I fell asleep into a speaker which was about the size of a small cave. I woke up after the concert and my hearing was off. I've been having trouble listening to the blues ever since."[13] This exemption from military service allowed the nineteen-year-old to spend the early years of the Vietnam War at the American College in Leysin, Switzerland, on a scholarship, acting in *Death of a Salesman* and teaching physical education to wealthy American girls.[14]

Despite this—or perhaps because of it—Stallone has come to a place of peace with himself and his image, whether boxer, soldier, cop, expendable, or one of the many other roles he has assumed. "You just take from your life experiences, and I've had many peaks and valleys. It's confounding because you think, at your age, you acquire a surety of choice and perception. Quite often it's just the opposite: you realize that, the older you get, the less certain everything is. I'm not sure if I trust my own impressions anymore."[15]

CHAPTER 4

Drawing First Blood

Hindsight being 20/20, *First Blood* was always a hit movie, it just took a decade to get made. In 1972, David Morrell's highly praised novel was immediately optioned for production, then embarked on a Toonerville Trolley tour of practically every studio in Hollywood before being saved by two independent producers who'd never done a picture before. The journey was as emotionally taxing as the one undertaken by its hero and just as fraught with danger.

Hollywood was reluctant to make any film set in Vietnam while the increasingly unpopular war was raging. Marshall Thompson's formulaic *A Yank in Viet Nam* (1964), Will Zens's *To the Shores of Hell* (1966), and John Wayne's hawkish *The Green Berets* (1968) were notable exceptions, particularly *The Green Berets*, which was released by a major studio, Warner Bros. By contrast, when *First Blood* was published, it was attractive not only for its storytelling skill but also because it was set, not in Southeast Asia, but in America, though Vietnam was never more than an emotional click away. Significantly, it showed the human ravages of the war rather than the war itself.

This did not, however, make it a slam dunk in Hollywood. While Morrell's intent was to show the effects of the war on those who had fought it, and the cost to the society that had sent them there, a film adaptation would need to be careful about how it approached these incendiary themes.

Producer-director Stanley Kramer was the first to take

aim. The fiercely independent Kramer, known for films that deliver a social message as well as entertainment, originally expressed interest in *First Blood* in early 1972 prior to the book's publication. Kramer had suffered two flops in a row (*R.P.M.* in 1970 and *Bless the Beasts & Children* in 1971) and was looking for a hit. He agreed to option the novel, inspiring the publisher, M. Evans and Company, to take out a display ad in *Publishers Weekly* announcing the Kramer deal. Then Kramer withdrew[1] and poured his energies instead into the action-romance *Oklahoma Crude* (1973), which did only slight business for its studio, Columbia Pictures. Producer Lawrence Turman (*The Graduate*) then heard about the novel's availability and took it to Columbia on his own. The studio purchased it for the estimable writer-director Richard Brooks. Brooks had recently made *Lord Jim* in 1965, *The Professionals* in 1966, and *In Cold Blood* in 1967, all for Columbia, although he stumbled with his next two films, the failed love story *The Happy Ending* (1969, for United Artists) and, back at Columbia, the clumsy 1971 romantic heist comedy *$*. Brooks was eager to return to thoughtful drama.

"What makes it a story damned well worth telling," Brooks told A. H. Weiler of the *New York Times*, "is the confrontation between a hunter—a veteran of World War II, a so-called 'just war' [Brooks misidentified Teasle's combat experience, which was in Korea]—and the hunted, a Vietnam hero who has killed some people upon his return from the war. The subject of the film is man against his time, a theme I feel very deeply about."[2]

Morrell, then twenty-nine, flew from the University of Iowa, where he was teaching, to meet with Turman and Brooks at Brooks's home in Los Angeles. Morrell described the awkward encounter to Brooks's biographer Douglass K. Daniel, who reported that the director, alluding to an altercation with his daughter (which the daughter said never occurred), wanted to explore the generational conflict in Morrell's novel. In the end, the townspeople and the National Guard would side with Teasle, Brooks reasoned, and Rambo would stand alone. As Teasle tried to talk to Rambo, a wild shot would ring out and both Rambo and the chief would take shelter in the same ditch (aka foxhole) against an unseen common enemy. As bullets tore at the top of the ditch, Teasle would turn to Rambo and say, "You know, none of this would have happened if we'd talked to one another," and both men would live. Casting ideas included Lee Marvin or Burt Lancaster for Teasle and Bette Davis to play the invented character of a psychiatrist. Choices to play Rambo were undesignated.

In the meeting, Brooks made the mistake of asking Morrell what he thought of the idea, and Morrell made the mistake of telling him, "It sort of sounds like I've seen it before in a cavalry movie." "Before Turman and I knew it," he says, "we were on the street."[3] Then, Morrell adds, "A few days later my agent phoned me to say that the head of Columbia Pictures had called him relaying a message from Brooks that the next time I'd have anything to do with the picture was when I bought a ticket to see it."[4]

Columbia paid Morrell $90,000[5] for the rights. Soon Turman was no longer associated with the project. After a location scout in several states and the writing of seventy-five pages of script, all of it paid for by the studio, either Brooks or Columbia called it quits, and Columbia sold the property to Warner Bros. in 1973 for $125,000. Two years later, Brooks made the Western hit *Bite the Bullet* (1975) for Columbia, and any hard feelings vanished in the flurry of profits.

Enter Canadian director Ted Kotcheff. "Robert Shapiro, who'd been my agent, was then vice president of Warner Bros.," says Kotcheff, who would ultimately direct the film, but not right away, "and he came to me one day and said, 'Would you like to develop this script?' I read the script and I read the book, and there was a whole bunch of scripts, but the best script was the one written by Michael Kozoll and William Sackheim."[6]

Ted Kotcheff, a Canadian of Eastern European descent, was attracted to *First Blood* for personal and political reasons. "All wars are stupid," he said, "but the Vietnam War was especially stupid." He spoke of a vet who, on the last day of his tour of duty, machine-gunned dozens of Viet Cong, then flew home to America to be dumped on the street without anyone to help him readjust to home life. "After finishing the book," Kotcheff continued, "I immediately agreed to take on the project. The story had a strong metaphor: An engine of violence like Rambo, once created, goes on existing and can wreak damage on the people who created it, despite the fact that he is trying to return to a normal state."[7] "Then after I had been working on it for three months, [producer] Robert Shapiro said, 'We're not going to make this film'" because it was too close to the Vietnam War and Shapiro felt the American people—who had just elected Ronald Reagan as president—didn't want to hear about it anymore.[8]

First Blood soon became the Hollywood starlet that everyone wanted to date but no one wanted to marry. In January 1973, Warner Bros.' production vice president Richard Shepherd announced that he had bought it for Martin Ritt,[9] who had been signed to direct,[10] followed by the studio's head John Calley saying that he was trying to entice Robert De Niro and Clint Eastwood to star. Producer Frederick Rollin "Buzz" Feitshans, who had just turned in *Big Wednesday* for the studio, asked that film's director/cowriter John Milius to script it. Milius passed at the time but would return later; Feitshans would remain. John Huston was briefly interested[11] but backed off when he heard that Walter Newman (*Ace in the Hole, Cat Ballou*) had written a script for Martin Ritt and didn't want to become involved with another director's project.[12] Ritt, one of the few progressive filmmakers able to get financing for controversial subjects, wanted to make *First Blood* as a commentary on Vietnam and the military mentality that created Rambos, with Trautman being the villain. He wanted Paul Newman as Rambo and Robert Mitchum as Teasle. "I can never condone murder," Ritt said, "so I cannot think of Rambo as a hero."[13]

The project next passed through Sydney Pollack's hands with Steve McQueen as Rambo and Burt Lancaster as Teasle, except McQueen, then forty-two, would have been too old.[14] By 1975 it was agent-turned-producer Martin Bregman who suggested his former client Al Pacino as Rambo with a screenplay by David Rabe that eliminated Trautman and ended with Teasle killing Rambo.[15] Pacino, who had just done *Dog Day Afternoon* with Bregman,[16] thought Rambo was too violent and left the project.[17] The Rabe script intrigued Mike Nichols for a brief time, and then Martin Ritt reentered when producer Ray Stark took over the Rambo reins. In 1977, there was a breakthrough when the Michael Kozoll and William Sackheim[18] screenplay drew John Badham's (*War Games*) attention. Badham wanted John Travolta (with whom he had just worked on *Saturday Night Fever*) as Rambo and George C. Scott as Trautman (drawing on Scott's *Patton* brand) with Gene Hackman and Charles Durning vying for Teasle. This got producer Carter DeHaven involved. DeHaven arranged an option from Warner Bros.,[19] had Kozoll change the ending to make Rambo live, and, with financing from the investment company Cinema Group,[20] brought John Frankenheimer to the table. Frankenheimer wanted Brad Davis, hot from *Midnight Express* (1978), although Powers Boothe,

Michael Douglas, and Nick Nolte were also considered.[21]
He even chased Gene Hackman through Hackman's agent,
Sue Mengers.[22] Frankenheimer had David Giler (*The Paral-
lax View*) briefly work on the script for five days. Said Giler,
"There's hardly anyone in town who wasn't involved."[23]

The project was on the boards at Filmways, an independent company that had absorbed American International
Pictures, when Filmways was itself taken over by Orion Pictures, who killed it.[24] Ironically, Orion would wind up distributing the finished film in 1982.

Enter Andrew Vajna and Mario Kassar, whose Carolco
Pictures was a foreign sales company and had been looking to
expand into producing their own product instead of distributing that of others.[25] "We started to find out how to option it
and we found out it was already at Warner Bros.," recalls Kassar. "They'd had it for a few years and done many different
screenplays for every actor in Hollywood. You name it; they
tried every A-list actor and it didn't work. And it's interesting:
In those days, when you wanted to buy something from one
of the studios that they had on the shelf gathering dust, you'd
go and negotiate and try to buy it. But years later a movie
called *Home Alone* (1990) happened that Warners had and
they [decided not to go forward] and Fox picked it up and
made a fortune on it. So what happens now is that you can get
something out of [Warner Bros.], but when you go to do it on
your own, you have to come back and give them first shot at
distributing it because they don't want to lose face anymore.
But they were very happy [with *First Blood*]; they asked me
for $350,000 with all the rights, all the script drafts, and I
took it, and they couldn't wait to get out."[26] Carolco also paid
Cinema Group $150,000 for the Sackheim-Kozoll script.[27]

(As for where the money came from, see Chapter 5,
"Rambo Unleashed: The Carolco Adventure.")

At one point, Vajna asked John Milius (*Apocalypse Now*) to return and do some script work,[28] as well as Larry Gross (*48 HRS.*).[29] It was Gross who added the idea that Rambo would steal a two-way radio from one of the sheriff's deputies through which he and Trautman would later communicate.[30]

With the 1978 release of both *The Deer Hunter* and *Go Tell the Spartans* and the 1979 release of *Apocalypse Now*, Vajna and Kassar reasoned that the public was beginning to accept films about Vietnam.[31] That's when Sylvester Stallone's name came up.

Continues Kassar, "We had just arrived in town; I didn't know anybody. It's a very social kind of thing. The first person I approached was [lawyer] Jake Bloom. I knew Jake Bloom and his partner, Tom Pollack. I knew a writer called David Giler. I met a director called Ted Kotcheff. Through Jake I said, 'You know, I think Stallone would be perfect for this thing.' Jake took it to him and Sly showed interest and slowly, slowly we got through it—even though, at one time, he changed his mind, then he went back into it. It's a long story; it's a whole chapter on its own. Stallone was not at the height of his career. He made *Rocky*, but then he made a couple of movies that didn't do very well or did [just] okay, *F.I.S.T.* and *Paradise Alley*. Of course, I'm a newcomer and I have to pay my dues to get anybody, so they asked me for a lot of money for Stallone in those days."

Stallone seemed eager to play Rambo but wanted $3.5 million. Carolco's counteroffer was the same $3.5 million but divided into $2 million for the movie and $1.5 million from eventual television sales. "I agreed to it," Kassar says. "We made a deal and he said, 'I have to fix the role' and write on it. Fine; the guy can write, there's no question about it. But after a while I got a call from his business manager, Herb Nanas, that Sly had changed his mind and he didn't want to do it anymore. I said, 'Okay,' and we went to a meeting, and on the way down in the elevator afterward I said to my partner, 'You know what? Let's go back up. I have this idea that maybe I can bring up something.' So we went back up and said to Herb, 'It's okay that he doesn't want to act in it. That's fine; we'll find another actor. But he's the only one that knows the character so well, and he wrote it so well, can we make a deal that he keeps on writing the character?' I had a feeling that if he started getting into it, he could come back. He started work and after that he said, 'I want to do it.' I said, 'Fine, perfect.' That's how we got him.[32] Of course everybody in town thought, 'Here are the two foreigners, what are they doing?' In fact, we asked ourselves, 'What *are* we doing?'"[33]

Now multiple recollections begin to intersect. Kotcheff had wanted Stallone all along. "I thought Stallone had both the toughness that the role demanded but, more importantly, the poignancy," the director said. "And, watching all of his performances, I thought that, with the right material and me as director, he could give as outstanding a performance as Robert De Niro or Al Pacino." He was surprised when Stallone accepted the day after he was sent the script.[34]

Stallone had different concerns. His recent non-*Rocky* projects had indeed done poorly, and he needed a hit that demonstrated his acting range.[35] Rambo fit the bill. Stallone had heard of *First Blood* in 1980 as he was wrapping *Nighthawks*, and became attracted to the ideas of a super soldier who waged undeclared war on the people who had created him. There were Frankenstein elements about it where the monster, Rambo, turned on his maker, Trautman. According to Hollywood protocol, there was just one problem: The script had been through more hands than a relay-race baton. That didn't deter Stallone, who had been nominated for an Oscar for writing *Rocky*, from adding his own touches. With the exception of John Huston's

Victory (aka *Escape to Victory*, 1981), Stallone had been rewriting the films in which he appeared, and for *First Blood* he turned in seven rewrites of the Kozoll-Sackheim script between July and November 1981.[36] His goal (according to a note on the 2002 *First Blood* DVD) was to make Rambo less psychotic, a conclusion reinforced by Stallone's charismatic portrayal.

"I said if I'm going to get involved in this, I want to rewrite the screenplay," Stallone recalled. "I want him to go right to the edge . . . a kind of feral ferocity that even shocks me, this contorted face and rage. Not hard to figure out where that came from; my father was Rambo in reality. Nothing was ever settled verbally. You did not mess with this guy. Look, it was genetic. I saw the opportunity to do what I considered the first pure action film, that this thing is completely done kinetically, there's just so much movement that dialogue can't be handled by the star, it has to be handled by Trautman and other people."[37]

Finally, director Ted Kotcheff, who had been approached in 1976, was hired. He recalls, "One day they said to me, 'We'd like you to make a film for us. Do you have anything you want to make?' I said, 'Yeah, I worked on and developed a script at Warner Bros., which is a great property called *First Blood*. We sent [the script] to [Stallone] on a Monday and on Tuesday afternoon Sylvester Stallone answered that he was going to do it. In the whole history of my filmmaking, forty years of directing films, this is the first time that: (a) I got my first choice; (b) that I got it within twenty-four hours."[38]

"We chose Ted Kotcheff as a director for two very simple reasons," Mario Kassar states, "and that's very honest. He was one of the very few directors we met in Hollywood when we'd just arrived here. He was very funny, very nice. He did a movie which we like very much with Richard Dreyfuss, *The*

Apprenticeship of Duddy Kravitz (1974). And also there were those Canadian tax deals, so it kind of worked out."[39]

By this time, nine years, eighteen drafts (if not more), and at least $650,000 (not counting salaries) had been spent that would never show up on the screen. What Stallone added, however, was something that only an actor-writer can provide: audience empathy. Explaining that, in Morrell's book, Rambo is so damaged by the trauma of his Vietnam experiences that he had to die in the end and had to be put out of his misery, Stallone thought with his heart instead of his head. He used emotion. He also felt that it would be constructive for veterans watching the film to see that, as bad as life may be treating them, there can be redemption, there can be a way out other than being executed or committing suicide. Because of this positive message, Rambo had to live. Even though the story may have led logically to the conclusion that Rambo needed to die, he would inject hope that rehabilitation was possible.

And there was something else that impressed the actor. "It was the first time that I recall a character, an American, attacking America," he said, "and this was coming along at a time when we were going through a very, very right-wing era. It was a time when Republicans were coming to the forefront, even though the Democrats were in power [the 1980s]. The country was shifting, and Rambo was sort of shifting with it. He represented the seething undertone of a lot of forgotten soldiers. I didn't know that was going to happen. . . . Rambo became a symbol for jingoistic, right-wing might, when just the opposite is true. Rambo, if anything, despises his affiliation with the military."[40]

Stallone held out on this point during shooting when it came time to film the final Rambo-Trautman showdown. "At the very end, originally," he tells it, "the way it was in the script [was that] I am shot by Colonel Trautman, and I die in slow motion. And I said to the director, 'This is not good. I don't want everyone who was a Vietnam vet to see this film, and then see me shot, and then realize, 'Oh, so there's no hope for me at all. None.'" And I left, and they were screaming if I don't come back, it was a breach of contract. They screened it in Las Vegas. It tested so badly they put in the one that you see. Cuz at that time they were losing twenty thousand vets to suicide a month and I don't want to be a part of that."[41]

"Rambo's treatment by the redneck sheriff and his deputies was a microcosm of the way America had treated their returning veterans," said Ted Kotcheff. "I think the film touched a nerve of guilt and shame. Indeed, many veterans thanked me personally for what the film had to say."[42]

This was the key to making *First Blood* viewer friendly. In the book, Rambo kills scores of people; in the movie, he doesn't kill anybody, he only wounds them or they die by their own misadventure. This was a decision made by Kotcheff and Stallone to reflect how the Vietnamese did not wish to kill American soldiers but only to incapacitate them so they would be seen in wheelchairs in every American city as living reproach to the USA's involvement. This is why Rambo immobilizes but does not kill.[43] Of the four on-screen deaths—Deputy Galt and three riders in a police car chasing Rambo in his stolen army truck—all die by their own folly in the course of trying to kill him. Rambo goes out of his way not to kill anyone. Hurting them, however, is quite another matter.

Not everyone would come to agree with this decision. Quentin Tarantino, no stranger to violence in films and a passionate fan who toyed with making his own *Rambo* movie, says, "I had read David Morrell's original book. The whole point of the book is that if you take this super weapon killing machine, when the war is over keeping that switch turned off isn't so easy. That entire concept is thrown away in *First Blood*. The changing of it from Rambo murdering the posse to wounding the posse was Stallone's idea."[44]

Vajna and Kassar were prepping the shoot in Vancouver when their line producer, Ed Carlin, suffered a heart attack. To replace him, they called Buzz Feitshans, whom they had known from earlier discussions on another project. (Carlin would go on to produce three other films before his death in 1996 at age sixty-four.) Feitshans, who had been the buffer between filmmaker John Milius and executive producer Dino DeLaurentiis on *Conan the Barbarian* (1982), kept *First Blood* moving.

On November 16, 1981, the trade papers reported that the production, budgeted at $15 million, had begun in Hope, British Columbia, Canada, standing in for the novel's Madison, Kentucky.[45] Although the terrains were similar for dramatic purposes, the four thousand miles between the two locations caused weather-related problems. The filmmakers wanted grey skies for mood, but Canada provided sun—that is, when it wasn't freezing or snowing, making it difficult to match shots.[46] The higher latitude also meant shorter days, particularly in the fall and winter weeks. The production lost two months as storms swept through the Fraser Valley, dropping so much snow that to match previous shots, crews had to melt the icy deposits with butane torches[47] All told, Mother Nature stretched the shoot to five months.[48]

The delay frustrated Stallone. *First Blood* relied almost entirely on location exteriors; there were few indoor sets in which to work when weather interfered. The wasted days not only tried his patience, but they also pushed off the start of *Rocky III*. "They promised him the film would shoot for three months," said Ted Kotcheff. "He was really pissed off. One night, right in the middle of this small town in Canada, Stallone started ranting and raving and swearing a blue streak. Andy and Mario had never had to deal with a big star like this. Herb Nanas was beside me watching, and he said to me, *sotto voce,* 'In the big leagues, the fast ball comes in at ninety miles an hour.' I think that was their first experience with big-league pitching."[49]

There was another storm on the way: Kirk Douglas. The veteran star had been recruited to play Trautman after Kotcheff and Kassar had flown to San Francisco to watch him and Burt Lancaster in a production of a play about Tom Sawyer and Huckleberry Finn in their later years, *The Boys in Autumn.* The show never made it to Broadway, but Douglas made it to Vancouver for *First Blood.* Carolco even took out a double-page display ad in *Variety* announcing Douglas as Trautman.[50] But when Douglas arrived on location in full costume and ready to shoot, he carried with him a script rewrite reflecting his creative input.[51] This pleased no one except Douglas, who kept referring to himself in the third person, such as saying "Kirk Douglas wouldn't do that." In Douglas's script, Rambo died.

This disagreement followed the one that had been taking place since before production started, and the two trains were heading for a Canadian collision. "We got Kirk Douglas," Mario Kassar recalls, "and everything is in place, and I tell Stallone, 'We're going to do like the book says, you're going to die at the end.' He said, 'No, I'm not dying at the end.' I told the director, 'Well, you work it out. The book says he dies.' But Stallone doesn't want to die. He's smart, he's done *Rocky I* and *II* and he believes in sequels and franchises. I didn't think this way, I was just making my first movie and wanted to make the best movie I can. We all took it for granted that they would work it out. So now we go on location to Hope in Canada, next to Vancouver, and the night before shooting we have a big dinner and everybody's eating and drinking and I go to Ted and say, 'Ted, do me a favor. You better go see Sly and tell him Kirk wants him to die at the end and he doesn't want to die at the end. We have a problem here. So Ted goes, and I wait one or two hours, and he comes back and Ted gives me a smile. I go, okay, that must have been resolved. The next morning, six-thirty or seven, very early, it's cold and snowy in the woods, I get a call that Kirk is on his way to the airport, he's leaving. What? Well, the first scene that Kirk was to do, he went to Sly's trailer and said, 'You know, I'm going to kill you at the end,' and Sly said, 'No, you're not,' and Douglas said, 'Okay,' and went to the airport and left the city and went to LA."[52]

Contradicting this account, Army Archerd, writing for *Daily Variety*, said that Douglas (who arrived December 11 after they'd been shooting for a month[53]) was gone so fast that Stallone—who had been on location since November 14[54]—didn't have the chance to meet him, and quoted Stallone as explaining, "He wanted to approach his character (with me) as a father-son arrangement rather than as a general and the disposable combat soldier. [Otherwise] I got along fine with him."[55]

By any version of events, this was a disaster. "Kirk Douglas in the foreign marketplace was more important than Stallone," Vajna said, "so when we tried to put together this package that we were going to sell, Kirk Douglas was an important part of it. When Kirk Douglas walked out that deal fell apart—thank God, because we got a much better deal later. Kirk actually wanted to kill [Rambo] at the end. He said, 'The only way I'll do this role is for me to kill him.' So he came up and of course we didn't want to kill him at the end, even though dramatically it really worked. It became more interesting because we kept him alive. But [Douglas] left because he wanted to kill him, and we said no."[56]

At that point three versions of the ending had been scripted by various people: Rambo is killed, Rambo causes Trautman to kill him, and Rambo lives. (The second and third were shot, neither of them from Douglas's material.)

"I idolized Kirk Douglas as a young man," said Sylvester Stallone in a 2002 interview, "and still consider him a brilliant force in the acting community." (Douglas died in 2020 at age 104.) "He is a very opinionated guy. He basically accepted the script and then rewrote it. And he did a good job, but it wasn't what we had agreed to do. He shows up on the set and he has a script with thousands of, it looks like, yellow pages. He'd rewritten the whole script." Douglas's concept was that Trautman and Rambo are the same person and, at the end, Trautman becomes Rambo and Rambo gets tied to a radiator. He goes, 'No, no, no, Rambo must die.' I said, 'I understand that, but not in this movie. I just don't think it should be done. It sends out the wrong message. Every Vietnam vet who sees this will go, 'Oh, the only solution is death; death is the only thing that awaits us at the end of the tunnel.' I don't think that's the right way to do it.' He goes, 'Yes, but it's artistic.' I said, 'You're right [but] I don't think this is going to work,' and [Douglas] says, 'Okay, I quit.'" Years later, Stallone recounted, he ran into Douglas socially and brought up *First Blood*. "You know what?" he reported Douglas saying, "My way was still the better way, Sly. It was artistic. But then again, it would have cost you about a billion dollars, so maybe I'm wrong. If you'd listened to me, you would have been broke but politically and artistically correct."[57]

With Douglas gone, they needed a Trautman, and fast. William Devane's name was floated, but the producers finally agreed with Kotcheff (in consultation with casting director

Lynn Stalmaster) on Richard Crenna, who had just finished another film. How fast could he get to Canada?[58]

"I got a call from my agent on a Sunday night," Crenna said, "and he told me, 'There's a script on the way to your house. I want you to read it and get back to me.' I said, 'Fine, I'll call you tomorrow.' He says, 'Not tomorrow, tonight.' I said, 'It's eight o'clock; when is it going to be here?' He said, 'Whenever you finish it, call me.' I called him about one o'clock in the morning. I had read *First Blood* and said, 'It's a terrific script, it's great, it's wonderful; tell me.' He said, 'It's good news and bad news. Number one, they want you to play Colonel Trautman. And the bad news is, they want you to start tomorrow.' I said, 'Wait a minute, tell me what happened.' He said, 'Never mind what happened, do you want it?' I said, 'Sure, I want to play the role, it's a wonderful role.' The first actor was Kirk Douglas. It may have been 'artistic differences,' it's none of my business, I never even asked why. But to my good fortune I was the one who was selected to come in and put on the green beret."[59] It had been casting legend Lynn Stalmaster who suggested Crenna once Douglas dropped out.

Andy Vajna and Mario Kassar later issued an apology to Douglas for giving the impression, in announcing his departure on December 15, 1981, that he had breached his contract. It was "honest and professional differences" that caused the split, they told the press.[60] In the meantime, Crenna flew to Vancouver on Tuesday, December 15.[61] On Wednesday, they rushed him to the set, where they fitted him into Douglas's wardrobe, fed him his first lines from off-camera, and told him, "Action." History has shown that, in *First Blood* and two sequels, Crenna and the public were the beneficiaries of Douglas's intransigence.

"I walked into a role that hadn't been shot yet," Crenna said, "so it was a matter of Ted Kotcheff putting me into his image. Trautman was a by-the-book guy. Pure military, pure soldier. I had played that before, but never to the degree I played it here. I had a little different focus than Ted Kotcheff had, and I started to play it differently, and he really led me by the hand to what he wanted me to be in this character. I'm still not sure I agree with him entirely, but it worked."[62]

"He's so consummately professional," Morrell says of Crenna. "Nothing fazes the guy. You ask him, 'Listen, can you be in Canada on Monday and start this role?' And Richard says, 'Sure, I can do that.' I can't imagine many actors who have the experience and confidence to be able to do that. Without any preparation, he brought a kind of stillness and, at the same time, a kind of deadliness to the role."[63]

The other crucial element in *First Blood*—the Inspector Javert to Rambo's Jean Valjean, the unstoppable force against the immovable object—is Brian Dennehy's Sheriff Wilfred "Will" Teasle. Gruff but beloved by the people of Hope, Teasle, in the book, is in a crumbling marriage and compensates by focusing on his job to the extent of being suspicious of drifters. When he spots Rambo, he assumes the worst. To him, Rambo represents the soldiers who fought in Vietnam and returned home to receive attention, whereas his Korean War service has been long forgotten.[64] The film eliminates Teasle's backstory. "He has a very difficult problem in this picture," Morrell states of Dennehy, "because he really has, unlike the novel, no role to play. [He is a] very excellent actor who has to create all kinds of gestures and facial expressions in order to become a character that doesn't exist on the page."[65]

"Brian Dennehy was a man's man and an actor's actor," praised Sylvester Stallone. "The way it was scripted, the dialogue was so sparse that you had to speak with your eyes and your body and your hands. Brian Dennehy was great because he would fill in the blanks."[66]

Stallone's first scene shot for the film was supposed to be an easy one: Rambo hurrying down a woody incline and bracing himself against a tree to survey the land below. In the process of shooting it, however, Stallone pounded his side hard against the tree, bruising himself and setting the stage for the injuries to come. It got worse. Next came the spectacular stunt in which Rambo jumps off a ledge over Chapman Gorge and breaks his fall by passing through several tree branches. Buddy Joe Hooker and another stunt performer began the fall, and Stallone finished it in the next shot, landing on the ground in front of the camera. On the third take, Stallone hit the limb wrong and broke his lower rib, rupturing his spleen when he hit the ground full force; his groan of pain is real and stayed in the film.[67] Stallone should have had a premonition about the danger; while poised at the slippery, mossy edge of the precipice, he reported that he was tethered by his feet just in case he slipped, then looked around and noticed that the director and crew members were all tied to trees so they wouldn't fall with him. To make it worse, Stallone (who would later appear in two *Cliffhangers*) suffers from acrophobia.

Not that there weren't lighter moments of pain. On his Blu-ray commentary, Stallone recounts the time, just for fun, he went to a local hospital emergency room wearing the makeup appliance of his right biceps slashed open. A pump under his armpit oozed blood when he flexed. The medics went crazy when all he asked for was some aspirin, making everyone in the ER praise him for toughness. "I became an emergency room legend in Hope, Canada," he joked.[68] On a more serious note, Stallone very nearly lost his thumb when an explosive squib, representing a gunshot to the strut of the mine that Stallone was entering to escape the National Guard, went off just as he was touching it.

In the days before CGI gunshots and fire, *First Blood* used practical (real) effects that, regardless of how many safety measures were taken, might have gone awry.[69] And not just guns and fire; for a scene where Rambo emerges from a flowing river to avoid both a contingent of National Guard and to throw the tracking dogs off his scent, Stallone had to submerge himself in the bone-chilling thirty-eight-degree stream wearing only a canvas top and fatigue jeans, placing himself at risk of hypothermia.

He wasn't alone suffering for the cause. The intense gloomy, wet chill in British Columbia was oppressive. At one time or another, everyone came down with a cold or worse. Shooting in the forest was also a hazard; everyone was cautioned not to wander more than fifty yards from the group because the risk was so high of getting lost among the trees, all of which looked alike. Additionally, the steep, rocky terrain made hauling equipment a Sisyphean endeavor.

To make things even worse, there was a weapons theft. Over the weekend of January 23–24, 1982, someone got into the company's locked five-ton truck that was being guarded by four people and stole fourteen M-16 twenty-shot fully automatic rifles, three 11-gauge Remington shotguns, two 44-caliber Smith & Wesson Magnum revolvers, and eleven Colt semi-automatic AR-15s. The locks on the truck were not forced open, and although the weapons had been disabled to be used as props, "a relatively minor operation would make most of them fully operative again," said RCMP superintendent Roy Byrne. The weapons' value was placed at $50,000.[70]

Against all this off-screen drama, the actors had to find their characters. It took Stallone a few days to do so. Not until what became the opening scene of the film—Rambo shows up at Delmar's home looking for his army buddy—did it come together. Always a man of few words and containing his Vietnam experience tightly, when Rambo learns that his last remaining friend has died, his past is forever shut off to him. Shattered and alone by the time Teasle confronts him as a vagrant, Rambo reverts to his war mentality.

He fights his way out of the Hope jail and commandeers a motorcycle.[71] Stallone did his own riding until reaching the town limits, then a professional took over. And a good thing, too; speeding after the motorcycle on Hope's cold and icy streets, and then heading into the woods, the stunt driver in Teasle's squad car shot past a curve and rolled down a hill. The stunt driver was unharmed, and Dennehy squeezed into the car to replace him for close-ups.[72]

One of the traditions introduced in *First Blood* that became a fetish throughout the series was the amazing variety of ways in which Rambo dispatches his foes. (This reached its apotheosis in 2008's *Rambo IV*.) Inasmuch as Rambo doesn't directly kill people in the first film, he finds other ways to elude his pursuers, as mentioned earlier— cutting the hamstring of one, impaling another with sharpened sticks, jumping from a high tree trunk onto a third, tricking a deputy into shooting another deputy tied to a tree, and so forth. One of the most satisfying has Rambo leaping out of the brush disguised like Birnam Wood to hold his celebrated Rambo knife to Teasle's throat, warning him to call off the pursuit. (Of course, the sheriff doesn't stop or the film would end in reel three.)

Director Kotcheff and cinematographer Andrew Laszlo make the foreboding wilderness into a character; Rambo must survive the landscape as ardently as he must elude Teasle's posse. All he wants is to be left alone, but that becomes impossible once Colonel Trautman enters at the midpoint. The setting is the base camp where the state police and National Guard units have deployed their weapons (the extras are actual Hope residents who had been laid off when the area's lumber mills closed). Richard Crenna's arrival is presented by Kotcheff and Laszlo as if he is a savior entering church, his backlit form gracing the entrance of the large headquarters tent, his stern voice commanding attention. Arrogant and forceful, he speaks the truth to Teasle and the state troopers that he was the one who created Rambo and is therefore the man who can and should take him down. Crenna's characterization—remember, he was searching for it as film was running through the camera—runs in contrast to what would have been Kirk Douglas's concept of the hunter.[73]

First Blood is an elegantly photographed film. Andrew Laszlo (*The Warriors, Streets of Fire*) worked under dreadful conditions: short days, shadowy forests, minimal light inside Rambo's cave—contrasting the primeval setting and the violence within it. Kotcheff, whose directorial range goes from comedies such as *Fun with Dick and Jane* (1977) and *Weekend at Bernie's* (1989) to dramas like *Uncommon Valor* (1983) and *The Apprenticeship of Duddy Kravitz* (1974), was at home in his native Canada, guiding the film with invisible firmness.

As with all effective action films, the location became a character. When Rambo is forced into an abandoned mine by the National Guardsmen who blast the entrance closed with a rocket, the interior was shot, according to Stallone's Blu-ray commentary track, in an actual cave. Kotcheff, Laszlo, and a minimal crew followed him inside, lighting the scenes with no more than matches and a torch. It was hazardous; taking a tumble into one of the chambers, Stallone fell heavily against his cracked rib but grabbed his wounded arm to make it look like that's what hurt. His actual groans from pain were recorded and used in the film.

As he proceeds through the cave/mine, he encounters water and a vast colony of rats. In the book, the chamber is full of bats, and he must trudge through a mountain of reeking bat guano. The setting recalls his POW detention. For the logistics of the film, bats became rats. "Friendly" white rats were dyed brown and substituted (Diane Minshall is billed as the rat wrangler). "They're friendly until you show up," Stallone said on the DVD commentary track, "and as soon as they hit the water, they flip out. It's ice cold and guess what they do: They go to the first warm thing, which is you." When Rambo finally feels the breeze that leads him to the mine's back exit, he climbs up a ladder to the surface. It is as if he is being reborn. Shooting from above, Kotcheff had the star pull himself up the final rungs using only his arms and letting his legs dangle. Said Stallone, "If I was offered this script today, I would have to say 'Pasadena' (pass). It's really something for a young man with a death wish."[74] He was thirty-five when he shot *First Blood*.

Rambo's single-handed destruction of the town, which comprises the film's last third, involved blowing up a huge street set that was built on the location. He hijacks a National Guard munitions truck and, wanting more firepower, raids a guns and ammo shop. The conflagration that Rambo prepares all around the town (which is notably deserted) is his effort to distract Teasle from shooting him first. Filmed with actual, old-fashioned explosives, before the days of CGI, the resulting fireballs were extended by shooting them with several cameras and cutting between angles to make it look like there were more of them.

Despite the weather and sunlight challenges, producer Buzz Feitshans kept the production on track, if not on schedule. Looking back, Mario Kassar warmly recalled, "Buzz is a very good line producer. He's very down to earth, no Hollywood. And we needed help. We were kind of ignorant in a way; we were learning—maybe the hard way or the expensive way.

We needed somebody, and we always work with people that we trust and we believe in because at the end of the day a set is like airport traffic. It's a confusion. There's so many things going on—things are happening here, this guy's eating a sandwich here, a truck is here, this guy's doing nothing here, this guy's on the phone. But somehow if you look at it as a first-timer, you say, 'Is this going to be a movie?' Then at the end of the day you look at the dailies, or at the end of this eight or twelve months, you say, 'It's a movie and it looks good.' We needed that sanity and kind of check and balance kind of thing, and at the end of the day they thought we were geniuses. But it could have turned out real bad."[75]

The film was edited by Joan E. Chapman, who was, like Kotcheff, a Canadian. *First Blood* was her first job as full editor, and she would work with him again on *Weekend at Bernie's* (1989). Later Jerry Goldsmith would be brought in to score the film (see the sidebar "The Song of Rambo," about Jerry Goldsmith).

The next goal was getting the film released. Ordinarily, all post-production efforts focus on a specific opening release date coordinated between a film's distributor and its waiting exhibitors. At the time *First Blood* wrapped, however, it had neither, and the interest on its $15 to $18 million budget was increasing. The story of how Carolco hitched their wagon to Rambo's star is an adventure all its own.

SIDEBAR

Synopsis of the Film *First Blood*

A slightly ragged-looking man (Sylvester Stallone) of about thirty, wearing a green military jacket and carrying a rolled-up sleeping bag, ambles into the outskirts of the town of Hope. There is a determination to his pace but nothing that reveals his purpose. He walks down to a lakeside house where a woman of color[76] and her daughter are hanging laundry. The man, polite to the point of deference, asks if Delmar Barry lives there. When he sees the woman's protective reaction, he shows her a small notebook in which Delmar wrote this address. Then he hands her a photograph of the military unit in which they both served in the Vietnam War. The woman dismisses her daughter and tells the stranger that Delmar died of cancer that he got from Agent Orange in Vietnam. The stranger is stunned and, as he leaves, tosses away his address book.

Now aimless, he walks into Hope and is almost immediately intercepted by Sheriff Wilfred "Will" Teasle (Brian Dennehy). [In the novel, he's a police chief. In the movie, he's a sheriff.] Teasle, assuming that the silent, sullen man is a drifter, drives him to the edge of town and tells him to keep walking. When the stranger instead turns and heads back into Hope, Teasle hauls him in for vagrancy, for carrying a hunting knife, and for resisting arrest.

Hope is decorated for Christmas, but the mood is not festive among the sheriff's deputies, who drag the stranger—whose military dog tags identify him as John J. Rambo—into a basement holding area. There he is demeaned by the deputies, including Art Galt (Jack Starrett). They make Rambo strip off his shirt, revealing scars on his back and chest, and hose him down in a stark cell. But when Deputy Ward (Chris Mulkey) approaches with a razor to shave off Rambo's barely existent beard, Rambo has a flashback to his confinement and torture by the North Vietnamese. He fights and escapes, beating deputies Galt, Ward, Balford (Michael Talbott), Mitch Rogers (David Caruso), Lester (Alf Humphreys),

Shingleton (David L. Crowley), and Preston (Don MacKay) on his way out.

   In the street he commandeers a motorcycle and takes off for the woods. Teasle follows in his patrol car, which proves unfit for the rocky, mountainous terrain and overturns. Teasle climbs out safely and radios for deputies Lester and Rogers to fetch Orval Kellerman (John McLiam), who owns hunting dogs, to join him in tracking Rambo. The posse chases Rambo to the edge of steep Chapman Gorge. Rambo is surprised when Galt shows up, riding in a helicopter and bent on shooting him with a high-powered rifle. Galt fires at Rambo despite Teasle's orders to take him alive. Rambo jumps into the gorge, breaking his fall on tree branches on the way down but gashing his arm open. When Galt orders the pilot (Charles A. Tamburro) to descend so he can get a better shot at Rambo, the updrafts make the copter unstable. Galt unhooks his seat belt so he can lean out of the cabin to get a better shot. Rambo throws a rock at the copter, cracking the window and causing the pilot to swerve, sending Galt tumbling to his death on the rocks below.[77]

   Now emotionally back in Vietnam, Rambo takes the rifle, two-way radio, and warm coat off Galt's body. When Teasle and his men arrive at the rim of the canyon and call down to him, Rambo calls back that he wants to end the pursuit. Instead, everybody but Teasle shoots at him, and he runs off into the wilderness.

   As the posse assembles at the bottom of the gorge, word comes over the walkie-talkie that John Rambo is a Vietnam veteran, a Green Beret, and a Medal of Honor recipient. Teasle ignores this and continues the manhunt. Out of pride, he refuses to call in the state police.

   Orval lets two of his three Dobermans loose among trees where they sense Rambo is hiding, but Rambo, who now has

Galt's rifle, fires back and wounds Orval. He also kills Orval's three dogs.

Rambo now hunts the posse one by one. He springs from camouflage and slices Mitch's hamstring. He dives from a tree and fells Ward. Another deputy is speared by a booby trap. Shingleton is shot by his own men when a deputy shoots at Rambo, and Rambo dodges, revealing Shingleton behind him tied to a tree. Significantly, the men's injuries are debilitating but not fatal. Finally, Rambo bursts from the foliage and grabs Teasle, pressing a knife to his throat and telling him, "Don't push it. Don't push it or I'll give you a war you won't believe." He releases Teasle and flees into the woods. Teasle weeps.

By now Washington State Police Captain Dave Kern (Bill McKinney) and his men have set up a field headquarters. Teasle and the state police collectively wonder where Rambo came from. Colonel Samuel Trautman (Richard Crenna) appears from nowhere and says, "God didn't make Rambo, I made him." He explains that he created the Special Forces unit of which Rambo is now the sole survivor and that no matter how many men they throw at him, Rambo will win. Further, they will need Trautman's help to bring him in.

Rambo puts his wilderness training to use. He uses his all-purpose knife to kill a wild pig. He then sutures his arm wound. He has taken Galt's two-way radio and thus can hear everything the police are saying to each other. Trautman again suggests letting Rambo go, confident that sooner or later he'll turn up working in a car wash in Seattle where it will be safer to bring him in.[78] This doesn't convince Teasle; he now wants vengeance.

Trautman calls Rambo on the walkie-talkie. The two Vietnam survivors resume their father-son relationship, but when Trautman wants to bring his deadly scion in, Rambo says it's gone too far to surrender.

The National Guard shows up the next day. They are almost comically ill-equipped to deal with a Green Beret in survival mode. As Rambo dodges the troops, he encounters a teenage boy who's carrying a gun. He tackles the boy, frightening him, then lets him go.[79]

Guardsmen spot Rambo and give chase. Rambo takes cover in an abandoned mine. The guardsmen know he's there and fire a rocket[80] into the opening, then stand proudly over the rubble to take souvenir photos. When Teasle arrives and witnesses this, he chastises them. Meanwhile, Rambo, unhurt, goes deeper into the mine, braving rats and filth before feeling the wind from an exit shaft and climbing out to freedom.

In a local bar, Teasle and Trautman have drinks and talk. Trautman says that Teasle can go back to his wife and kids whereas Trautman and Rambo are without such personal anchors. (Trautman and the audience, of course, have no idea that Teasle cannot, in fact, return to his family, because that's not in the movie.)

Eluding the Guard, Rambo jumps atop a truck hauling M-60 machine guns, throws the driver (Robert A. Cathcart) safely onto the road, and heads back into Hope fully armed. A squad car pulls alongside Rambo trying to force him off the road, but Rambo pushes it off first.

Arriving in Hope, he blows up a gas station, a car dealership, and a sporting goods store. Teasle is preparing for a gunfight when Trautman arrives and tells him, "I've got more of a chance than you do because he trusts me."[81] Teasle rejects Trautman's offer.

Rambo wields the M-60 as if he is a human tank, shooting up the police station and hitting Teasle, who is trying to snipe him from the roof of the building. When Teasle fires at Rambo, Rambo shoots upward and hits Teasle, who falls through the skylight onto the floor of the sheriff's station.[82] Before Rambo can finish Teasle, Trautman arrives. Rambo breaks down and displays the trauma of so many returning Vietnam vets. "Civilian life is nothing," he cries out. "There I could fly a gunship, drive a tank, was in charge of million-dollar equipment. Back here I can't even hold a job parking cars." He falls into Trautman's arms and Trautman walks him from the building to be taken away by the authorities.[83]

SIDEBAR

Alternate Ending

No one ever thought there would be a sequel to *First Blood*. After what Rambo did to Hope—even though he never killed anyone—John Rambo had to die, if not for legal justice, then for poetic justice. The original Kozoll-Sackheim script ends with him in the jail vestibule as Teasle fires shots into the room where Rambo has gone. From the action described in the script:

> Rambo springs from his cover, prepares to return the fire when a voice calls out to him from behind: "Johnny!" Rambo spins around, his eyes catching a fleeting glimpse of Trautman framed in the doorway. Trautman FIRES. The gunshots melding with Teasle also firing. Rambo almost speaks as the full force of the two, deft rounds takes his heart. He is dead before his incredulous face strikes the floor close to the loft stairway. And now the only sound is the clicking of

the hammer on Teasle's empty pistol as he compulsively pulls at the trigger.[84]

This screenplay ends as Teasle, mortally wounded, crawls to the edge of the gaping hole in the ceiling to look down at Rambo and falls through onto the floor. He reaches to touch Rambo's body. Trautman goes to Rambo and "gently closes the lids over the accusing eyes that stare at him."

In the first cut of the film, despite Stallone's protests, they included Rambo's death, although it's a contrived suicide in which Trautman aims a pistol at close range and Rambo reaches over and pulls the trigger on himself. It is done "with a slight suggestion," writes David Morrell, "that Trautman might have helped him." The deleted footage first appeared on the film's 2002 Blu-ray release and is included in later editions.

As noted earlier, Stallone shot the scene as contracted but held out for the alternate he preferred. Stallone huddled with Kotcheff and told the director, "Ted, we've put the character through so much, the audience is really going to hate this."[85] At this point the two men conspired to shoot the more benign ending in which Rambo lives and is escorted from the building by Trautman to meet his legal fate. This is the "happy" ending that fans of First Blood know and cherish, but—after all the back-and-forth during preproduction—there are still differing accounts of how long it survived in the editing and previewing process.

"I'm looking at the end," Kassar recounts, "and we put on the music of Jerry Goldsmith and I'm looking at the last five minutes of the movie in my office and I put the tape recorder with the music and am watching the ending and nobody could convince me that he shouldn't die. It was one of the best scenes in the whole movie that he died, it was perfect. People told me this and that, and then Sly said, 'What are you doing? Are you out of your mind? There are sequels.' He was basically saying that you don't want to kill your hero, he didn't want to die. And I have a month of really torturing myself [to let him live]. Financially I made the right decision, but dramatically I liked where he died at the end. Who knows?"[86]

According to Kotcheff's memoirs, when he began shooting the "Rambo lives" version, the producers ran up and "went nuts," complaining that Rambo's suicide mission was being contradicted. "When the American distributor wants a happy ending, which I'm sure they will," Kotcheff argued, "then you won't have to spend all the money to bring the whole cast and crew back here three months from now. You'll be kissing my ass in gratitude." So they shot "he lives."

Unable to resolve the ending between themselves, the producers screened the "he dies" version for a preview audience in Las Vegas. The crowd, who had become increasingly supportive of Rambo during the film, "nearly rioted," according to both Stallone and Kotcheff, when they saw the downbeat ending. Wrote Kotcheff in his memoir, "The theater went dead silent for a full minute. The credits began to roll. Then a voice in the crowd yelled, 'If the director of this film is in the theater, let's string him up from the nearest lamppost!' We rushed out of the theater."[87]

In later interviews, the producers said that they quickly returned to Hope, British Columbia, with a skeleton crew and reshot the ending. That's not how Richard Crenna remembered it. Speaking in a 2002 interview, the actor recalled that the ending was very much like *Of Mice and Men*.[88] Rambo was emotionally distraught, and Trautman, seeking to have him avoid the harshness of a military court-martial, decided, like George in the Steinbeck story, to kill Rambo to put him out of his misery. Indeed, as the picture was being shot,

everyone began to realize that the audience, after identifying with Rambo and what he had lived through, would
not accept his execution, even as a mercy killing. Stallone
and Kotcheff huddled. Kotcheff wanted to shoot the scripted
ending, then shoot the one in which he lives.[89] In an interview, Crenna said that the "he lives" version was the only
one that was shot. He misremembered this, as the Blu-ray
footage reveals.

Producer Buzz Feitshans, who disliked movies in which
the hero dies at the end, also believed that Rambo had to
live. Like everyone else, he had no idea that there would be
a sequel. His recollection of the shooting schedule, however,
was that the "he lives" version was shot on one day and a
few days later the "he dies" version was committed to film.
By this account, therefore, both endings were shot during
the original production period, not later with a pickup crew
after a test screening. This jibes with Kotcheff's account in
which the director tells the producers, who were nervously
pacing the lobby as the grumbling crowd left the theater,
"Well boys, not to worry! I just happen to have this other
ending in my back pocket."[90]

Vajna told another version about the ending. "We shot
several endings and we, by the way, tested these endings. It was
one of the funniest things. Mario and I got into huge arguments
about what is the right ending for this movie, and Mario felt
for a long time that dramatically we should kill him because,
you know, he's done all this harm. And I sort of thought, and I
said, 'Yeah, but emotionally it doesn't work. You want this poor
guy to go on.' And we fought back and forth, and we tested the
movies. We put on one ending and then [judged] the audience
reaction, and then we played the other ending. Of course, none
of it made any sense because we got just as much response to
the ending where he dies as to the ending where he lives, just

because of the circumstances by which we were trying to test the film. And we just ultimately decided that making him live was the right way to go."[91]

Unfortunately, the production records are not available to determine how the decision was made. The bottom line of all of this is that success has many fathers and that there was never a thought of a sequel; Kassar and Vajna just wanted to make a movie that didn't let the audience down. Consequently, *First Blood* now and forever ends with John Rambo being led from the ruins of the sheriff's office in custody while his embittered bête noir, Teasle, is lifted, still alive, into an ambulance.

This hasty but effective revision enabled *Rambo: First Blood Part II* to exist, but it posed a problem for Morrell, who had to explain his hero's resurrection when he novelized the sequel script. His solution, suggested by his writer-friend Max Allan Collins, was remarkably simple:

Author's Note

In my novel *First Blood*, Rambo died. In the films, he lives.

SIDEBAR

The Frankenheimer Take

John Frankenheimer was a directorial prodigy. One of the brightest talents of what has been called, for good reason, the Golden Age of Television in the 1950s, he easily transitioned to motion pictures with *Birdman of Alcatraz* and *The Manchurian Candidate* (both 1962), *Seven Days in May* and *The Train* (both 1964), and *Seconds* (1966). He was shattered emotionally after the 1968 assassination of Robert F. Kennedy, who was a close friend and on whose media campaign he had worked. He drifted through the 1970s, although he still had a firm hand on his craft. When he was offered *First Blood*, it must have seemed like a gift: a character study, a political statement, and an action film all rolled into one.

The script that he worked on with screenwriters Michael Kozoll and William Sackheim is a model of understatement, even at 122 pages, and it is instructive to consider how different a Frankenheimer *First Blood* may have looked even though it would still have been David Morrell's *First Blood*.

It starts with the very first sequence in which Rambo walks down a backroad highway, only here he is passed by a convoy of National Guardsmen who mock his hippie-like appearance. This sets the stage for Chief (not Sheriff) Teasle doing the same thing and sets up audience sympathies, especially where some soldiers were known to mock men who joined the National Guard as an alternative to probable Vietnam service.

Here, too, is the first appearance of the new scene where Rambo stops at a home seeking his army buddy Delmar only to learn that his friend had died. The scene is extended from what appears in the film, going inside the home and meeting other family members who are still mourning Delmar's death. Part of this scene was kept in the *First Blood* script as a friendlier character introduction, and the next action paragraph says it all as Rambo walks away:

> With each step, the pain is building in Rambo, contorting his face, filling his eyes—his fist reflexively strikes his thigh, once, twice, again, again—the sleeping bag falls away as he turns his rage and anguish on a tree truck [sic], pounding it repeatedly, pounding

it harder before butting it with his forehead, again, again, again, beating off the pain with pain—

Then we meet Teasle, at home and awash in police paperwork, watching as his wife, Elaine, packs to leave him and stay with her sister in Chicago, where they came from. It appears to be an amicable separation (she can't stand small town life any longer), but the tension is great and everyone in the police station is talking about it by the time Teasle shows up for work. This being a small town, his first duty is warning a teenage boy who has been caught masturbating to do it in the bedroom from now on and to lock the door. That's the measure of local excitement. But then Rambo is brought in by Shingleton and Galt, who proceed to book him. They, not Teasle, are Rambo's first antagonists.

The tonal difference between this early script and the final one quickly becomes apparent. Frankenheimer wanted a more textured, character-driven film; Kotcheff, Vajna, and Kassar wanted the mano-a-mano to start as soon as possible and never let up.

The opening scene at the lakeside house where Rambo looks for Delmar was invented for the movie. The novel's author, David Morrell, thinks it was a good decision: "Movies are different from books. In my novel, Rambo and Teasle receive equal attention. I wanted readers to be unable to choose between them. But the scripts I read seemed to want to choose one or the other as the main character. In one of the early scripts, Teasle got most of the attention while Rambo was reduced to being a guy who broke into a commercial cave and survived by looting the candy-bar machines. In my novel, Rambo is furious about how his Vietnam experience trained him to be a killer. But in the later movie scripts, he became a sad-eyed victim. Once you do that, you need an early scene in which the audience quickly loves the character. Sly has the most sympathetic eyes, they're like the eyes of a deer. That ability is what turns movie actors into movie stars, and Sly has such wonderfully sympathetic eyes that all he had to do was look so sad about poor Delmar dead from Agent Orange and the audience was on his side. Given the way my character was reinterpreted, I thought this was an interesting solution."[92]

The ending to the script for the never-made Frankenheimer version is closer to the book. Rambo mortally wounds Teasle. Trautman kills Rambo. Teasle lives long enough to see that Rambo is dead. A reporter (Murray) who has been covering the carnage looks at Rambo's body, shakes his head, and says, "'I wonder how many more like him are out there right now.' Trautman pauses, ices Murray with a look, then indicates Teasle and says, 'I wonder how many more like *him* are out there right now.'" The implication is clear that not only are there hundreds, perhaps thousands, of traumatized veterans who are living at the mercy of hair-trigger violence, but there are also authority figures like Teasle who don't understand the ticking time bombs that are coming home from battle, who live on the edge of starting another one.[93]

A major Hollywood movie of the 1980s could not afford such ironies. If it had been made in the 1970s, when audiences sought textures and ambiguities, the Frankenheimer version probably could have explored these themes. *First Blood* synthesized the novel wisely and sensitively. Stallone's portrayal gave Rambo something more commercially important than depth—it gave him audience sympathy. While it's impossible to know whether a more complicated character study would have had the same box office results—or what would have happened if the producers had listened to Kirk Douglas or if John Frankenheimer could have brought his dynamism to the mix—it's interesting to ponder the Rambo that might have been.

Differences Between Novel and Film

The Kozoll-Sackheim adaptation notwithstanding, no one realistically ever expects a direct translation from book to film. Beyond the obvious considerations of budget and running time, there are stylistic differences between a novel's capacity for internal monologue versus the automatic objectivity of cinema. In the case of *First Blood*, many decisions, creative and financial, had to be made when turning David Morrell's novel into Ted Kotcheff's film. (The use of possessives is the first clue.) There are dozens of changes, but those that draw a sharp distinction between the two mediums are:

- In the book, Rambo is walking into town when he is met by Teasle. In the film, he is first seen visiting Delmar's family. This scene was created for the film to introduce his character in a positive light, to give him a starting point for a clearly defined character arc, and to explain his emotional shutdown on learning that his last human contact with Vietnam has died. After hearing of Delmar's passing, he discards his address book, having presumably exhausted its listing of his wartime friends.

- In the book, Rambo has no first name. In the film, he is given the first name of John.

- In the book, Rambo escapes naked from the

police chief's office. In the film, he wears jeans and a tank top.

- In the book, Rambo kills many people. In the film, he never kills anyone. Deputy Galt's death is the result of his own clumsiness and aggressiveness, and, later, three people die in a car trying to stop Rambo's truck.

- In the book, Rambo kills an owl, and the other dogs die pulling a deputy over a cliff. In the film, he kills three dogs and a pig, all off-screen.

- In the book, Rambo, escaping through the woods, gets clothing and a weapon from a bootlegger and his son, then uses his scent to distract the police tracking dogs away from their still. (He will use this tactic again in *Rambo* [2008] when he tears a scrap of fabric from missionary Sarah's dress and puts it on his shoe to mislead their SPDC trackers.) In *First Blood*, he clothes himself in discarded burlap that he finds in a dump.

- In the book, Teasle's Korean War background forms the backstory for his enmity toward Rambo. In the film, it is indicated only by a plaque on his office wall. No reason is given for his persecution of Rambo other than Rambo's long hair.

- In the book, Rambo has long hair and a beard. In the film he has long-ish hair and no beard.

- In the book, Rambo navigates through a cave of bats. In the film it's rats.

- In the book, Teasle's marriage is falling apart. In the film, it is not mentioned.

- In the book, Rambo and Trautman have no communication until their final confrontation. In the film, they speak via Galt's purloined walkie-talkie. Film continuity error: Rambo is seen taking Galt's insulated jacket off his corpse but is not seen taking the walkie-talkie. Later Rambo has seemingly disposed of the jacket to create a scarecrow-like figure that fools his pursuers.

- In the book, the National Guardsmen are well-trained. In the film, they are comic relief.

- In the book, Teasle dies after his shoot-out with Rambo. In the film, Teasles lives albeit barely.

- In the book, Trautman executes Rambo. In the film, Trautman walks him out to his fate in the hands of the law.

CHAPTER 5

Rambo Unleashed: The Carolco Adventure

"**W**e were two young kids in a candy store," Andy Vajna remembers about the early days of Carolco Pictures, the company he cofounded in 1976 with Mario Kassar. For the next nineteen years, the two men would ride one of the biggest roller coasters in Hollywood. "Mario and I met in Cannes in the early 1970s," Vajna continues. "I was then a distributor in Southeast Asia and Mario was a buying agent in Europe where he was helping me to buy films for my theatrical circuit in Hong Kong. And we sort of got together. We liked each other and then we decided to start a company together."[1]

At the time, Vajna was the owner of a pair of theaters in Hong Kong and, in 1973, had invested $100,000 in a martial arts picture titled *The Deadly China Doll*. The picture grossed $3.7 million and whetted his appetite to move from being an exhibitor to becoming a producer.

The early- to mid-1970s were a time of restructuring in the international film industry. The old-line Hollywood studios were folding, merging, or becoming corporate conglomerates. The international industry was a patchwork of territories, each sold separately at Cannes, MIFED, MIPCOM, and other film markets. Ironically, despite the financial shifts, the era has come to be regarded as one of the most vital in the history of cinema, perhaps because desperate film companies were trying new ways to reach increasingly elusive young audiences.

Vajna and Kassar were beneficiaries of the newly opened

doors. In 1976, they produced *The Sicilian Cross*, which was distributed by American International Pictures and ITC Entertainment[2] with input from Canadian Cineplex mogul Garth Drabinsky. To handle it, they created Carolco. "It has no meaning," Kassar said of the name. "It was a defunct company in Panama. It sounded good and the company was already done. No other reason."[3] Adds Vajna, "It was just a name off the shelf of an attorney. It was nothing. There were no girlfriends involved."[4]

In a world where individual producers could not afford to set up offices around the world, Carolco generated income by brokering the sale of foreign rights for their clients' productions. Then it hit them that they were in the wrong end of things.

"We figured that that was a business where you were always wrong," recalls Vajna, "because you're either selling a movie that's not good enough and they're paying too much for it, or it's too good, in which case they're not paying enough for it. Either the producer or the guy that bought it is always unhappy. So we said, well, we've got to get out of the middle, so maybe we ought to just make our own movie and at least that way we only have to worry about one side of the equation.[5] If we are going to risk our money, we might as well be there for the harvest as owners of the film rather than just sales agents."[6]

As recounted earlier, their studio connections led them to *First Blood* even though the project had passed through the hands of so many other producers. "I guess it goes by cycles in Hollywood," Kassar says. "There's always something, one project that's been around forever, and for whatever reason—many studios, many actors, many drafts—they never get it made."[7]

While they were putting together the picture, they were also straining to find financing. They wound up assembling the budget with the same preselling strategy they had used repping other filmmakers.

"*First Blood* was very strangely financed," Kassar reveals. "My godfather was a banker in France. [I had] a good relationship with him. I went to see him at the bank, and I said, 'Will you do me a favor?' He said, 'What?' I said, 'I believe a lot in this book that I want to make into a movie, and I need a loan.' He said, 'How much is the loan?' I had to take a deep breath because I had never asked for so much money; it used to be half a million, seven hundred [thousand], three hundred [thousand], things like this. I said, 'eighteen.' I stopped at 'eighteen' because I couldn't pronounce 'million,' but he understood 'million' and he said, 'Are you sure you can do it? Can you presell? Can you cover? Will you be okay?' I said, 'Oh, sure. No problem,' because in my mind I was going for it. Worst case, I can survive being thrown out of the window. And he agreed! I couldn't believe my eyes and ears, and actually, I didn't even sign any papers or any documents. He went out, he called the manager, and said, 'I need an open letter of credit for $18 million to the Union Bank of California that I could draw whatever I needed whenever I needed it and that's how I got the financing for the movie. There was no collateral. My collateral was me. I'd never seen it happen anywhere before. I don't know, it just *happened*."[8]

By the time their film was nearing completion, Kassar and Vajna were eager, if not desperate, to repay the loan using the promised presales. Traditionally, however, it is difficult, if not impossible, to get US distribution until international distribution is in place. They cut together an eighteen-minute preview promo from their footage and showed it to Warner Bros., who had first option to distribute. Warners passed but retained their contractual share of any profits. Twentieth Century-Fox also passed.[9] The brevity of the preview reel was hurting them. Says Vajna, "When they saw it, they thought, 'Eighteen minutes? Anybody can put together eighteen minutes. What's the rest of the movie like?' So Mario and I looked at this long and hard, and before the American Film Market, we cut together a fifty-five-minute promo reel [mostly action] that we showed. It got a standing ovation and the film got sold around the world within five minutes."[10]

That's not an exaggeration. Richard Crenna was also at the AFM screening and recalled that it was like the New York Stock Exchange with exhibitors actually on their feet yelling across the room at Vajna and Kassar and making bids for the picture. The seasoned Crenna said that he had never seen anything quite like it.

"Stallone was there," says Vajna. "He had seen an earlier cut that was very long that he was not very happy with,[11] and we invited him to this screening where he wasn't sure what he was going to see. We had a temp score with Jerry Goldsmith music, so it had the same emotional impact. Then when it got the standing ovation, [Stallone] was in heaven."[12]

There was one more step before diving into the distribution shark tank, and that was the ending. They still weren't sure which one to put on *First Blood*; would Rambo live or die? They held a final sneak preview at the Parkway Theater in Las Vegas and asked the audience to watch both endings to help them decide which to use. As has been noted, the audience overwhelmingly preferred the ending where Rambo lives and said so on enthusiastic comment cards filled out in the lobby.[13]

With the world in their hands, so to speak, Kassar and Vajna resumed talks with US companies for domestic distribution rights. They were already in the black from foreign sales and were prepared to talk tough to the Hollywood boys. They approached Universal, who offered Carolco $4 million up front to distribute *First Blood* but wanted all rights, including lucrative television and cable. Carolco rejected Universal's offer and shopped the film to Orion Pictures, who declined to give them

advance payment but promised to spend $5 million on market-
ing and let them hold on to TV and cable rights.[14] Orion was
attractive because, although it was a new company, it had been
formed by men who had just left the management of United
Artists and benefited from their keen institutional memory
versus Vajna and Kassar's lack of marketing experience.

"Because that was our first movie, we knew very little about
what to do," Vajna admitted, "other than approving the poster
and that sort of thing."[15] One of the challenges was selling an
R-rated film to a wide audience. Rather than fight it, Carolco
embraced it. "All those controversies were very good for us,
frankly," Vajna said, "because that kind of publicity actually
helps sell whatever you're selling because it's bringing attention
to its existence."[16]

First Blood opened on October 22, 1982, and grossed more
than $9.2 million on its first weekend in the United States alone
(a considerable amount at the time).[17] On its original release,
foreign and domestic, it grossed more than $125 million.[18]

Buoyed, if not flabbergasted, by the kind of grosses that
independent films seldom achieve—and emboldened by cash
flow—Carolco embarked on an ambitious slate of productions.
They also moved up in the world, literally. They had begun
their company in a small office on Melrose Avenue, a Hollywood street known for trendy shops and fashion salons, with
Vajna's wife and Kassar's girlfriend as their secretaries. With
money, they moved to a bigger building on Sunset Boulevard
at the edge of Beverly Hills, where they took over a few floors.
Finally, they built their own multistory office building on the
Sunset Strip across from Tower Records and Spago restaurant.
They attracted attention by overpaying for talent, including
gifting Arnold Schwarzenegger a $14 million Gulfstream jet
to appear in *Terminator 2*. Agents and managers were thrilled;
studios and competing producers were appalled.[19]

Then the lawsuits started.

On August 2, 1984, Warner Bros., Cinema Group, and David Morrell filed a brief against Vajna, Carolco, and Carolco's subsidiary Anabasis Investments, maintaining that the company's accounting was "faulty."[20]

Lawsuits are de rigueur in the film business,[21] and this did not deter Carolco from greenlighting such films as *Angel Heart*, *Extreme Prejudice*, *Red Heat*, *They Live*, *Iron Eagle II*, and other titles that would come to fruition with the cash flow from *First Blood* and its sequel, *Rambo: First Blood Part II*. Indeed, it was after *Rambo: First Blood Part II* was released on May 22, 1985, generating over $300 million worldwide,[22] that the legal briefs began. On September 17 of that year, *Weekly Variety* reported that David Morrell claimed the producers had failed to pay him his full share of net profits. The suit said that Carolco assessed $250,000 for unperformed script consulting services by an unaffiliated company, $400,000 for a completion bond fee that was not paid, and $250,000 for legal and accounting costs unrelated to the Rambo films. Morrell also sought royalties for merchandising and damages of $1 million actual and another $1 million punitive as well as an injunction against the further exploitation of his novel's copyright.[23]

Not to be outdone, a year later Carolco and Anabasis sued Orion Pictures in a disagreement over profit distribution, asking $3 million in actual damages and $20 million in punitive damages.[24]

"We had an argument with Orion because they were not following the contract," Kassar reports. "They had no incentive to spend more money on advertising because I would make more than them at the end of the day. I worked with Mike Medavoy—he was really a champion—but it was the old guys in the back room, Arthur Krim, who were not too happy. Mike Medavoy was really nice. He was all behind the movie; he's a good guy, I like him very much."[25]

Orion, which had been formed in 1978 by five top United Artists executives who left UA in a dispute with its parent company, Transamerica, was hurting from a string of failed 1985 non-*Rambo* releases. While the suit was in progress, Kassar and Vajna attempted to buy $55 million of Orion's stock.[26] They lost their bid to Viacom and other companies. (There is no record of how that suit was settled.) Carolco also purchased the former Dino De Laurentiis studio ("Dinocitta") in Wilmington, North Carolina, which had become a haven for runaway studio production in that right-to-work state.[27]

The IRS got involved around 1996, eventually demanding back taxes and fines of $109.7 million from Vajna and Kassar. The IRS also went after the company's CEO Peter Hoffman, who had been hired to stem the hemorrhage of money, claiming that he had diverted close to a million dollars from the company to his own account sans taxes. Hoffman was indicted in December 1996[28] and would eventually pay a fine after Vajna testified that the money was a no-interest loan. Vajna also lent Hoffman money for lawyers and paid his own IRS tax bill of $6.5 million in 2001.[29]

Andrew Vajna left Carolco in December 1989, selling his share to Mario Kassar for $106 million.[30] Once free of Kassar, Vajna formed Cinergi Pictures, which released box office successes such as *Tombstone* and *Die Hard with a Vengeance* but also money losers such as *Color of Night* and *Judge Dredd*.

Meanwhile, Carolco remained in the Rambo business. On May 25, 1988, they released *Rambo III* through distributor Tri-Star Pictures, grossing $189 million on a reported budget of between $58 to $63 million.[31]

Managing Carolco on his own (though he held only 62

percent of the company's stock),[32] Kassar tried to broaden the company's brand by making smaller, more artistic films (*Mountains of the Moon, Jacob's Ladder, Hamlet*, all 1990) in addition to blockbusters (*Total Recall*, 1990, *Terminator 2* and *Basic Instinct*, both 1991) and the bizarre (*Showgirls*, 1995). *Showgirls* (a Las Vegas story to end them all) wasn't the nail in Carolco's coffin. The film, a semi-porn backstage drama about Las Vegas performers, is still talked about as being "so bad it's good." But even *Showgirls* wasn't enough to doom Carolco. What did it was *Cutthroat Island* (1995), a pirate movie starring Matthew Modine and Geena Davis, wife of the film's director, Renny Harlin. A legendary flop at a $10 million return on a $98 million budget,[33] in November 1995 its failure forced Carolco into bankruptcy. At a March 1996 auction, Canal+ acquired most of the company's assets for $58 million[34] after Fox initially offered $50 million, then reneged and dropped to $47.5 million.[35]

Meanwhile, the Rambo property went on the block. In spring 1996, the Los Angeles Bankruptcy Court announced a May 13 auction of sequel rights. Applicants would have to bid a minimum of $500,000 with advances at levels of $50,000 and a requirement of a $50,000 deposit just to enter the competition. Miramax led off with a $500,000 offer on behalf of their Dimension Films subsidiary. Legendary (and legendarily parsimonious) producer Roger Corman's Concorde/New Horizons[36] agreed to put up $550,000 for the sequel rights. Finally, a joint venture between Yoram Pelman and HSI Productions (a TV commercial/video company) promised the court $600,000.[37] On May 13, as promised, the court made its decision and awarded the Rambo sequel rights to Miramax/Dimension for a very clear, simple reason: Neither Corman nor Pelman/HIS bothered to show up. "While we are disappointed that overbidding didn't take place, both Carolco and the creditors committee were very satisfied with the sale price," said Howard Weg, the lawyer representing Carolco and its affiliates in their bankruptcy case.[38] How this interfaced with the Canal+ acquisition is not known.

This was not, of course, the end of the Rambo legend. In a world where Rambo can live after being killed, so could Carolco. In 1998 Kassar and Vajna reestablished their relationship by forming C2 Pictures, producing *Terminator 3: Rise of the Machines*, *Basic Instinct 2*, the feature version of the sixties TV series *I Spy*, and, for Fox television, *Terminator: The Sarah Connor Chronicles*.

In his later years, Andrew Vajna returned to his native Hungary. From 2011, he was government commissioner in charge of the Hungarian film industry. Among his strengths was arranging international financing and distribution through the Hungarian National Film Fund. He also bought into the nation's television system. Vajna died on January 20, 2019 (from "a long illness," some obituaries indicated), and is survived by his widow, Timea Palacsik.

In 2015, Mario Kassar returned to head the newly configured Carolco Pictures, renaming it Recall Studios in 2017. At this writing, he lives in Los Angeles with his wife Denise Richard-Kassar and their three daughters Natasha, Tatiana, and Anastasia.

Peter M. Hoffman left Carolco and became CEO of Seven Arts Entertainment. In 2015, he and two other defendants were convicted of a 2009 $1.1 million wire fraud scheme involving the conversion of a Louisiana mansion into a postproduction facility for which they received state tax credits for expenditures they never made.[39] Facing up to 175 years in prison, Hoffman and his codefendants were given probation by US District Judge Martin Feldman.[40]

Reviewing *Rambo*

The reviews of *First Blood* were mixed-to-positive, but there was more behind them than the aesthetics of cinema. It was politics. *First Blood* gave mainstream film critics a chance to write about Vietnam, a subject their newspapers generally restricted to editorial writers and opinion columnists. Finally permitted to share their views about America's involvement in the war, many of them held the filmmakers and Sylvester Stallone personally responsible for whatever outrages they had been feeling regardless of whether the affronts had anything to do with the film.

Some of the reviews—testy at best if not downright accusatory—ranged from Marc Wainberg's pan in UCLA's *Daily Bruin* ("A Leech on the Side of Movie Vietnam" ran the headline)[41] to Janet Maslin's *New York Times* review saying "as a tough, powerful, silent presence, [Stallone] is unexpectedly commanding"[42] and going on to correctly predict a career for him as an action film star.

In the *Village Voice*, then a bastion of antiwar thinking, Joy Gould Boyum condescended that *First Blood* was "another film of dubious morality and doubtful attitudes, but it is likely to find an audience and sweep viewers up in its violent action and muddled thinking. Directed by Ted Kotcheff, who provides the whole with considerable energy, and starring Sylvester Stallone, who is compelling as long as he remains silent (which fortunately he does for most of the movie), *First Blood* takes the form of a classic tale of violence and revenge."[43]

An unsigned review in the trade paper *Screen International* turned out to be more accurate, praising "93 [*sic*] well-packed minutes of first-rate entertainment," adding that "Stallone's John Rambo is a Jack the Giantkiller whose lack of words to use as weapons makes him blood brother to every man who feels inadequate when confronted by the insolence of office. But a Jack whose good looks and powerful physique make him a 'lonely Prince Charming' that women in the audience would gladly kiss to free him from the spell of having to live like a frog. *Rambo* is *Rocky* in an updated Western."[44]

Box Office, the American exhibitors' trade publication, was more cynical. Their Jimmy Summers wrote, "You probably thought stories in which Vietnam vets were presented as walking time bombs had been done away with years ago. But here's one more. Like all the rest, it pretends to be a compassionate portrayal of a mentally wounded veteran ignored by society. But once again, it's actually only a hook for an action-adventure movie that needs an explanation for the hero's resilience."[45]

The most astute analysis came from Peter Rainer of the *Los Angeles Herald-Examiner*, who noted that, in the construction of the story, "Rambo is meant to be sympathetic. Director Ted Kotcheff and his writers . . . have rigged the movie so that we share Rambo's moral outrage. The cops—who, of course, drew 'first blood'—are mostly piggy little sadists, the guardsmen are wimps who wouldn't last a day fighting in a real war for their country." Moreover, "Stallone's *Rocky* association gives Rambo the sympathy of a maligned underdog."[46]

Roger Ebert took issue with what he perceived as the film's flawed logic. "The ending doesn't work in *First Blood*," he said. "It doesn't necessarily work as action, either. By the end of the film, Stallone has taken on a whole town and has become a one-man army, laying siege to the police station and the hardware store and exploding the pumps at the gas station. This sort of spectacular conclusion has become so commonplace in action movies that I kind of wonder, sometimes, what it would be like to see one end with a whimper rather than a bang."[47]

But it took "Har" (Jim Harwood) in his *Weekly Variety* review to predict the key to Rambo's enduring popularity by relating both the film and the character to society at large. Appearing under a snarky *Variety* headline that *First Blood* was "anemic," Harwood wrote, "It's dangerous to label a film as socially irresponsible but *First Blood* is certainly on the borderline. There are enough nuts out there already without offering them a hero to cheer for."[48]

It was, as history shows, a prescient sentiment. Rambo—rather, Sylvester Stallone's portrayal of Rambo—made him, quite literally, the poster child for vengeance. Understandably, Stallone himself had a different perspective: He didn't consider it random, gratuitous violence. Rather, he saw the controversy over the violence as a way for antiwar protestors to seize the limelight and he criticized them for dumping on a movie while there were real-life—not cartoon or mythical characters—who didn't do actual damage. Stallone denied that Rambo was responsible for setting a new trend or new wave of violence. "Rambo has taken on an importance that I never thought," he said, "a message to the American people that they must not stand still for oppression."[49] This reasoning would follow Stallone throughout his Rambo films.

There was another undercurrent that emerged that had nothing to do with Rambo: a resentment of Stallone's relatively fast rise from small-part actor (*The Prisoner of Second Avenue*, 1975) to underdog (*Rocky*, 1976) to auteur.

"They always come down on Stallone," muses Richard Crenna. "They don't come down critically on Schwarzenegger or Chuck Norris. They don't come down on the other people who make"—he chooses his words carefully— "action films with the violence and the bloodshed. The word *Rambo* is now in the American dictionary."[50]

But after *Rambo: First Blood Part II*, all bets were off. Stallone's embodiment of what Rambo had become—as opposed to how he had been originally designed—became the lightning rod for a broad range of reactions including wish fulfillment, racism, jingoism, PTSD, veterans' rights, right-wing politics, and left-wing we-told-you-sos—all despite Stallone's insistence that Rambo was not supposed to be political.

"These movies have become controversial for all the wrong reasons," Crenna continued. "More often than not, what was branded as being 'Ramboism' is directly opposed to what he, as a character, stands for. As for the arguments about violence, why isn't there any controversy over movies like *The Untouchables* and *Lethal Weapon*?"[51] "I kind of laugh at that," he told another reporter. "What about the Arnold Schwarzenegger and Chuck Norris movies? They're infinitely more violent. Rambo has come to mean senseless violence and that's not true. Rambo is a man who fights *against* violence."[52]

Why do people give Arnold a pass and come down on Sly? "I think it might have had to do with the fact that Arnold is more careful with his personal life," suggests Pat H. Broeske, a reporter who has covered them both. "Arnold didn't have a reputation for firing people on his set. It was before we heard about his personal life. Also, Arnold has a playfulness that we pick up on, that we don't quite pick up with Sly. But Arnold, until that whole mess with his nanny,[53] kept a lid on his personal life. Arnie was shrewd and didn't show [his ambition] but Sly couldn't hide it. He wanted to succeed. He was taking charge, and perhaps started directing too early, and people resented him for that. A lot of people didn't like him at the time. Critics *really* didn't like him."[54]

As the man who created Rambo, David Morrell has this take. "I was on the set of *Rambo III* with Richard Crenna, who was a wonderful man and very, very open. We got to talking about Sly's and Richard's careers. What he told me was that in Richard's long career from when he'd been a child actor through all the different things he'd done in television and movies and all the people he'd worked with, there were only two male actors whom he'd worked with who knew what to do in front of a camera. They might not be good on Broadway, they might not be like Paul Newman, where there's a lot of intellectualizing, but they knew what to do in front of the camera. They knew it was about eyes. They knew it was about props. They knew it was about visual effect. Richard said those two guys were Steve McQueen and Sylvester Stallone. Richard had worked with Steve in *The Sand Pebbles*. He said, 'Their inventiveness, and their use of their eyes, and the props,' he said, 'It was just amazing to see them work.' I'm not trying to belittle Arnold, who has terrific presence. Given the *Terminator* movies alone, he's made his place in movie history. In a way, it's apples and oranges, but in a way, it's not really because we sense, I think, that Sly goes deeper, that if he wants to, you can just sense a terrible quiet anguish in him."[55]

Time has been good to *First Blood*. Not only is it possible to view it as the most benign and focused of the *Rambo* quintet, it also offers the greatest range of Stallone's acting, and his skill must be acknowledged. From the hurt puppy he plays at the beginning, to the attack dog who gives Teasle the chance to live, and finally to the emotionally naked veteran who collapses in front of the man who created him, it's an inspired performance that has been overlooked, if not obscured, by the blood sport of the sequels. Only in the first outing does Rambo let his opponents survive. Of course, this was done to keep the audience sympathy with the character and the star, but it also works to forgive the viewer for enjoying malicious people getting what they deserve.

Cinematically, the film is a remarkable achievement. Andrew Laszlo's photography is lush yet realistic; the fog creeping through the primordial landscape isn't from special effects smudge pots, it's from Canada's challenging weather. The camera's mobility in the woods is invisible, yet anyone who has ever had to lay track or set up lighting in a tree-strewn location knows how difficult it is. Shooting in Rambo's cave with, quite literally, a single match providing illumination was a breakthrough, and the sound design was appropriate for the action and not overdone like so many modern films where every bullet casing can be heard hitting the ground. The Rambo films have a polish that elevates them above genre films of earlier generations (*Billy Jack*, *The Losers*, *Devil's 8*, etc.) which, as exciting as they were, tended to record action in a perfunctory way rather than exploiting the vocabulary of the medium.

Binding it together is Jerry Goldsmith's perceptive score. He manages to combine a sense of militarism with a profound melancholy, and its reuse in subsequent Rambo entries proves how versatile and timeless this master composer's work turned out to be.

With the hindsight of history and a knowledge of what followed, *First Blood* emerges as the touchstone from which the Rambo legend came to life. With each subsequent film, however, the critics became increasingly hostile. Their hostility was couched in distaste for the films, yet there was something else at work, something in the dynamic between filmmakers and audiences that critics pounced on, rightly or wrongly. The movies became more than movies, they became moral and political statements. Rambo was changing and so was America, and the friction from those changes was being played out on the screen.

CHAPTER 6

Rambo Returns

As convoluted as the road to the screen had been for *First Blood*, the path for *Rambo: First Blood Part II* should have been a superhighway. But it wasn't.

"The first film," Andrew Vajna recounts, "was financed through this loan from a bank. We had promised the guy that we would be able to sell rights all along to sort of help with his financing, of course, which didn't happen, so he found himself on a limb for the entire movie by the time we finished with it. Even though he came out okay and made a lot of money with it ultimately at the end, he was not willing to come in and help finance number two." Thus, in March 1983, with *First Blood* on the way to a $125 million worldwide gross, Vajna and Mario Kassar set out for the American Film Market to presell the foreign rights to the sequel which, unlike the first film two years earlier, didn't yet exist.[1]

At this point, the practical decision to keep Rambo alive at the end of *First Blood* paid off. "As soon as we kept him alive," Vajna says, "we thought that there would be a sequel in it." They decided to hire James Cameron, whose screenplay for *The Terminator* was attracting attention, to try his hand at writing it.[2] Cameron accepted, it was later reported, because he said he wanted to learn what it was like to write a script for someone else to direct.[3]

Kevin Jarre (*Glory*, 1989) also wrote a script, but his work was arbitrated to "story by" in the course of the film's multiple rewrites and reconceptions.

David Morrell, who novelized the eventual screenplay (of which there were several drafts), recalled, "The James Cameron screenplay was rich in description. It read almost like a novel. But . . . in the finished shooting script, in which other hands were involved, a lot of the texture of the Cameron script was removed."[4]

"The big difference in Cameron's script," Vajna adds, "was that he wanted to start him out in a mental institution—sort of reminds you of *Terminator 2*—where he escapes and then does this mission. But other than that, the story and the characters were the same. We were thinking about buddies but we felt ultimately that this was the single white male, you know? So we went with just Rambo."[5]

Titled *First Blood II: The Mission* and dated December 22, 1983, Cameron's 127-page script does indeed open with Trautman visiting Rambo in a mental institution. Not only is Rambo in an isolation cell, but the attendants also stand by to shoot him with a tranquilizer gun of the kind ordinarily used on animals. Contrasted with the rock pile sequence in the produced film, this scripted reunion in a cell in the mental institution's basement shows Rambo reverting to military obedience (even though he was discharged and is now a civilian) when Trautman shows up. Seeing his self-induced squalor, Trautman tells him sarcastically, "You shoot up one little town in Oregon with a fifty-caliber machine gun, one little Dogpatch town, and everybody figures your wrapper's broken. No sense of humor." This is Trautman's attempt at bonhomie. Rambo remains stoic, however, and repeats his impassioned speech from the end of *First Blood* about flying gunships in 'Nam and not being trusted to park cars back in America.[6] The contrast is at once disarming and bitter, and Trautman finally tells Rambo, "You just picked the wrong war to be a hero in." The scene's larger function is to bring new viewers quickly up to speed. While

Stallone's production script denudes the encounter of friendly banter and keeps the rock pile encounter formal, Cameron's script has Trautman reel off Rambo's honors to him as a tactic to persuade him to take on the mission. This is contrasted with Murdock (Charles Napier, here named Kirkhill) who later does the same recitation out of a dossier when Rambo shows up in Thailand. The crucial difference is that Trautman is trying to challenge Rambo while Murdock is clumsily telling him things both men already know solely for the benefit of the audience.

One major aspect of Cameron's script is that Rambo parachutes into 'Nam with a CIA man, Brewer, whose ineptitude is comic, if not dangerous, and retains his tech equipment. In his rewrite, Stallone wisely loses Brewer but keeps the strong female character of Co, whom Cameron created. This not only strikes a blow for female empowerment (a Cameron trademark throughout his films), it also positions Co as a possible romantic interest.

"Between Sly, Cameron, and everybody," Mario Kassar adds, "the idea was to go and rescue prisoners of war in Vietnam. That's how it started and slowly, slowly there was a screenplay. And then came the point of who's going to direct this movie."[7]

"Ted Kotcheff was considered," Vajna continues, "but I think he was busy doing other things and, strangely enough, he made another movie, *Uncommon Valor*, that was very similar in storyline. We thought that he was stealing our idea for Rambo, and we went in another direction."[8] That other direction was also with a different director, George Cosmatos.

"I was hired by the producers and Stallone to do the movie after they had seen a small movie I did called *Of Unknown Origin* (1983) which won the best-in-festival award [at the 1983 Paris Film Festival]," said Cosmatos.[9]

Said Vajna, "We met George through friends of ours in

Rome, where he was living at the time. When we decided to do the sequel, we thought he's a very good visualist and we thought if we could get him to do it and get Sly to agree to it we would be able to deliver the kind of film we wanted. Initially he wasn't sure. Then of course he was involved in part of the conversations about keeping Rambo alive because obviously he had seen all the [script] versions. Stallone was very excited about going forward with it and recreating this American hero. I mean he was GI Joe. He's been very successful with his *Rocky* series, so this added another character for him to hang on to. Sly ultimately agreed to it and it worked out fine."[10] On Stallone's insistence, once Cosmatos was aboard, they discarded the somewhat realistic Cameron approach in favor of one developed by star and director that resulted in what some critics called a "$34 million right-wing fantasy"[11] that divided the press but united conservative fans (including, as will be shown, President Ronald Reagan). Then there was the trouble with the title. Given the confusion that was to come with the three future films—*Rambo III*, then *Rambo*, then *Last Blood*, in that nonconsecutive order—how did the producers decide on the unwieldy *Rambo: First Blood Part II*?

"[That was] the big drama," Kassar acknowledges, "because, in America, everybody understands what *First Blood* is and there was the book and things like this. But the first country that released the film in Europe, if my memory is correct, was Italy, and they just called it *Rambo*. So all of a sudden there was no more *First Blood* around the world, it was *Rambo 1, Rambo 2, Rambo 3*—everything was *Rambo*."[12] Eventually *Rambo* (2008) was called *John Rambo* internationally, but the confusion remains.

Although *Rambo: First Blood Part II* wasn't scheduled to start shooting until August 1, 1984, in June of that year, Vajna and Kassar, through their company, Anabasis Investments, shot and distributed a teaser trailer that appeared on some three thousand screens.[13] This was daring in that the pair had not yet made a distribution deal for the film's American release. "We were involved in everything that could be done in a movie," Kassar explains.[14] "We shot an advance trailer of the movie before we shot the movie. I was flying from one place to another and one day it just came all into my head and I kind of wrote it down and I said, 'Why don't we do this as a teaser, even before the movie started shooting?' There's a whole thing where you start seeing somebody putting his boots on, putting a knife on, putting the bullets on, putting the bandana on, you know, and then turns around—'Coming This Summer.' We shot that on a stage here in LA."[15]

The film's idea for a "show mission" had a basis in reality. On November 27, 1982, acting on information from Laotian refugees that 120 American POWs were still being held captive near Tchepone, former US Army Special Forces officer Lieutenant Colonel James G. "Bo" Gritz went to Thailand with four Americans and fifteen Laotian guerillas toting Israeli-made Uzi submachine guns. They crossed over into Laos at night and were almost immediately ambushed by Laotian paramilitary forces. One American was wounded and taken prisoner, later to be ransomed and released. The raid was financed, in part, by actor William Shatner (who said he was only buying the rights to Gritz's story), businessman Ross Perot, and, supposedly, Clint Eastwood.[16] Gritz was deported by the Thai authorities and later testified before a House committee headed by Representative Stephen Solarz that he had no evidence of the existence of the POWs.[17]

Gritz's escapade fed the national controversy over forgotten troops, and its newsworthy fervor seemed perfect for Rambo's next assignment. What could be more harrowing for a hero than to confront devils from his own past? With Stallone aboard, the producers approached Richard Crenna to return as Trautman. He was instantly in.

"I love playing the character," Crenna said. "I love working with all those people, you know, Andy, Mario, Buzz, the whole bunch. I mean I just enjoyed coming to the set. I enjoyed working. We had many of the crew go through all of the films. This was a family." It also didn't hurt that the movie would be shot in the vacation town of Acapulco.[18]

Mexico was not Vancouver. Crenna recalled the heat, compared with the cold of Canada. Yet he didn't sweat, which both confused and irritated Stallone in the scenes they played together. Crenna explained simply that he refused to allow himself to sweat, claiming he went into a Zen mode. On the other hand, he said, Acapulco, despite being a lovely area, was fraught with bugs and high humidity. The jungle was always near. But it was hard for an actor to complain about the accommodations.[19]

The script gave Crenna the chance to flex his political as well as his acting muscles. Although Trautman must defer to his CIA superior, Murdock, he gets to lecture him on the hypocrisy of the MIA-POW status. At the time the film was made, many men were still missing from the war.[20] It's a controversy that exploded in 2008 when journalist Sydney H. Schanberg broke a story that Senator John McCain, whose political career was based on his having been a Vietnam POW, was hindering searches for remaining POW-MIAs.[21] *Rambo: First Blood Part II* was prescient, even revolutionary, for statements such as this:

TRAUTMAN: In '72 we were supposed to pay the
Cong four-and-a-half billion in war
reparations. We reneged, they kept

the POWs. And you're doing the same
thing all over again.

MURDOCK: And what the hell would you do,
Trautman? Pay blackmail money to
ransom our own men and finance the
war effort against our allies? What
if some burnt-out POW shows up
on the six-o'clock news? What do
you want to do, start the war all over
again? You wanna bomb Hanoi? You
want everybody screaming for armed
invasion? Do you honestly think
somebody's gonna get up on the floor
of the United States Senate and ask
for billions of dollars for a couple of
forgotten ghosts?

TRAUTMAN: Men, Goddamn it! Men who fought for
their country!!

Playing Murdock, the bad guy, Charles Napier knew he
had a choice part. Napier, whose two-hundred-plus screen
credits included appearances in almost every TV series since
1968 and a gallery of small roles in the films of Jonathan
Demme, knew that being cast in a big-budget action film would
help his career. But when he heard that Lee Marvin had already
won the role, he didn't abandon hope. He begged his agent to
just let him show up for a meeting. When he got to the studio
lot, he discovered that he was the only one in the office, which
meant that the part had already been cast. Then by chance
Stallone walked into the room and recognized him from an
old *Kojak* episode they had done together at the start of their
careers.[22] Stallone took him into a back room and introduced

him to director George Cosmatos. When Napier left, he felt so buoyed that he called his agent to say how well it went. Five minutes after they hung up, his agent called back to tell him he'd landed the role.

Napier would revel in playing the bureaucratic villain, Murdock. Over the years, whenever he was recognized in public, he took actorly pride in telling people who said they hated him that *of course* they were *supposed* to hate him. When Roger Ebert of the *Chicago Sun-Times* called him "the man Rambo fans love to hate," Napier gleefully reported that, despite this, no one had ever bothered him about it. People understood.

One person who didn't make it into the cast was Dolph Lundgren. He was originally hired to play Yushin, Rambo's Russian tormentor. But when Stallone saw Lundgren's screen presence, the role of Yushin seemed to be a comedown, so he decided to cast him as his antagonist, Drago, in *Rocky IV*. As a result, Lundgren, who had already been signed as Yushin, was paid off and went on to greater fame pummeling the Italian Stallion in the fourth Rocky epic.[23]

Julia Nickson, playing Rambo's doomed love interest, Co, was also new to the franchise. A top model in Hawaii, Nickson had not seen *First Blood* until right before she went into her audition room for *Rambo II*. Stallone was there, and she was so captivated by him that she forgot there were other people present.

"It's kind of embarrassing," she admits, "because [later], Mario Kassar said to me, 'Do you remember when we were in the room?' And I honestly had to say 'No' because all I could think of was Stallone. He was the one sitting in front of me and I was looking into his eyes and, you know, basically nothing else existed in that moment. I had been in love with him for years, and then actually being in a room, acting with him. . . And I hadn't a clue what I was doing. I felt like I faked my way through the entire film. But I have to say that he was a teacher and a mentor all the way."[24]

An example of this occurs in a scene by a lagoon as Nickson and Stallone are fleeing Russian and Vietnamese forces. She asks him to bring her back to America, but he hesitates, knowing what a damaged protector he would be. Their exchange is front-loaded with backstory and comes to a tragic head when Co is assassinated.

"Before I die I become more intimate with Sly," Nickson recounts. "And, you know, you can't be that intimate. It's a jungle and we're running away from the bad guys. Co Bao and Rambo have a moment and make plans for the possibility of something in the future." They kiss. "Sly wanted to remove the kiss but I requested it be kept as written. I thought the film needed a moment of intimacy and calm amidst the explosive gunfire. I really fought to keep a kiss in there because I felt that my character should have a possibility of what could happen between them, some sense of a dream that was in the making and some sense that they really mattered to each other. And Sly acquiesced to it, so it came into being. It was beautiful and a very important part because right after that, she doesn't make it through the rest of the movie. It led to more of an emotional investment for Rambo as the possibilities of a life together are destroyed. In actual fact, he is still in the war. It is not done with him yet. He can go home, if he survives, but there will be no peace. I think that is a particularly touching moment.[25] She only sees the vulnerability. That's what moves her and touches her. There's a line in the movie where he says he's expendable. And she says, 'you're not expendable.' It's a line that moves me so much and obviously had great impact on other people."[26]

This dichotomy—a man of action containing a man in

pain—is key to the evolving Rambo character, and many observers fail (or refuse) to see this. Nickson read an early draft of the script and recalls "a couple of scenes in it that James [Cameron] had written that I thought were so beautiful. There was one scene, particularly, about an orchid. I see this orchid and I say that it has been nourished on the blood of soldiers, on the blood of people that have been killed to fight for their country.[27] That got taken out. I think it was just too feminine an approach for Sly and it wasn't the concept that he was interested in. I fought for it but I didn't get to keep it."[28]

"One thing that helped this *Rambo* from all the other *Rambo*s," said George Cosmatos, "is that he had this relationship with this woman, and it made him more vulnerable. And when he loses her, he becomes very powerful, very emotional."[29]

Nickson's character of Co Phuong Bao is significant. Of all the five Rambo films, she is his only potential love interest. Although, in Morrell's novelization, Rambo cautions himself not to become sexually involved with her because it would erode his ability to concentrate on his mission, the hint of it provides audiences with a glimpse of salvation for him. Alas, it is not to be; once she is killed, he channels his grief into revenge.[30]

Nickson's casting is also significant in that she is an actress of mixed racial heritage. "If it was being made today," she recalled in a 2013 interview, "I wouldn't have landed the part as I am half-Caucasian. I would not have been considered ethnically authentic enough."[31] As for Stallone's portrayal, she says, "Rambo is the epitome of the hero, the mythological hero. And along with that aloneness is that sense of the warrior's journey that he takes by himself. He carries the burden alone. I think one of the great things about my character is that, just for a short time, she takes that journey with him and is responsible for him being able to continue with it. She is saying, this is life. Which is a very empowering thing—a very empowering ability or responsibility to give to a female lead in a movie. And probably that character is one of the precursors to all the female action stars that are so rampant in films today."[32]

Nickson notes that the seed of *Rambo: First Blood Part II* is the script by James Cameron. Cameron's belief in strong female characters was already apparent. "Co Bao is the only character in all the Rambo films who rescues him from torture and likely death," Nickson notes. "Her action foreshadows the resolve that Cameron later exhibited in *Aliens* and *Terminator 2: Judgment Day* to create fierce, strong female leads." She notes that John Travolta was, at one point, proffered as Rambo's comic relief but "the producers decided to nix that pairing and my character was then created."[33]

Despite her screen chemistry with Stallone, Nickson remains puzzled (but pleased) about why she was cast. "I was told I exhibited a certain strength that they felt they needed for the character and, obviously, some athletic qualities were needed for the role." Unlike Stallone's obsessive physical training, however, Nickson "had about fifteen minutes of weapons training and that was it. I was a dancer and runner so I was lean, and due to having played field hockey and polo for years, I could be mean and aggressive. I never felt that Co Bao was a trained soldier. She was picked out of a CIA office because she was smart, athletic, and could speak some English. She was sent to deliver a message, lead him to the camps, and then go home; after all, the war had been over for many years."[34]

Acting opposite Stallone in only her third film, Nickson found him "a fabulous actor to work with because he has the ability to control all aspects of filming. If something isn't working, he can make the changes, whereas normally that is the director's purview. He taught me camera angles and the difference between masters and close-ups as well as different lenses. He made me feel comfortable in making suggestions if I felt something was important. For example, when we make our way to the pirate camp, I mentioned they might have a lookout. He incorporated that by putting a guard in a tree. I thought of adding the lookout, but [Sly's] putting that character up in the tree is an element that added danger to the scene. Sly was very good at creating tension.[35]

Although the cast and crew stayed in hotels in glamorous Acapulco, there was precious little time for recreation. Because it was a location shoot, they worked six-day weeks in settings where temperatures and humidity both hovered at ninety-five degrees. The Mexican latitude allowed longer shooting hours than had British Columbia for *First Blood*, and the film's crew were amazed that, despite the tough schedule, Stallone made time to work out before and after each shooting day to maintain his Rambo physique. "I have to say," Nickson adds, "it's probably one of the few movies I've done where the guy looks better than the girl."

Despite this dedication, Stallone still had time to cavort. Reports Nickson, "There were a few nights where we took the Sly-mobile. We would just all pile in, and the bodyguards Norm and Tony were with us and we'd go to a disco. I had never experienced a discotheque such as those in Acapulco. You couldn't get in unless you were a really important person, but I was with the important person so I was okay. Stallone became like the unofficial Mayor of Acapulco. I mean, we would go to one disco after another and drink these little tequila and 7-Up things called slammers. And they would slam 'em on the table and we'd chug. I don't drink at all so it takes about two for me to be totally unlike who I really am in life. That was our way of unleashing during the weekend. I don't really remember the producers ever coming with us. I think they were doing much more important things, like making sure we were on budget and our locations hadn't been swept away."[36]

"I'm always asked about this as if there is more to share, but this was a very professional shoot. No one took drugs or smoked pot. There were no scantily clad dancers or women of the night. Nobody misbehaved or was ever arrested. We drank tequila and then went home to our hotels."[37]

One particular memory that George Cosmatos had of the shoot was "seeing Sly between takes sitting on a rock in a tropical rain forest writing the script of *Rocky IV*."[38]

Thanks to *First Blood*'s profits, Carolco was able to turn Mexico into Vietnam. This involved building huts, planting rice paddies and fields of elephant grass, borrowing a Mexican Air Force Base to use as one in the film, and finding terrain that could look like the Southeast Asian settings in the script. They hired three thousand Mexican extras, put them in Vietnamese costumes, and passed them off as Asians.[39]

Director George Cosmatos liked to shoot with two blimped (silenced) cameras on dollies and a third handheld camera to pick up assorted wild (catch-as-catch-can) shots. For scenes with explosions, he commandeered as many as seven cameras to give editors Mark Kornblatt and Mark Helfrich enough coverage footage to work with. In scenes where Rambo exploded a number of grass huts, the editors extended the sequence by flipping footage right to left and reusing it.

David Morrell, who was novelizing the screenplay while the film was being shot, was kept abreast of the production by Andy Vajna, who sent him VHS cassettes of the footage.

"Andy thought I would benefit from seeing early versions of some of the scenes, particularly an argument between Trautman and Murdock," Morrell reports. "I watched George shoot those scenes several ways, telling Richard Crenna and Charles Napier to vary the speed of their dialogue to give the editors more to work with in terms of pacing."[40]

"George Cosmatos was an extremely intense being," Nickson remembers. "This film meant a lot to him, and he was constantly thinking and pacing and smoking. He was very kind to me and always communicated as if I had been working for years. I never saw any ego. There was some screaming and shouting," she notes, "but fortunately I was never the reason for it."[41]

Film companies making war movies often ask for Pentagon help in getting free military equipment. There is no indication that the producers of *Rambo II* requested or received any—the Pentagon only supports films whose philosophies they approve. The company had to acquire their Hueys from Texas, not Washington, and the Pentagon received no acknowledgment in the end credits. "I never thought of the movie politically, to be honest with you," George Cosmatos said, "I just thought of this hero in the jungle, a warrior fighting the enemy, and it never crossed my mind to create such a political uproar."[42] To serve Cosmatos's demand that aerial sequences be thrilling, producer Buzz Feitshans was able to arrange for low-level helicopter flyovers (sometimes called flat-hatting) for the final showdown.

A mock-up of a jet was used in the scene where Rambo is deployed alone at night over North Vietnam. Prepared to be "inserted" with weapons, communications devices, and other gear, he gets hung up with his parachute cord on the door of the jet and is forced to cut himself loose. The tense sequence was shot indoors in an aircraft hangar with a painted night sky hung in the background and the plane safely on the ground. Says Cosmatos, "So now we have the wind machines blowing, we intercut for reality with a real plane, intercut with a mock-up with a wind machine to give you the feeling of reality, lights, et cetera. He jumps out, intercut with the real plane. He's by the mock-up. He's hanging now in the air. We're hanging him from wires, which you had to paint black, so you don't see them. And thank God for Jerry Goldsmith's music to keep it going. You see all the intercutting of the helicopter shots moving across mountains and valleys give you the feeling that it's the plane flying. Now a [stunt performer] jumps out . . . a real jump from a real plane."[43]

Other production challenges were more down-to-earth, so to speak. Stallone had to slog through bogs and later be suspended in a mud pit after being captured by the North Vietnamese. The bogs and pits were dug out by the company, but they were filled with local water, which, to be charitable, was not potable. Additionally, to achieve the proper color, prop men added instant coffee. Then they made it gloppier with oatmeal. Other Hollywood tricks included barbed wire made out of rubber and a knife that glowed red-hot from having a translucent blade with a red light inside. It smoked, not from heat, but from chemicals that produced smoke at room temperature.

The compound bow and arrows that Rambo shoots at his pursuers were launched with what the film editors called "Rambo time." Ordinarily, if someone shoots an arrow from one camera angle, the picture then cuts to where the arrow is going; it leaves the frame in one shot and enters it precisely in the next. Mark Kornblatt and Mark Helfrich thought it would be more effective to add a few frames at the end of one shot and at the beginning of the next to increase the visual drama of the weapon's flight, and it worked. Arrows that were shot into people, following a decades-old moviemaking trick, were guided to their victims on wires and the editing is so fast (and the sound of *thwump!* so overwhelming) that it looks real even though one never actually sees the blade go in.

As with *First Blood*, Mother Nature took her toll on *Rambo II*. A hurricane destroyed sets and shut down shooting for several days, but Cosmatos kept going by shooting inserts (close-ups of maps, knives, papers, etc.) in a hotel room with acclaimed cinematographer Jack Cardiff. Other delays included the scene in which Rambo dispatches a boat full of river pirates. The sampan that was being used was strong enough to hold the actors, but when the crew and their equipment were loaded aboard, it sank. This happened three times.

Kassar, Vajna, and Feitshans faced not only the exigencies of location filming but also the diplomacy of getting permission to shoot in another country under the gaze and ego of local politicians. Charles Napier reported that the company was using a Mexican Air Force hangar and that, while they were there, a Mexican army captain invited them all to have drinks with the general. When Stallone explained that they were busy filming, the captain made it clear that the general would cut off their electricity, so how about that drink? Without delay, they assembled an entourage and went over to the general's house. After that, Napier recalled, they could do anything they wanted. The only hitch was that the general wanted to keep a huge Styrofoam Buddha statue that was part of the set decoration. When the cast and crew left Mexico, Buddha became nationalized.

It wasn't all fun and games; there was also tragedy. The pyrotechnics in the film indirectly led to loss of life. The explosions that leveled the Vietnamese prison camp included 300 gallons of gasoline, 200 pounds of black powder, 5,000 feet of primer cord, and 15,000 feet of wire connected to all of it to set it off on command. An even bigger explosion involved the destruction of a waterfall (from which Rambo, of course, escapes). On December 1, 1984, it was reported that Cliff Wenger, Jr., had fallen to his death after checking the aftermath of the waterfall explosion. Wenger had climbed the slippery rocks to make sure that all sparks and flames from the blast were safely out when he tripped and fell to the bottom of the waterfall. Crew members immediately rushed to help him, but he succumbed to multiple skull fractures on top of possible drowning.[44] The film is dedicated to him.

Rambo: First Blood Part II was ready to go, and this time, the world was primed for it. Mario Kassar and Andy Vajna had little trouble finding a distributor, but rather than go back to Orion Pictures, and armed with the box office success of *First Blood*, they shopped around. Recalled Vajna, "After the release of the first one ... we did a deal with Tri-Star where Tri-Star had the US and we had the foreign, and so there was no more paranoia about what to do, who's going to buy what, how do we do with the screenings, like we did in *First Blood*."[45]

On May 21, 1985, *Rambo: First Blood Part II* opened on 2,074 American screens, exceeding the saturation opening of the previous year's *Beverly Hills Cop* (in which Stallone almost starred; q.v.) by sixty-four screens.[46] Its worldwide gross to date exceeds $300 million. The budget, however, remains a matter of conjecture. *Variety* says it cost $21 million plus an undisclosed advertising-publicity expense.[47] Aljean Harmetz in the *New York Times* puts it at $25.5 million.[48] *Entertainment* Weekly pegs it at $34 million.[49] Some sources insist that the budget was $27 million, and BoxOfficeMojo doesn't have a clue.[50] Considering, however, that it grossed over $300 million, it confirms Hollywood's addled hindsight that "nothing is as cheap to produce as a hit." It would, however, be the last *Rambo* film to show a profit (as opposed to making money).

Moreover, "It became the quintessential movie of the eighties about war and Vietnam," director Cosmatos says, "and it was very controversial. Most people loved it, some people found it a guilty pleasure, but it was a huge hit all over the world. Everywhere they felt the same about this warrior Rambo. I think it was really a surprise when this happened. But we found out through time that it was a story of this underdog that goes against all odds and survives, and that's any man in the world today. So the movie, although it's a movie from the eighties, is, in a way, eternal."[51]

Rambo: First Blood Part II was widely attacked as being racist for its impersonal portrayal of the Vietnamese soldiers. Its sequels would be cited for similar shorthand. This is a controversial subject. A distinction might be made between the second, third, and fourth entries, in which Rambo fights organized government armies (Vietnamese, Afghan Communists, and Burmese), and *Last Blood*, where he vanquishes a Mexican sex trafficking cartel. National armies are usually, by definition, ethnically homogeneous. In terms of drama, they are the enemy and must be vanquished as impersonally as possible. This is war. *Last Blood* will pose another issue.

Summarizing this debate on FilmReference.com, Douglas Kellner, distinguished research professor of education at UCLA, wrote, "The Vietnamese are portrayed as duplicitous bandits, ineffectual dupes of the evil Soviets, and cannon fodder for Rambo's exploits, while the Soviets are presented as sadistic torturers and inhuman, mechanistic bureaucrats. The stereotypes of race and gender in *Rambo* are so exaggerated, so crude, that they point to the artificial and socially constructed nature of all ideals of masculinity, femininity, race, and ethnicity."⁵² Part of the controversy stemmed from President Ronald Reagan's statement, after screening *Rambo: First Blood Part II* at the White House, that Rambo was a Republican.⁵³ This troubled Sylvester Stallone. "I went, 'Uh-oh,'" he told the *Hollywood Reporter*, "Rambo is totally neutral. He doesn't even live in this country . . . People assume I'm the same as my character . . . Do I really need this controversy?"⁵⁴

First Blood and *Rambo: First Blood Part II* were influential as genre changers. In previous action films, the action tended to be restricted to three or five major sequences with considerable dialogue between them, but the Rambo films were mostly action with a minimum of dialogue, and action movies thereafter tended to imitate this pattern. Also, in many subsequent non-Rambo action films, such as 1988's *Die Hard*, the main characters were explicitly compared to Rambo.

The Rambo movies also introduced an element of visual elegance that would soon become an industry standard. These days it's hard to find an action film, no matter how low the budget, that doesn't look exquisite. *First Blood* and *Rambo: First Blood Part II* enjoyed the eye of cinematographer Andrew Laszlo in the first and famed Jack Cardiff in the second. Cardiff was renowned as one of the world's greatest cinematographers, especially when depicting color. His credits included the incomparably photographed *Black Narcissus* (1947), *The Red Shoes* (1948), *The African Queen* (1951), *The Brave One* (1956), and numerous other classics, each with a different yet appropriate style. At the same time, the elegance of the photography does not distract from the muscular action; indeed, it gives it a legitimacy that makes the action all the more effective. Combined with Jerry Goldsmith's impressive score, which recalls themes from

First Blood and adds Asian tones, *Rambo: First Blood Part II* is a cinematic step above its predecessor, which already hit high marks. Its philosophy, however, was not to be so highly praised, and its success at both the box office and as a phenomenon of popular culture, as shall be seen, has yet to fade.

SIDEBAR

Synopsis of the Film
Rambo: First Blood Part II

Having single-handedly caused the destruction of Hope three years earlier, John Rambo (Sylvester Stallone) is called away from his hard labor on a prison rock pile to be greeted by his creator, Colonel Sam Trautman (Richard Crenna). Trautman offers him reprieve from the rest of his eight-year sentence and a possible presidential pardon if he will take part in a special mission involving Vietnam. Rambo agrees, bitterly asking Trautman, "Do we get to win this time?" In the Thailand staging base, Rambo is told by the mission director Murdock (Charles Napier) that he will be dropped into North Vietnam to gather photographic proof of whether POWs are still imprisoned in a particular camp despite the peace treaty between the US and Hanoi that provided for their release. Rambo is perplexed about why he should only photograph the camp rather than free any prisoners he may find there. Worse, this is the camp where Rambo himself was held prisoner when he was captured in 'Nam. Murdock, who is a CIA spook, assures him that Trautman will later lead an extraction force to free any prisoners once Rambo returns with evidence of their presence. Later dialogue between Murdock and Trautman explains that this action is being cynically taken to placate public doubt whether soldiers are still held in Vietnam, and Trautman lectures Murdock that, if they are, it is because the US broke its promise to Hanoi about reparations.

After warning Trautman that Murdock is not to be trusted, Rambo is flown covertly into North Vietnam at night with a backpack full of weapons, communications technology, and instructions that he will be met somewhere on the ground by an operative named Co Phuong Bao. Bailing out of the insertion plane, however, he gets hung up on the airplane door. He cuts himself loose with his all-purpose Rambo knife and parachutes to the ground without his weapons and communication package. All he has left are his bow and arrows, gun, knife, and wits.

Making his way carefully through the jungle, he almost cuts the throat of a Vietnamese woman, who, it turns out, is his contact, Agent Co Phuong Bao (Julia Nickson). Co has arranged for river pirates to transport them upriver to the POW camp. On arrival, they discover that the camp has not been abandoned but is crawling with Vietnamese soldiers guarding a hut full of US prisoners whom they use as slave labor.

Ignoring his mission orders, Rambo frees one of the prisoners, Banks (Andy Wood), and kills seventeen Viet Cong as he, Co, and Banks head back to the pirate sampan ahead of a patrol of pursuing Viet Cong. Once onboard, they learn that the pirates have sold them out. As an armed enemy boat approaches, Rambo kills all the pirates.[56] Co and Banks jump into the river while Rambo stays to fire a grenade launcher at the boat, blowing it up. Rambo tells Co to stay behind even though the two of them have become attracted to each other.

At the Thai base, Trautman, Ericson (Martin Kove), and

Lifer (Steve Williams) take off to extract Rambo despite Murdock's objections. Once Trautman radios that he sees Rambo
and Banks at the rendezvous, however, Murdock gives orders
to abort the mission and return to base. Trautman protests.
One of the men flying with him, Lifer, who is a mercenary
working with the CIA, holds a pistol to his head and forces
him to accede.[57] The copter flies off, abandoning Rambo and
Banks, who are captured.

Arriving back in Thailand, Trautman confronts Murdock, who reveals that the mission has all been a show to get
Congress and the POW/MIA lobby off "their" (presumably
the State or Defense Department's) backs. Even if Rambo
returned with proof, it would have been "lost" in the bureau-
cracy, and nothing would ever be done about saving the
remaining captives, who would be abandoned.

In the prison camp, Rambo is confined to a slime pit. A
contingent of Russian soldiers arrives led by Lieutenant Colonel Sergei Podovsky (Steven Berkoff).[58] That night, despite
being confronted with a transcript of broadcasts from US HQ
about his reconnaissance mission, Rambo refuses to make
a radio broadcast confessing to his mission. He is tortured
with electric shocks by the beefy Russian Sergeant Yushin
(Vojislav Govedarica) and resists until Yushin threatens to
mutilate Banks with a red-hot knife. Rambo agrees to make
the broadcast, and the first message he sends is to Murdock,
seething, "I'm coming to get you." Then he takes the microphone and bashes the Russians. With the help of Co, who has
surreptitiously slipped underneath the cabin's floorboards
and shoots through the wooden planks, he escapes with the
Russian brigade and Lieutenant Tay's (George Kee Cheung)
Viet Cong contingent in pursuit.

Come morning, making their way to Thailand, Rambo
and Co reach a stream where they enjoy a romantic respite.

They discuss her coming to America. The two of them grow closer—then she is shot by Tay, who has been tracking them. Co dies in Rambo's arms. He takes from her neck a necklace with a jade Buddha amulet.

At base, Trautman wants to go back and save Rambo. Murdock has him placed under arrest.

Rambo is now out for pure revenge. He dons a headband and wears Co's necklace. He takes his bow and kills the pursuing Russians one by one using a variety of methods, never running out of regular arrows and saving his incendiary arrowheads for later. He leads the Russian and Viet Cong patrols through a peasant village, noticing a chicken along the way. He lures Tay's forces into elephant grass, following a trail of blood, which, they learn too late, is from the slain chicken, not him. Rambo torches the field, burning the troops alive, then uses incendiary arrows to blow up huts and troop trucks. Confronting Tay across a waterfall, he uses his one last explosive arrow to take his revenge for Co, blowing him apart.

Now he is pursued by a Russian helicopter commanded by Yushin. They bomb the waterfall and Rambo saves himself by diving into the water with the copter shooting after him. When the copter descends to look for his body, Rambo reaches out of the water and drags a Russian soldier out of the open side door and to his death. Then he climbs aboard the copter to fight Yushin, whom he flips out onto the ground, after which he tosses out the pilot and takes command of the unit himself.

Rambo flies back to the prison compound and destroys it. He frees the POWs, who climb aboard his helicopter to fly back to Bangkok. They are almost immediately pursued by another Russian helicopter. After they exchange shots, the Russian pilot finds that Rambo has landed in a stream and is apparently dead behind the controls. But Rambo was just playing possum and blows the Russian chopper apart. He then flies the rescued prisoners back to the base in Thailand.

There, Rambo overcomes Ericson and bursts into the operations room after Murdock, restraining himself from killing Murdock with his Rambo knife. Trautman thanks Rambo. Rambo tells him that he and his fellow veterans wish their country loved them as much as they love their country. Then he walks off to an uncertain future.

SIDEBAR

Why and How Morrell Novelized
Rambo II and *III*

For years, novelizations of movies were seen as an advertising adjunct, a way before the arrival of home video for fans of a particular film to own a form of it. Novelizations were usually adapted from screenplays well before the film was shot, in order to meet publishing deadlines, and were little more than retyping the script's action description and adding "he said" and "she said" to the dialogue.

This changed with David Morrell's novelizing of *Rambo: First Blood Part II* and *Rambo III*. Instead of simply translating the screenplays into prose, Morrell combined several different script drafts—some of them widely disparate—and added his own material to create enriched, yet faithful, reading experiences.

When Andy Vajna and Mario Kassar approached Morrell, he had an advantage: "In the movie contract, no one can do books about Rambo except me," he reports. "Carolco came to me, in the days when novelizations were a big deal. My first reaction was that it was a derivative kind of writing and that I didn't want to be associated with it. Then I got to thinking because I like to try everything and see if I can make it new. I looked around, and I thought, 'Maybe there is a way to do a novelization that's never been done before.'

"The shooting script for *Rambo II* was maybe eighty-seven pages. I didn't see a book in it. I asked Andy, 'Do you have anything else? Because I can't write a book with this. It's just too thin.' Andy said, 'Well, we have the James Cameron script.' At that time, James Cameron was not 'James Cameron,' but I'd seen *The Terminator* and knew what a great storyteller he is.

"The next morning, through the magic of my first experience with FedEx, I received the script and oh my God, what a wonderful script. There was a problem with the comical sidekick, who would probably have been John Travolta. That was all wrong, but oh my God, the opening in the mental institution, with Rambo in a cell in the basement with a guard. It was so wonderful. I got back to Andy and said, 'All right, I'll do it. But this novelization will not be the movie. It'll be in large part the movie, but it will not be a carbon copy of the shooting script. It's going to be a third Cameron, a third shooting script, and a third me.'"

The book was on the *New York Times* bestseller list for six weeks. "I'm very proud of my Rambo novelizations," he says. "They go back to the character as I imagined him in my novel *First Blood* and at the same time go with what Andy and Mario were trying to do. What really interested me was that Rambo, in order to redeem himself, goes back to the very POW camp where he was tortured and from which he escaped. This is a guy who's haunted by his past. His return to the scene of his nightmares is barely mentioned in the movie. I wondered, *What would it feel like to go back there?* That was

the emotion that made me really want to write the novelization for *Rambo II*.

"For *Rambo III*, the process was different, but the result
was similar. The first scripts I received were epical, with
a massive sandstorm and a Dutch female doctor and war
orphans and an escape over blizzardy mountains. It was truly
Rambo of Arabia. Then I received a new draft and another
draft after that and another. Each script reduced the scope of
the plot. I was told that the reduction was for budget reasons.
Soon the sandstorm was gone. The Dutch female doctor was
gone. So were the war orphans whom Rambo and Trautman
take across the snow-drifted mountains to escape the pursuing Russian soldiers. The mountains were gone.

"Finally, I received so many scripts and they were so
different that I phoned Andy and told him that the only
way I could meet the publisher's deadline was by choosing
what I thought was the best script (an early one) and using
it as the basis for the book. If you look at the movie, it can
be condensed as: Act One, Trautman gets kidnapped; Act
Two, Rambo tries to rescue him and fails; Act Three, Rambo
tries to rescue him and succeeds. The second and third acts
are similar. But the script I chose had a huge third act that
involved rescuing the war orphans and gave Trautman a lot
more to do. Also, I wanted to explore the idea that Afghanistan was Russia's Vietnam. I invented a mirror image of
Rambo, a Russian special-operations soldier who thought the
way Rambo did about the futility of wars.

"I may have made a contribution to the *Rambo III* movie,"
Morrell continues. "In all the many scripts I read in writing
my novelization of *Rambo III*, the sequence involving the
game with the goat carcass didn't exist. But after I sent the
manuscript of my novelization to Carolco, the next script I
read included that sequence.

"In the end, my novelization was a combination of the shooting script, that wonderful early Cameron script, and my own additions. Even more than the book for *Rambo II*, the novelization for *Rambo III* expanded the possibilities for writing movie adaptations."

SIDEBAR

Synopsis of the Novelization of *Rambo: First Blood Part II*

The Quarry

Time-present is 1985. Rambo, sentenced to the penitentiary for his destruction of Hope, breaks big stones into little ones on a prison rock pile, keeping his sanity through Zen meditation. He is approached by Colonel Trautman, who wants him to return to North Vietnam, where Rambo was once a captive, on a mission to get photographic evidence of POWs still being held there—a mission that Murdock, the CIA man who has come along with Trautman, tells him will never exist. Rambo agrees. In his cell before departing, bitter that, for all his sacrifice in 'Nam, no one ever thanked him or his fellow vets, he drops all his service medals down the crude toilet in the floor and sets fire to his personal photos lest someone find them if he doesn't return. His memories are now confined within him, along with his pain.

The Wolf Den

Arriving at Fort Bragg, North Carolina, Rambo gets his first briefing from Murdock, who tells him that some 2,400 American servicemen are thought to be missing in action in Vietnam, Laos, and Cambodia and that Congress and the

League of American Families are demanding proof. Rambo is stunned when he realizes that Murdock wants him to go back to Ban Kia Na, the very POW camp where he was held during the war. He becomes angry when he realizes that his familiarity with the area is why the CIA wanted him and not someone else. Murdock explains to him that the reason he should only photograph any POWs but not rescue them is because of Son Tay. (In 1970, Special Forces carried out a mission to the Son Tay POW camp in North Vietnam only to discover that its prisoners had been moved. Filmmaker John Milius, in his as-yet-unproduced screenplay *The Greatest Raid of All*, contends that Special Forces' ability to reach Son Tay drove North Vietnam to the Paris Peace Talks. Therefore, despite not saving any prisoners, the US saved all of them.)

Rambo flies to Bangkok. Noticing that he is being followed from the airport, he eludes his trackers and reaches the field where there has been a Huey helicopter waiting for his arrival. He flies the Huey to the Wolf Den, a tech-heavy HQ from which he will depart for 'Nam. Murdock greets him there, and Rambo tears into him that he had to lose the "spooks" (CIA agents) who were tailing him, and that, if they could follow him, so could the enemy. The distrust between Rambo and Murdock is palpable.

Rambo is issued a wealth of high-tech equipment as well as a special compound bow. He is also handed a camera and cautioned that he is only to take photos of any POWs he may find. He is told that his ground contact will be Co Phuong Bao, that his code name is "Lone Wolf," and that his mission is called "Dragonfly."

After Rambo leaves them alone, Trautman and Murdock argue about the war and its aftermath, with Trautman saying, "Lies were told to start the war, lies were told to cover

mistakes," and that the US lost because it tried to fight guerillas with traditional tactics. Murdock tolerates this outburst.

The Wat

Before he gets aboard the plane, Rambo tells Trautman that
Murdock is a fraud because he bragged about being at a battle
at Con Thien in 1966 that actually took place at Kud Sank.

Flying under the radar into Vietnam, as Rambo parachutes from the jet, he hangs up on its open door. Ericson
and Downy, two men assigned to fly him in, urgently radio
Murdock back at Wolf Den. Murdock is set to abort the mission when Rambo frees himself with his knife. He floats to
the ground, however, without his special tech equipment and
camera, saving only what he had on his person: the knife, a
pistol, and a bow and arrows.

Slogging through the rain forest, he assumes a Buddhist
frame of mind. He kills a viper and, after several miles' hiking, meets his contact, Co Phuong Bao, who is a woman. This
surprises him. They pass an abandoned Buddhist temple
and make their way to the sampan where pirates are waiting
to take them upriver into North Vietnam. Although Co is
attractive, Rambo rejects any personal involvement with her.
He recalls his training discipline which included forsaking
sex because, during sex, one loses control.

Rambo and Co finally link with the pirates and set out for
their destination.

The Compound

Having lost communication with Rambo, Murdock wants
to call off the mission and leave him to survive on his own.
Trautman is astonished at Murdock's callousness and wants
to return to the extraction point with Ericson as planned and
retrieve Rambo, against Murdock's wishes.

On the sampan, Rambo gets close to Co and admires a necklace she wears that has a small Buddha pendant. A Vietnamese army patrol boat pulls close and demands to board and inspect them, not knowing that they carry a grenade launcher. Rambo hides and Kinh, the lead pirate, successfully bluffs away the patrol boat.

Kinh deposits Rambo and Co on the shore and promises to wait for them. The pair wades through a marsh full of human skeletons whose frames Rambo determines are large enough to have been Caucasian. Soon they cross a ridge and come upon the prison camp hidden from detection by aerial reconnaissance under a canopy of trees. It appears to be deserted, but then they see a sentry on duty and know that the camp is still operational.

Rambo's thoughts go to the powerful three-string compound bow that he carries, the bow that he taught himself to fire, drawing on his part-Navajo heritage. Avoiding the tripwire of a Claymore land mine, Rambo tells Co that, lacking a camera, he now needs to go into the camp to see if it holds anyone. "When I lost the camera," he tells Co, "orders stopped. People began."

Infiltrating the camp, Rambo hears a scream and sees two guards merrily swapping gossip. He sees Tay, his tormentor from when he was a captive there. The old barracks are empty, but soon he sees, caged behind bamboo, five sickly prisoners. Rambo is vexed; with no camera, will Murdock believe him? He dares not break them out because they'll all surely be killed, and the men are too weak to endure the rigors of a jungle trek. Then he hears another prisoner (Banks) moaning, hanging from a cross and near death. Rambo frees him from his torturous restraints and carries him, on the way shooting one guard with an arrow and slicing the throat of another. Then Co is discovered, but Rambo shoots the soldier who is about to shoot her. Carrying Banks, Rambo leads Co away.

On schedule from base, Trautman and airmen Ericson and Doyle set out in a copter to extract Rambo, counting on him and his training to reach the meeting spot even without communication.

Rambo, Co, and Banks make it to the sampan and head down the river toward rendezvous.

The Slime Pit

Before long, a US Navy gunboat intercepts them. Only it isn't the US Navy—it's Vietnamese Communists who found the abandoned vessel after the US left their country. Rambo and Co learn that Kinh, the lead pirate, sold them out to save his crew's lives. Rambo insults Kinh to trick him into slapping his face. He uses his flinch from the slap to cover grabbing the rifle that another pirate is holding on him. In due course, Rambo kills all of the pirates on the sampan and escapes from the approaching gunboat.

In the air, Trautman, Ericson, and Doyle fly the copter to the extraction point.

As Rambo, Banks, and Co rush to the pickup spot, Rambo tries to persuade Co to come back to America with him. She declines and leaves them so they can be rescued. The Viet Cong from the prison camp start to catch up, and Rambo shoots them with an AK-47 as Co disappears into the jungle and safety.

When the chopper arrives and sees that Rambo has Banks, Trautman orders the pickup. Hearing this on the radio back at base, Murdock tells Ericson to abort the project and abandon Rambo. When Trautman objects, Doyle aims a rifle at his head and the chopper flies away. On the ground, Rambo and Banks are captured.

When an enraged Trautman returns to the base, Murdock explains to him that the whole mission was just a cover to give Congress an excuse to stop looking for POWs. No matter what evidence Rambo might have found, it would be "lost."

Now returned to the camp where he was once a prisoner, Rambo is tied to a cross, tormented by Tay, and lowered into a slime pit. He attempts to use Zen to deal with it. He emerges from the mud covered with leeches.

Then a team of Russian advisors appears led by Sergeant Yushin and Lieutenant Podovsky. Banks, now back with the other prisoners, warns them that if you're ever tortured by Russians, you should hope that they kill you by mistake.

The Grave

Rambo is told by Podovsky, while the brutish Yushin stands by, that the torture will make him consent to broadcast a radio message to US headquarters that he found no prisoners, and thus the operation is a failure.[59] The Russians electrocute Rambo on a metal box spring connected to a generator. Co sneaks into camp, pretending to be a prostitute. Podovsky shows Rambo a transcript of Trautman's broadcast to headquarters, revealing that he saw Rambo, and smarmily asks Rambo if he wouldn't enjoy getting even for being abandoned. While Podovsky says this, Yushin heats Rambo's knife to a red-hot glow.

It starts to rain as Co kills a guard with her knife and crawls under the raised floor of the command cabin where Rambo is being held.

Rambo wonders how long he can bear the pain when Tay enters with Banks and throws him to the floor. Yushin takes the red-hot knife and presses it into Rambo's cheek. When even this does not inspire Rambo to make the broadcast, Podovsky orders Yushin to cut out Banks's eye. To save Banks,

Rambo agrees, and begins the broadcast, "Murdock, I'm coming to get you." Murdock hears him. Podovsky increases the generator's power, electrocuting Rambo further. Instead, Rambo, in supreme anger, breaks free of his restraints and leaps forward, throwing Podovsky toward the generator. He grabs the microphone and uses it to pound Yushin's face. As Tay and a guard reach for their guns, the floor explodes as Co fires her AK-47 up at them, killing the guard. Tay escapes. Co tosses Rambo his bow and quiver and the pair make their way out into the camp.

Podovsky orders Tay to find the escapees. Yushin, his mouth crushed, demands revenge. Podovsky summons his Soviet patrol and sees Yushin and two of his men heading toward a helicopter as the rain and lightning continue. Yushin takes off in search of Rambo and Co.

Rambo and Co continue through the night. They rest by a body of water. After what they have been through, Co decides she wants to come to America. There is a hint that she also wishes to marry Rambo. Meanwhile, Tay, ridiculed by his superior for letting Rambo escape not only during the war but again just now, sets out to track them as a matter of personal revenge.

At dawn, Rambo and Co find a clearing, only to be spotted by Yushin in his Huey. The Huey has a "dragon," an M-134 minigun that fires six thousand 7.62 rounds per minute seeded with tracers so the stream looks like a tongue of fire. Fleeing into the jungle, Rambo suddenly realizes that he has lost Co. He doubles back, finds that she has been shot by Tay, and holds her as she dies in Rambo's arms.

Tay now tracks Rambo as he carries Co's body into the woods and rests her in a crude grave. He takes her Buddha medallion necklace and puts it on himself for a memento. He ties a strip of her clothing around his forehead as a headband

and screams, "I'm through fighting other people's wars! This time, no one's going to stop me from winning!"

The Blood Zone

Rambo, tracked by Tay's men, picks them off one by one with arrows, which they cannot hear because the firing of nearby AK-47s deafens them to their sounds.

AWACS reports to Murdock and Trautman indicates that someone is killing Vietnamese soldiers with a bow and arrow. Trautman knows it's Rambo and warns Murdock that the Soviets are about to get a taste of what Rambo did to the sheriff back home, and when he's finished with the Soviet commander, he will come for him.

Rambo commandeers an old man's chicken truck and takes a can of gasoline. Tay vies with another officer, Vinh, in pursuing Rambo. They lead their unit into a field of elephant grass, following a trail of blood, presuming it's from a wounded Rambo. Suddenly the field explodes in flames, and all the men are caught in the fire. Many are incinerated. As the Huey continues its search, Rambo fashions incendiary arrows from C-4 plastic explosive. He blows up a truck but misses the Huey. (The blood that the men followed came from a slaughtered chicken.)

Tay comes across some of his men, who have been killed by Rambo in various horrible ways. Finally, Tay himself is shot by Rambo using a final explosive arrow that blows him to bits.

Still pursued by the Huey, Rambo ducks for cover as two cannisters of napalm are launched toward him. He dives into water to avoid the flames. Then he grabs onto the skids of the Huey, pulling it off balance as the pilot tries to fly away. Rambo hoists himself into the cockpit and throws a Russian crew member to the ground, grabbing the man's M-60 on the way. Dangling from the copter and firing the weapon, Rambo blows Yushin apart. The pilot bails out and Rambo grabs the controls.

At the Wolf Den, Murdock places Trautman under arrest and orders his men to destroy all the equipment to leave no evidence of his covert operation. They hear that Rambo has used the Huey to level the prison camp and retrieve all the POWs. Another Russian Huey appears as Rambo is trying to leave with the freed men. There is a copter-copter stand-off, and Rambo fires the dragon at the Russian bird. The sky explodes.

Murdock orders Ericson to shoot down Rambo's helicopter once it crosses into Thailand. Ericson refuses because, this time, Trautman is holding a gun to his head and Doyle has been knocked unconscious.

Rambo and the POWs land at the US base in Thailand. The soldiers there are prepared to shoot them until Colonel Trautman orders them to stand down. With Trautman's implied permission, Rambo seeks out Murdock, who tries to justify his duplicity. Rambo aims his M-60 at him and pulls the trigger. It clicks, empty, and Murdock shits his pants. "More men are out there," Rambo says. "More prisoners. You find them or I'll find you and maybe, finally, this war will be over."

Trautman joins Rambo and tells him what he has long wanted to hear: "You did a good job."

From now on, however, all Rambo wants to do is survive.

CHAPTER 7

Rambo of Arabia

There were two wars going on in *Rambo III*: the one on the screen and the one behind the camera. The good guys won both of them, but they were Pyrrhic victories that stalled for nearly twenty years a fourth entry in the series. It was a lesson in "be careful what you wish for." The commercial returns on *Rambo: First Blood Part II* had been breathtaking: a gross of over $300 million from ticket sales alone on a budget of $27 million.[1] Even without knowing the advertising and publicity budget or allowing for Hollywood's byzantine bookkeeping, there was simply too much money for the distributors to hide. Reporting for *Variety*, Todd McCarthy noted that, between *First Blood* and *Rambo: First Blood Part II*, whose combined gross was $390 million worldwide, Carolco reaped $170 million in revenues.[2] With that in fist, as noted elsewhere, they went on a spending spree not unlike a lottery winner who forgets that the IRS is waiting in the wings.

The flower of success was in full bloom, and intoxicated by its scent, it would have been ludicrous not to go for a third outing. Moreover, Carolco and Sylvester Stallone had created what is today known as a franchise, a concept in which film companies knock out reboots, remakes, and extensions without having to use the pejorative word *sequel*, even though that's what they're making. Studios started doing this during the 2010s,[3] infatuated with the concept of "branding" that created public awareness of a name in the same way that McDonald's, Subway, KFC, and 7-11 are generically known.

The difference is that business franchisees buy into an ongoing brand and are supported by the franchisor, whereas film franchises enter the market to live or die on opening weekend.

By the time *Rambo: First Blood Part II* transitioned into *Rambo III*, the franchise had become formulaic. Rambo had turned into an avenger, morally correct, politically neutral, killing bad guys, and saving good guys. The highly trained Special Forces prodigy, whose mind was as agile as his body, now seldom spoke. He still meted out justice to those deserving of it, but now it was in service of others, not his own psychological liberation.

If a journey of a thousand miles begins with a single step, the journey of *Rambo III* began in December of 1985 when Carolco hired David Morrell to write a screenplay for a third Rambo film. "I flew to Los Angeles and spent two long mornings with Andy Vajna, Mario Kassar, and Buzz Feitshans, discussing possible directions," he says. "In the end, we agreed on what I believe was the first of the Trautman rescue plots, with Trautman being a US military advisor in a Central American country where rebels are plotting to take down the government. The rebels kidnap Trautman during an attack on the US embassy. The central dilemma in the post–*First Blood* Rambo movies is how to motivate him to become a warrior again when his killing skills are what he hates about himself. His loyalty to Trautman, who by now in the series is a father figure (quite different from how I depict him in my novel and how he is mostly depicted in the first movie), drives Rambo to want to rescue him. In my conversations with Andy, Mario, and Buzz on those two mornings, no one ever mentioned that they'd considered an early version of the Trautman rescue plot.

"Eventually, with other writers, that plot device was transferred from Central America to Afghanistan, where it took a totally different direction from what I discussed with them. The geography not only changed, and the surrounding characters not only changed, but also the one element that I most liked never got out of the discussion stage, and that was to bring in a strong female character, Trautman's wife, who would have her own military background and who in the climax would stand next to Rambo, each of them firing automatic weapons at Trautman's abductors. I remember being told that audiences wouldn't accept that sort of female character in an action movie. Then James Cameron's *Aliens* came out in 1986 and his *Terminator 2: Judgment Day* in 1991, with Sigourney Weaver in the first and Linda Hamilton in the second, playing exceedingly capable action women. But this was in 1985."

In May of 1986, Carolco announced that it would begin shooting a sequel in October or November of 1987,[4] that it would be written by veteran scribe Harry Kleiner (*House of Bamboo*, 1955; *Fantastic Voyage*, 1966; *Bullitt*, 1968, all co-credits) and that the budget would be $30 million.[5]

Working with Stallone on the script, Kleiner took an analytical approach, trying to humanize Rambo and provide him with a credible, formidable antagonist. "Your protagonist is only as good as his antagonist," Kleiner explained. "The problem you have today is cardboard antagonists that are just blown away. There's no suspense. The antagonist has to be real, like a human being." By July of 1986, the start date was now October 1986 or January 1987 for a July 4, 1987 release through Tri-Star Pictures.[6] The release date turned out to be optimistic and was later revised to "sometime around Thanksgiving."[7] Russell Mulcahy (*Highlander*, 1986) was signed to direct.[8]

Initial plans were to start shooting the picture in the spring of 1987 in the United States because Stallone wanted to avoid the extreme conditions he'd experienced when shooting *First Blood* in British Columbia and *Rambo: First Blood Part II* in Mexico. "I wanted to shoot the third one here," he told reporter Claudia Eller. "There is a large contingent of Afghanis outside their homeland in the US and doing the film here would add a sense of reality.[9] Two months later, the plans had changed to shooting in Mexico starting on April 7, then in May.[10] By the time principal photography finally began on August 30, 1987, it was in Morocco, then Guaymas, Mexico. When Guaymas proved "unworkable," according to Carolco's marketing vice president Kathryn Linclau, the company migrated to Israel, Bangkok, Thailand, and Yuma, Arizona.[11]

Before shooting began, Stallone had said, "For a while, we talked about doing this movie in Arizona or Nevada. But then I thought, hey, what's everyone going to do—hit the crap tables every night after filming? That's not quite the state of mind I thought we should have for a movie like this." That's why Israel was chosen after a location search. "I got off the plane," Stallone continued, "and said, 'Yeah, this is it. It feels like the kind of place where you should make *Rambo*.'"[12] Israel was finally selected as the primary location, doubling for Afghanistan.[13]

Nevertheless, a few days later, word came that filming would be moved to the United States and that Sylvester Stallone was rewriting Kleiner's script to make Rambo "more realistic and less of a cartoon figure."[14] This was a significant decision. At the end of 1986, Oliver Stone's stunning Vietnam drama *Platoon* had been released, and on March 30, 1987, it had won the Oscar for Best Picture, resetting the bar for war movies. Its effect was profound. Where *Rambo II* had been a fantasy, *Rambo III* needed its boots on the ground.[15] Most likely aware of this change, Sylvester Stallone performed what is known as a "page one rewrite," apparently starting from scratch, and, by January 2, 1987, he was confident enough of what he had produced to label it the "almost, could be, not quite sure, final draft." It wasn't, and Sheldon Lettich (*Russkies*, 1987; *Blood Sport*, 1988) was hired to rewrite Stallone. A new budget was drawn that had grown from $30 to $45 million, which included Stallone's $16 million fee.[16] The film would eventually cost $63 million ($25 million over budget) that would require a worldwide gross of perhaps three to four times that amount to break even.[17]

Rambo III headed to Israel after initially rejecting not only Morocco and Mexico but also Spain and Tunisia. The big attraction in Israel was the availability of fully equipped production facilities at G&G Studios, the home of flamboyant Israeli filmmakers Menahem Golan and Yoram Globus. When director Russell Mulcahy and his crew got to G&G's Jaffa studio, however, they discovered that it was an empty former fish warehouse with no equipment but plenty of schmutz and had to be cleaned and disinfected. Filmmaking equipment had to be flown in from England and the States. Lawsuits ensued, including one, surprisingly, from Golan and Globus against Carolco for passing $200,000 worth of bad checks.[18] By January 15, 1988, the amount was being touted as $666,000 (one million shekels) in bad checks. Carolco blamed Golan and Globus Studios, who failed to provide the production services. Those who knew Golan and Globus could relate.[19]

Not all the fighting was of the business variety. Israel is, after all, a country that has been at war since its founding in 1948. "We had a sense of the unrest that was surrounding us," Richard Crenna would later describe about their Israeli location. "While we never personally felt threatened, there were incidents that were occurring around us almost daily. There

were bombings, there were attacks by terrorists, and coun-
terattacks by Israeli forces in retribution, so you were always
aware of the terrible trouble that we found ourselves in the
midst of. The Israelis afforded us the best security we could
have found. We had Israeli forces that were guarding us the
whole time, particularly Sly, who was a pretty big target—not
only for critics but for terrorists. We had information that
attempts might be made during the picture, so there was
always a constant security around him."[20]

August 1987 was spent shooting the nighttime capture
of Colonel Trautman (Crenna) by the Russian-led Afghanis.
Stallone was not scheduled for this sequence. When the star
did arrive after Labor Day, he discovered that Mulcahy had
ignored the prepared storyboards and wasn't following the
agreed plan for scenes shot at the Dead Sea either. Consequently, Mulcahy, first assistant director Andy Stone, and
cinematographer Ric Waite (who had just worked with Stallone on *Cobra*, 1986) were sent packing.[21]

"Things weren't jelling," said Stallone. "There were creative differences. Personality differences. The key to *Rambo*
is emotion—if you don't find yourself wedded to the crusade,
the film won't work. Well, we had people who weren't in sync
with the crusade."[22] Stallone chose cameraman and second
unit director Peter MacDonald as the next director. Having
staged the fight scenes for *Rambo II*, MacDonald was the clear
choice to take over for Mulcahy, who left on a Tuesday with
MacDonald taking over smoothly the next day. Stallone also
brought in David Gurfinkle as director of photography. Soon
producer Buzz Feitshans was banned from the set, reportedly by the star himself. "Stallone's taken over," a source said.
"He's running the show now."[23] Feitshans remained the credited producer while Andy Vajna and Mario Kassar were the
credited executive producers.

Why didn't Stallone take over directing? "In my opinion, he wanted to be directed," says Kassar. "The whole movie was on his shoulders, so many things he had to do, he was already working on the screenplay. Sly knows everything; he knows where the camera should be, he knows what to do, he knows what the lines should be, he's done it all. I got him Kotcheff on the first one, I convinced him to take Cosmatos on the second one. The third one was out of my hands; he chose Russell, and then we changed to Peter MacDonald. We were shooting in Israel, and it was going on and on and at one point I said to Peter, 'We are going on and on, we're going now. We've done enough shooting; we have enough fighting. If there's anything [missing] we can do it in the States? It's getting too long and too expensive.' We finished it here [in the US] in the desert; I don't remember if it was Arizona or where. It's been a long time."[24]

Moving up the DGA roster to replace MacDonald was second unit (action sequence) director Andy Armstrong, who began filming troop movements and explosions at the Dead Sea. Armstrong lasted three weeks and was replaced by Ernest Day, whose credits included David Lean's *A Passage to India* (1985). Then Gurfinkle was released as director of photography, and John Stanier took his place. In all, it is estimated that some one hundred people were fired in the course of what became a taxing five-month shoot with scrapped film amounting to a $2 million irretrievable waste.[25]

Todd McCarthy and *Variety* had the knowledge and courage to print facts about the production that others either did not know or declined to publish:

- Inexperienced personnel did not produce call sheets for days on end, so no one knew when to report to the set;

- Dailies and film stock were lost;

- Equipment went missing;

- A $3,000 Panavision lens was thought to be lost when, in fact, it was sitting behind an office desk all along;

- Costumes were stored in hotels while the actors needed them on the set;

- Approximately fifty military vehicles were ordered for a battle sequence but only two batteries were ordered to run them;

- Vajna and Kassar reportedly received $17,500 apiece weekly expenses whether they were there or not.

Additional costs arose from the unusual catering situation: *Rambo III*'s crew consisted of Israeli (Jewish), Arab (Muslim), and American workers, so three caterers with separate dietary restrictions had to be engaged to satisfy religious and cultural preferences.

There was growing tension between the Israeli crews and the American and English crews. The final break happened when the company learned that it could not set off gasoline bombs in Israel's national parks, nor could helicopters be allowed to perform the stunts required by the script. The frustration built in Stallone to the point where, while the company was still in Israel, he summoned experienced production coordinator Richard Liebgott (*First Blood Part II, Cobra*) out of retirement to get the production back on track. Liebgott did, and without credit.

Firings continued when editors David and Tom Berlatzky were let go in November.[26] Moving to Thailand for the film's opening sequences, Liebgott found that it would take two hours to drive the cast and crew every day from their Bangkok hotel to the location, so he hired boats to sail them upriver to the set in twenty minutes. When it was time to leave Thailand after working seven-day weeks, fourteen hours a day, Liebgott discovered that there weren't enough flights to get everyone back to the States or to England for Christmas. The decision was made to send Stallone and the married couples to Tokyo, where billionaire Kirk Kirkorian, who had just sold the MGM Grand Hotels, lent his private jet to fly them stateside, where they could catch connecting domestic flights.

After the Christmas New Year break, the explosive battle sequence that ends the film was shot in early January 1988 on the California-Arizona border near Yuma. Here the local Native American tribes, unlike the Israelis, had no problem allowing their land to be wired for explosions. The Yuma location was also used for three days to reshoot Trautman's capture, but that footage was scrapped and reshot over six additional days in the same location.

The star's age was also a factor. Although only forty-two, Stallone was feeling the cumulative effects of four *Rocky*s, two *Rambo*s, a *Cobra*, *Nighthawks*, and *Victory*, not to mention the personal pressures that came with them.

"I made this picture at such a low ebb of my own emotional fortunes," he told Roger Ebert (Stallone had just divorced Brigitte Nielsen in July 1987), "that I didn't care if I lived or died." He did, however, feel a responsibility toward the investors and his crew. "There was an ambulance standing by at all times," he noted. "In any of those shots where I'm running toward the camera and the explosions are going off behind me, if the camera panned another two feet, you'd see the ambulance."[27]

David Morrell, who was on location near Eilat in Israel and Yuma, Arizona, noted that Stallone was an impressive horseman. In fact, the actor had grown up on a Potomac, Maryland, horse farm owned by his father, Frank Stallone, Sr., and would again demonstrate his equestrian prowess at the beginning of *Rambo: Last Blood* (2019). "I saw him on horseback for most of one day, and anybody who knows horses knows how hard that is. The muscle control required to be elegant on a horse for that long is extreme. On one occasion, he had his son, Sage, on the horse with him, and the boy was really enjoying it. When they filmed the scene where Sly gallops holding a flaming Molotov cocktail, the force of the wind generated by the horse's movement caused the flame to go back toward his arm. After the scene was finished, I saw burn blisters on that arm. A while later, he was required to drop from the horse onto the ground. He had to do this several times to allow for various camera angles. I was maybe thirty feet away from him, behind the camera. I remember looking at his back, thinking, 'Boy, the makeup people are really good. That looks like real blood.' In fact, the blood was real because of the number of times he had to drop onto his back."[28]

All told, the Yuma shoot took more than a month and raised the budget by an estimated $9 million. A few days of pickups (normal procedure once a film has been mostly edited and the director sees what else is needed) with Stallone in March 1988 brought production to a close.[29] By the end of it, the crew was sporting T-shirts that boasted, "I survived *Rambo III*."[30] Adding the final word, an exhausted Richard Crenna said, "If we do another Rambo, let's shoot it on the French Riviera."[31]

Although the shooting of the film was over, a different kind of shooting was only beginning.

The first ripple of dissatisfaction with the film was reported in early 1988 when the US Army, which had supported the film with a recruitment announcement after the credits, ordered their announcement removed. An unidentified army spokesperson explained, "We're looking for intelligent, well-adjusted soldiers. Rambo doesn't fit that image."[32]

The US release of *Rambo III* on May 25, 1988, was the occasion for some people to renew their displeasure with *First Blood Part II* and the ever-expanding Rambo mythos. Antiwar groups objected to the violence and protested in front of theaters in Los Angeles, Seattle, and Champaign, Illinois.[33] The *Los Angeles Times* reported that the National Coalition of Television Violence (NCTV) counted 245 separate acts of violence in the film.[34] On August 13 in Los Angeles, legendary peace activist Jerry Rubin, who had been on a hunger strike protest, ended a sixty-three-day fast (one day for each $1 million the film had reportedly cost) by delivering a giant pizza in the shape of a peace sign to Stallone's Malibu home.[35]

"I think movies like *Rambo III* are possibly the most ill-conceived idea at this time," said Michele Phillips, a member of the popular singing group the Mamas and the Papas, at a Memorial Day rally protesting the film. She appeared with Ron Kovic, author of *Born on the Fourth of July*. "There are signs that the Cold War is over and I think that warmongering for the sake of making a few million bucks at the box office is unconscionable." Actor Spiro Focas, who played the Afghan resistance leader in the film, passed out informational leaflets about the Russian exit from Afghanistan, "so the audience can know a little more than what they see . . . the war is not over with the withdrawal of Soviet troops and the country needs to be reconstructed."[36]

Censorship problems continued when the British Board of Film Classification ordered twenty-four cuts for scenes of violence and for "glamorizing" displays of weaponry.[37] Patrons at the Rio de Janeiro, Brazil, premiere rioted, and it took police tear gas to break them up.[38] Protestors in West Germany complained about that city's film classification board's rating of the film as "outstanding" despite its violence.[39] This may have been in reaction to Stallone's June visit to Berlin to promote the July release of the film when he was refused entry to Communist East Berlin because the occupying Russian forces thought his presence might foment violence. "So much for glasnost," the actor said at the time.[40]

By the beginning of 1989, the picture had grossed approximately $54 million.[41] Its final tally from ticket sales, foreign and domestic, as reported by BoxOfficeMojo, is just under $190 million. A second advertising campaign that idolized Stallone helped. David Rosenfelt, executive vice president of marketing for Tri-Star Pictures, took note that 40 percent of Rambo's patrons were women, so he instigated a campaign featuring a blond female model under the slogan, "You don't have to be macho to love Rambo."[42] This dichotomy is emphasized by the contrasting covers of the paperback editions of David Morrell's novelizations. The cover of *Rambo: First Blood Part II* displays a shirtless Stallone holding an anti-tank rocket launcher while the cover for *Rambo III* features only an extreme close-up of Stallone with a barely noticeable headband. In a similar contrast, the one-sheet poster for the movie *Rambo: First Blood Part II* displays Stallone wearing a torn T-shirt and holding a rocket launcher while the poster for *Rambo III* shows the star in a tank top, his hands braced on his hips, looking like an advertisement for a gymnasium franchise.

Despite the grosses, the film didn't earn a profit. A minimum of three times a film's budget is a standard ratio for estimating whether there's a profit after deducting production, distribution, and exhibition costs. Despite this, in the euphoria of cash flow, the producers optimistically approached Stallone while *Rambo III* was still in production to make *Rambo IV*, offering him $34 million if he would agree. "I turned down thirty-four," he later recalled with chagrin. "We were doing *Rambo III*. We thought it was going to be the biggest hit—this was before it came out. Then they go 'We want *Rambo IV*. Here it is: pay or play, thirty-four.' I go, 'Let's not jump the gun here.'" Thirty-four million in 1988 would be worth $85 million today. Hearing that, Stallone said, "What an idiot. Now I think about that and, wow."[43]

Not wanting their star to defect to another film company, Carolco, in addition, offered Stallone a ten-picture deal.[44] Producer Sir Run Run Shaw of Hong Kong promised him a blank check to make *Rambo IV* for his studio, starting at $20 million with cast and director approval, saying, "He's worth it. Rambo is the biggest box office smash in the history of the Orient."[45]

Stallone did, indeed, make *Rambo IV*, albeit twenty years later, and for a considerably smaller payday. He would direct and cowrite it himself and use it to come to terms with what the character and spirit of Rambo meant to him, what Rambo meant to the world, and how to reconcile the two.

In *Rambo III*, Stallone had a vision that is worth examining.[46] The screenplay, but not the film, begins with the capture of Trautman and his covert "documentary crew" by Russians at the Pakistani-Afghani border. In contrast, the finished film starts with Trautman asking Rambo to come to Afghanistan with him. Next, Griggs, who is attached to the US embassy in Thailand, asks Rambo to go into occupied Afghanistan to extract Trautman, who has been captured. The dynamic is different. In Stallone's script, Trautman gets himself captured and Rambo reluctantly reenters a war zone to get him out.

His exchange with Griggs, who finds him at his forge, shows how he has become hardened:

> **RAMBO:** My duty is over. My war is over. He
> shouldn't have gone in there.

> **GRIGGS:** All right, I've got the picture. You're a
> lost vet trying to get your act together;
> your friend means nothing and you're
> scared of combat because maybe the
> next blood you see will be your own.
> Hey, no problem, but keep running
> from reality because it hurts.

Griggs starts to go, but Rambo leaps on him and pins him backwards, snarling into his face.

> **RAMBO:** Don't ever talk to me about combat;
> I've buried more reality than you'll ever
> know.

> *Rambo turns away and faces the*
> *burning embers.*

> **RAMBO:** When do we go?

The difference between these two triggering scenes is essential to showing how Rambo has changed since his Vietnam foray three years earlier. In the production script (which is so detailed that all a director would need to do is follow what the writer has put on the page), Rambo equates Trautman with the futility of war and resists returning to feed the demon. He sees through Griggs's clearly manipulative insult but nonetheless decides, on his own terms, to rescue Trautman. He also assumes that Griggs is coming with him—and, in fact, Griggs does come with him. This sets up a buddy rivalry not unlike the one with Brewer that didn't make it into *Rambo: First Blood Part II*, and for the same reason: Loners don't have partners.

Richard Crenna saw the advantages of an Afghanistan story. "This time we defeat the entire Soviet Army, the two of us—with some help," he joked, but then became serious. "There was always the concern [that Gorbachev would pull all the troops out of Afghanistan], but it didn't concern us in terms of the audience response to the film because, you know, it's the same as making a film about the Civil War or Vietnam or about World War II. I think there's a certain segment of the population that would say, 'Well, that's old hat,' but that's very small. I think most people, even if they had no interest in the Afghanistan conflict, would still want to see the picture for Rambo. Second, they would maybe want to see the picture for what went down in Afghanistan, what was this all about, why was the Soviet Union there, and why were they leaving? While we're not a political film—we're an entertainment film— certainly some of those questions are addressed in the film."[47]

By the time the rewritten script was shot, Griggs has been reduced to a cameo by actor Kurtwood Smith, who stands around while Trautman tries to enlist Rambo to come with him into Afghanistan. Trautman is no longer involved with the faux documentary crew, but it's suggested that the off-screen documentary crew was spying. In the film, once Trautman is captured, Rambo demands to extract him and the mission becomes personal: Rambo is saving his friend, bailing out the government that screwed him over twice, and perhaps assuaging his guilt for not having gone with Traut- man in the first place.

Afghanistan became Stallone's personal cause. "It's hard for me to believe how little press this war has gotten," he said at the time, chiding the reporters who covered the film company's arrival in Yuma to shoot the desert scenes. It's "more important than anything I've ever done. It's a hideous, insidious war. It's a war primarily directed against women and children." Explaining that the Soviets want Afghanistan as a warm-weather port and for missile bases to control the Persian Gulf,[48] Stallone dismissed criticism that he was Russia-bashing: "I don't care." Speaking later, he said, "I made *Rambo III* because of the pain that the Afghan people have suffered as a result of the Soviets. Millions of people have been killed and maimed . . . so I don't think the question of whether Rambo commits a few violent acts versus millions of atrocities and brutal acts against a helpless people . . . are the ones that should be counted."[49]

He then added, perhaps speaking of himself as well as Rambo, "He learns to have a cause to live for. He purposefully seeks this final challenge, not so much because he wants to fight, he's doing it for himself. Rambo realizes this at the end of the movie. He is what he is."[50]

Stallone's take throughout the film is to personify the Russian occupation of Afghanistan and celebrate the resistance fighters. Notably, he is wounded at the end and is cradled by Trautman with dialogue that sounds as though both men have just come from a screening of *Casablanca*. David Morrell's novelization suggests that Rambo and Trautman might reunite at some future date, with the unspoken nihilistic message being that there will always be a war available to them.

Rambo III marks a change in the Rambo character. The first and second films involved Vietnam, and therefore touched directly and deeply on Rambo's pain, fears, and memories, as well as the American public's. The next three films, in which he supplies his skills to Afghanistan, Burma, and Mexico, strain to provide a similar personal motive with which both Rambo and the viewer can identify. In *Rambo III*, the motivation is rescuing Trautman. In *Rambo IV* (aka *Rambo*) it is more of an existential motivation where Rambo resolves to do what he does best almost as if to prove he can still do it. (More personally, for Stallone, it was to shine light on another conflict that he felt had not received enough public attention, Burma.) And in *Last Blood* (*Rambo V*), it is the swan song of a fighter who fails in his efforts to rescue a loved one and, because of this, loses his will to live, a decision that he turns into a holy sacrifice.

Rambo III became a turning point for John Rambo just as it was for the series. In comparing the Russian folly in Afghanistan to America's folly in Vietnam (and implying that America had no business occupying Afghanistan once the Russians left), it gets as close to politics as any of the five films. By attacking Russians and Afghanis, Rambo was no longer supplying catharsis to the audience that was still fighting Vietnam. Thirteen years ahead of the unthinkable events of September 11, 2001, the film cannot be accused of being reactionary toward Islam.[51] But it is a skillfully made action picture with enough carnage to satisfy the requirements of the genre, deliver a well-deserved blow to broadly drawn villains, and provide a sterling opportunity for Richard Crenna and Sylvester Stallone to enrich their screen relationship. In *First Blood*, Crenna's Trautman was Rambo's creator and surrogate father; in *Rambo III* he becomes not only a peer but beholden to him for saving his life, almost a role reversal. The change is profound and reflects the similarities between Rambo and Mary Shelley's *Frankenstein*. Where, in *First Blood*, Rambo is the monster to Trautman's Dr. Frankenstein who created him, by *Rambo III* the titular character becomes the philosophical monster from the latter half of Mary Shelley's novel. This is the half of *Frankenstein* that nobody remembers, the part where the doctor ruminates about the meaning of life and guilt and wishes to atone for what his skills have led him to do.

Rambo III marked the end of Carolco's involvement. "My favorite of the three we did, obviously, is *First Blood*," says producer Mario Kassar, whose company, with Andrew Vajna, was built on that film's success. "And the second one was okay because it was still about Vietnam and getting people out of Vietnam. The third one, we were too much ahead of our time. We went to Afghanistan, which is the cemetery of the world; nobody ever won in Afghanistan."[52]

There is an unusual footnote to *Rambo III*: In movies as in life, timing is everything, and *Rambo III*'s success may have been tarnished by geopolitics, according to director Peter MacDonald. "When we were making the film," he says, "the Russians were in Afghanistan about four weeks before the premiere. Of course, they pulled [out], which wasn't good news for us. Also at that period of time is when glasnost started and the friendship between America and Russia started. So, in a way, it harmed the film, I think, because the obvious enemy were no longer the enemy. We were all mates again, which is good. I like to think maybe we helped all of that, but I don't think people will go along with that. But we did get the Russians out of Afghanistan!" he jokes, then he adds, "One day someone should really make a film about what happened in Afghanistan, because it really was the most terrifying war."[53]

Continued Stallone, "Look at this as a positive attempt to expose what is an open wound and an unfair, unjust, genocidal situation that has no place on the face of this earth. What I'm hoping to do is to bring light to a horrible situation that is taking place in the world. But I'm not kidding myself. There'll be some people who'll be waiting to accuse me of Red-bashing." As for the film's violence, he said, "Oh, c'mon, *Rambo III* may have gotten scathing reviews, but it came in eleventh at the [1988] box office. And it did some good foreign box office. This is just another cycle of my career."[54]

But perhaps the greatest compliment, in a twisted way, was the fact that the film was so popular that pirated video-cassettes were a hot item in Afghanistan a few miles from the historic Khyber Pass. These bootleg VHS copies were renting for 15 rupees (80 cents) per day, according to a young Afghani boy whom reporter S. J. Mustin cornered for a quote. The boy then asked, "Why doesn't [Rambo] wear a shirt?" Then he answered his own question: "That's for the American woman, right?"[55]

SIDEBAR

Synopsis of the Film *Rambo III*

It's been several years since his escape from Vietnam with a group of rescued POWs whom the government had written off for cynical political purposes. Rambo (Sylvester Stallone) has retired to Thailand, having embraced Buddhism and living with the monks in a monastery in exchange for helping them build it.[56] He also earns money (and works off his enduring anger) by competitive krabi-krabong stick fighting. He is spotted during one such contest, which he handily wins, by Colonel Trautman (Richard Crenna) and US embassy attaché Robert Griggs (Kurtwood Smith). Trautman and Griggs want Rambo to venture into Afghanistan, which is under Soviet occupation, to help liberate a particular territory that remains in Russian hands despite a growing Mujahideen insurgency against them.[57] Rambo declines, saying, "This isn't my war," so Trautman goes off

"He was just some nothing kid
for all anybody knew."
Sylvester Stallone as
First Blood begins.
Orion/Photofest. © Orion Classics.

No longer some nothing kid.
Sylvester Stallone as Rambo.
Yoni S. Hamenahem/Wikimedia Commons.

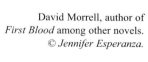

Rambo apples.
APictche/Wikimedia Commons.

David Morrell, author of
First Blood among other novels.
© *Jennifer Esperanza.*

David Morrell (LEFT) and Stirling Silliphant. Their friendship grew from a fan letter into a collaboration. *Tiana Silliphant.*

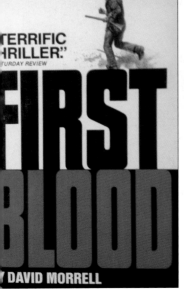

First US edition paperback of *First Blood.* *David Morrell.*

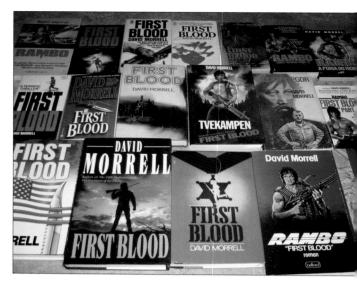

A sampling of the domestic and international editions of *First B[lood]*
David Morrell's 1972 novel that created Rambo. *David Mo[rrell]*

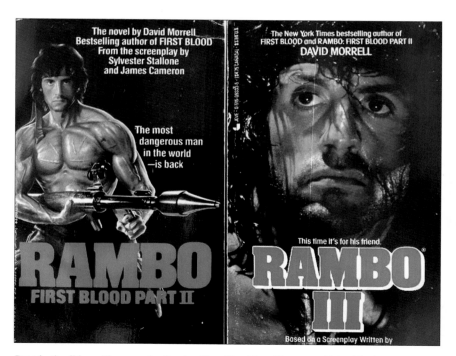

Paperback editions. The cover for *Rambo: First Blood Part II* was so criticized for its violent
appearance that the publisher used only a closeup of Sylvester Stallone on the cover of *Rambo III*.
Both books were novelizations written by *First Blood* author David Morrell.

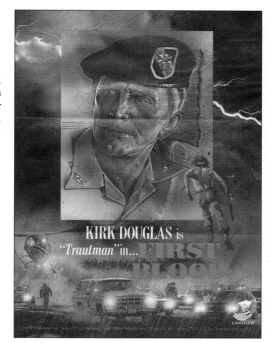

First Blood Kirk Douglas poster. Carolco bought trade advertisements announcing that Douglas would costar in *First Blood*. He decided not to. *David Morrell.*

KIRK DOUGLAS is "*Trautman*" in...

FIRST BLOOD

lone on top of the world at
Venice Film Festival, 2009.
olas Genin, Festival de Venise/
imedia Commons.

Brian Dennehy plays Sheriff Teasle, Rambo's *First Blood* antagonist whose reasons are explained in the boo but not in the movie.
Justin Hoch, Hudson Union Society/ Wikimedia Commons.

Rambo could have killed Teasl *First Blood* but relents, telling F instead, to call off his manh Teasle does not heed Rambo gets "a war like you won't belie *Orion/Photofest. © Orion Class*

Richard Crenna hit the ground acting when he took the role of Colonel Sam Trautman in *First Blood*. *n Mathew Smith/Wikimedia Commons. Richard Crenna.*

ard Crenna (LEFT) and id Morrell in Eilat, Israel, ng the *Rambo III* shoot, 1987. *id Morrell.*

David Morrell (LEFT) and
producer Andrew Vajna
of Carolco Pictures.
David Morrell.

Sylvester Stallone and
David Morrell on location
in Israel for *Rambo III*.
David Morrell.

Sylvester Stallone and Julia Nickson in *Rambo: First Blood Part II*.
This is the only instance in all five films where Rambo has a love interest.
TriStar/Photofest. © *TriStar Pictures.*

Richard Crenna (RIGHT) tangles with Charles Napier (CENTER) over the fake mission that has
dispatched Rambo back to Vietnam as Martin Kove looks on in *Rambo: First Blood Part II*.
Toho Company/Photofest. © *TriStar Pictures.*

David Morrell (RIGHT) and Gil Hibben, the knifesmith who crafted the knives for *Rambo III* and *Ran...* David Morrell.

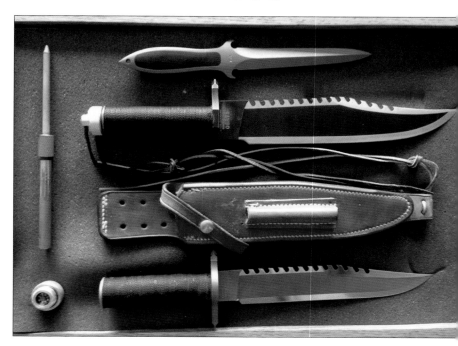

Knives made by Jimmy Lile. *Private collector.*

Knives made by Gil Hibben. *Private collector.*

Gil Hibben's mysterious now-you-see-it, now-you-don't "rescue" knife,
used briefly only once, when Rambo is probing for land mines in *Rambo III*.
© *Derek Hibben Photography.*

Sylvester Stallone comes to the aid of Richard Crenna in Afghanistan in *Rambo III*. *Artisan/Photofest.* © *Artisan Entertainment.*

Sylvester Stallone is the enigmatic "Boatman" who helps, then rescues, both missionaries and mercenaries in *Rambo. Lionsgate/Photofest.* © *Lionsgate.*

In an image paying homage to Sam Peckinpah's *The Wild Bunch,*
Rambo wields a machine gun against the enemy in *Rambo.*
Lionsgate/Photofest. © *Lionsgate.*

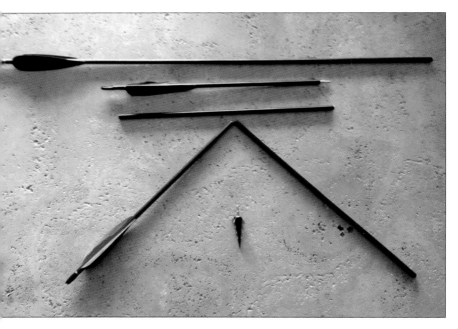

Collapsible arrows and detachable arrowhead for Rambo's compound bow. *Private collector.*

Sylvester Stallone prepares his deadly compound bow and arrow—bare-che of course.
TriStar/Photofest. © TriStar Pictures.

The Coquihalla River Bridge in British Columbia, where R was told by Teasle to keep wa If he had, there would be no le The bridge has been r after collapsing du weather event in *Wikimedia Com*

Reagan and Rambo: Visiting the White House on January 20, 1981, Sylvester Stallone sits at President Reagan's table. He later said he felt uncomfortable with Reagan's insistence that Rambo was a Republican. *Reagan White House Photographs/ Wikimedia Commons.*

ɔ graffiti on a wall in Bystrc, a suburb of Brno in ech Republic. Rambo was seen as a revolutionary figure mmunist bloc countries, and some credit him with icing the people's spread of democracy. *edia Commons.*

In a scene cut from the US release of *Last Blood*, Rambo tries to rescue hikers during a storm but fa
This feeling of powerlessness inspires him to redeem himself.
Lionsgate/Photofest. © Lionsgate.

on the mission without him. Almost immediately after crossing the Afghan border, Trautman is captured by Russian forces. When Griggs tells Rambo what has happened, Rambo insists on going to rescue his mentor.

Rambo arrives in Peshawar, Pakistan, and connects with arms dealer Mousa Ghani (Sasson Gabhi), who has been advised by Griggs of his arrival. Of course, he tells Rambo that he will disavow any knowledge of him should he be captured. Mousa supplies plastique and detonators even though he has no idea who Rambo truly is (at first, he thinks he's a tourist) and then cannot believe that Rambo is going alone to the village of Khost, next to the Russian compound where Trautman is being held.

At the Russian compound, Trautman meets his captor, Russian Colonel Alexi Zaysen (Marc de Jong), and his brutish henchman Sergeant Kourov (Randy Raney). Zaysen wants Trautman to tell him about the stinger missiles he was bringing to help the Mujahideen, suggesting that his cooperation will help them both get out of there.[58] Trautman lectures Zaysen that Russia's invasion of Afghanistan is as wrongheaded as America's equally futile invasion of Vietnam.

Trautman is beaten by Zaysen for information about where and when the stinger missiles are being delivered. He stops when a shifty-eyed man (whom we first saw working for Mousa and who already looked suspicious) turns out to be an informant who reveals that Rambo is on the way.

Rambo and Mousa trek together to where Trautman is being held. On the way, Mousa enlightens Rambo about Afghanistan's past. When they arrive at the village, Rambo sees the devastation caused by the Soviet attacks and is befriended by a small boy named Hamid (Doudi Shoua). The villagers advise Rambo that there are ten thousand Mujahideen warriors waiting at the border for the right time to enter and free their country. An elder, Masoud (Spiros Fokas), sermonizes about the Russian genocide against his country that the news media is not covering. "To us," he says softly, "death for our land and our god is an honor."

While the elders debate whether to accompany Rambo to the Russian fort, the younger men play *buzkashi,*[59] a game in which they try, from horseback, to carry a sheep carcass into a goal. While this is going on (Rambo, an excellent horseman playing the game for the first time, wins), two helicopters from Colonel Zaysen strafe the village, killing and wounding dozens of people and leveling the homes. Rambo grabs a machine gun and blows up one of the copters. Commandeering another one, Zaysen escapes.

One of the tribesmen tells Rambo, "This is not your war." Recalling his earlier dialogue, he replies, "It is now." When asked why he is doing it for Trautman, Rambo says, "Because he'd do it for me."[60]

Working together, Rambo and Mousa sneak into the Russian compound, crawling carefully through a minefield.[61] Suddenly little Hamid joins them, and he's armed. Rambo and Mousa plant timed charges all over the compound. Russian tanks arrive, and Rambo drags himself underneath one to get closer, unnoticed, to the prison. Inside, he hears people, including women, being tortured.

The explosive charges start going off. In the chaos, Rambo is pierced in his side by a rod. He, Hamid, and Mousa escape by going into the underground drainage system. They are followed by Zaysen's men. Rambo blows up all of them.

Zaysen beats Trautman to learn who Rambo is. "Is he god?" Answers Trautman, "God would have mercy. He won't."

Rambo goes back for Trautman but first gives Hamid the Buddha amulet that Co had worn in Vietnam. Rambo uses the powder from a bullet to cauterize his wound where the rod pierced him.

The next day, Zaysen and his men search the caves. His crony, Sergeant Kourov, threatens Trautman with a flamethrower. Rambo bursts into the cell and uses the krabi-krabong stick fighting technique to vanquish the guards.[62] He escapes with Trautman and the other prisoners and commandeers a Russian helicopter to fly everyone to safety, but Zaysen attacks in his helicopter and Rambo's chopper crashes. The prisoners flee their separate ways. Rambo and Trautman must now reach the Pakistan border while being chased by the entire Russian army unit.

Rambo uses his bow and incendiary arrows to explode the enemy. Trautman even gets to kill one of them. Rambo and Trautman escape into a cave, followed by a contingent of Russian soldiers while Zaysen communicates with his men from his copter. Many shoot-outs later, the Russians are killed, Trautman climbs to safety, and Rambo follows—except that, when he reaches to the top exit of the cave, hurting from his wound, Kourov is waiting for him. The men fight until Rambo throws Kourov down the hole and back into the cave, where he is hanged by his own cable. Then Rambo explodes him with a hand grenade for good measure.

This is when Zaysen and hundreds of troops, tanks, and armed vehicles show up to confront Rambo and Trautman, demanding their surrender. Rambo and Trautman decide to go out fighting when countless Mujahideen arrive to attack the Russians. It's a violent confrontation capped when Rambo takes over a tank and drives it straight into Zaysen's grounded copter, jumping to safety just before both vehicles explode.

Trautman and Rambo, both wounded, say goodbye to Mousa and Hamid and drive away.

The title appears: "This film is dedicated to the gallant people of Afghanistan."

Synopsis of David Morrell's Novelization of *Rambo III*

Part One: *The Anvil*

Rambo ponders the four truths of Buddha as he constructs a temple in Bangkok, Thailand, while reliving the memories of his past: the capture, the torture, the scars, the violence. And the conflict with the cop. And the colonel, the only man he can trust, who bought his freedom from captivity only to send him back into hell. That mission cost him his spirit and the woman Co, of whom the only physical memory is the tiny Buddha on the necklace round his neck. Weighing his heritage—Christian, Navajo, and now Buddhist—he wants to choose wisdom over war.

And yet here he is, one year after returning from his rescue mission in 'Nam, forging metal sheets to construct the temple and also stick-fighting men for prize money to finance its construction. In the crowd watching him he sees Trautman, looks away, wins the fight, and lets his beaten opponent live, a charitable deed met with roars of approval by the onlookers.

Trautman and a civilian, Robert Briggs, try to enlist Rambo to go to war-torn Afghanistan, and learn why an intelligence operative has disappeared while bringing weapons and medical supplies to anti-Soviet Mujahideen rebels. As with his previous mission, they also ask Rambo to glean photographic proof of Russian atrocities in the Soviet-occupied country. Rambo declines, saying, "Not my war."

Part Two: The Embassy

Trautman proceeds on his own to the Afghan-Pakistan border, from which he will train operatives. Rambo, in Bangkok, has second thoughts. When he hears that Trautman has been captured, he crashes the US embassy to find Briggs, who tells him that it would be an international incident if, under torture, Trautman reveals US presence in Afghanistan. (At this time, America was not publicly committed to help the Mujahideen.) In prison, Trautman is roused by Russian Colonel Zaysen, who demands he confess to being in country and adds that doing so would allow them both to leave. If he refuses, Zaysen says, he will turn him over to Sergeant Kourov. Trautman does refuse, and the beating begins.

Part Three: The Gunshop

Rambo arrives outside Peshawar, West Pakistan, to meet his contact. The 1979 Soviet invasion of 115,000 troops has devastated neighboring Afghanistan, killing a million people and displacing half a million others. Rambo decides that if God won't help these people, he will. The contact, a gun dealer named Mousa, will lead him into Afghanistan. In addition to the arms, Mousa gives him a compound bow improved from the one he used a year ago to rescue the POWs from Vietnam. Rambo changes clothes to look more Muslim than Buddhist, pockets Co's medallion, and departs on horseback. Along the way, Mousa and Rambo—but mostly Mousa—talk of war, death, and their beliefs. Finally, Mousa concludes, "Life is a test of worthiness."

The pair stop for tea in a peasant hut where Rambo learns that their Mujahideen hosts come and go as they wish and have their own ways of fighting the Russians. They reach a denuded wasteland and survive a dust storm. The land is barren. This is what war has made of Afghanistan. They cut loose the horses and bury the weapons they were packing.

Part Four: The Wasteland

Mousa nearly suffocated in the dust storm, but Rambo revives him. Mousa invites him to become Muslim. Rambo sees a child's toy and reaches to pick it up, but Mousa quickly stops him and warns that such toys are connected to explosives that the Russians leave to maim unsuspecting children. As they near a village, two Russian gunships attack. Rambo blows up one of the gunships with a grenade rifle. Then he destroys the second one, allowing a young girl who was targeted to flee to safety. Mousa is felled in the shock but is otherwise unhurt. Leaving behind the death and destruction of the village, Rambo continues alone, only to be surrounded by many Afghan horsemen who, seeing his Western features, believe he is a Russian. They start to tear him apart, only to be stopped by Mousa and then freed at the order of Khalid, the village leader. It was Khalid's daughter, Halima, whom Rambo saved back at the village. Rambo, Mousa, Khalid, and the men begin erecting protective barricades against the certain arrival of more Russian gunships.

In the Soviet prison, Trautman, beaten and sleep-deprived, is asked by Zaysen why he is here. In return, Trautman asks his captor, "Why are *you* here?"

The beatings resume.

Part Five: The Sanctuary

The Rambo-Mousa-Khalid team, with Khalid's daughter in tow, arrive at a camp removed from the village, far away from

Russian awareness. It has an infirmary, where Rambo learns that Trautman has been captured by the Russians.

At night, Rambo attends a guerilla counsel with the regal Rahim, the skeptical Akram, and other elders who doubt his intentions, saying that America has abandoned them. Mousa and three rebels leave to find the weapons cache that he and Rambo hid. Rambo watches the men play *buzkashi*, a brutal horseback game, which involves catching and carrying a goat carcass from one goal to another. Michelle, a Dutch woman from the infirmary, translates for him that the men want him to play their game or else they will brand him a coward. Rambo, summoning his Navajo heritage and years working on his family's horse farm, vies with Akram for the carcass, and wins. This victory by an infidel puts him in danger, but Akram agrees with Rambo and the men cheer this proof that he is not Russian.

Mousa returns with the weapons. The tribesmen vow to help Rambo.

In the Russian prison Zaysen, between Kourov's punches, tries to get Trautman to disclose his mission.

Part Six: *The Valley of Pain*

There is a wedding in the village, a positive sign amid all the death. Rambo learns that an armored Russian column is on the way, and the tribesmen want him to fight with them. He tells them he is here only to save his friend. They agree to help him if he in turn helps them. They lead him to the Valley of Pain, where they plant charges to destroy Russian tanks. Rambo is impressed with the men's guerilla expertise when the Russian Spetsnaz troops are thrown into disarray by the onslaught. A Soviet gunship arrives and fires, only to be destroyed by charges planted by Rambo and Mousa. After the battle, religious and cultural differences reemerge, and

Rambo finally demands that, in exchange for the help he has given them, the Mujahideen must help him find Trautman.

Russian Major Azov criticizes Colonel Zaysen for sending the troops into the valley to search for rebels. Captured rebels are executed.

Andreyev, a Russian defector now with the rebels, draws Rambo a map of the compound where Trautman is being held but warns that a rescue team would fail. Hearing this challenge, Rambo says he will go in alone.

Part Seven: The Fortress

Forcing Andreyev to come with them that night, Rambo and Mousa head to the Russian fortress. Approaching it in darkness during a dust storm, they cross a minefield. Entering the fort grounds, Rambo is prepared to kill Andreyev should he be a double agent and try to expose them. Instead, the defector proves his loyalty by killing a Russian guard.[63]

Trying to "motivate" Trautman, Zaysen has Kourov burn a captive child with acid to make him tell where rebel leader Akram Haidar can be found. Major Azov tells Zaysen that torture only makes the enemy more defiant. Stalking through the compound, Rambo kills guards with arrows. Andreyev is discovered by the Russians and lies to them that he has just returned, then kills a guard. Rambo takes keys from a dead guard and opens Trautman's cell. At the cost of Andreyev's life, Rambo, Trautman, and Mousa escape. They free other Afghan prisoners. Azov aims his pistol at Rambo, then lowers it, thinking, "This isn't my war."

Flinging Trautman over his shoulders, Rambo struggles toward the horses.

Part Eight: The Cave

Zaysen berates Azov in the wake of the raid: Forty Russians killed for four rebels? Zaysen orders Azov to lie that it was two hundred rebels. And to give chase.

A wounded Rambo helps Trautman to freedom. He has accepted his destiny. Mousa catches up with them. A Russian convoy pursues, led by Zaysen and Azov, both of whom have come to believe that the Soviet invasion of Afghanistan was a mistake. Rambo urges the exhausted Trautman to survive by staying awake and repeating song lyrics such as "When Johnny Comes Marching Home."

Sergeant Kourov hates his superior officers as he rides with Zaysen into battle on the personnel carrier.

Rambo and the others find their fellow rebels hiding in a cave. Akram tells him the tribes have left, fearing Soviet retribution. Michelle performs a blood transfusion between Rambo and the near-dead Trautman. As gunships approach, Rambo fashions a litter for Trautman. Hearing the gunships firing five miles away, they leave.

Part Nine: The Mountains

Leading the horses along mountain trails, pulling Trautman on his litter, weak from giving blood, Rambo worries that the Soviet gunships will strafe every place they think their prey might be.

In pursuit, Zaysen pushes his gunships onward. In their flight, Rambo and a delirious Trautman reminisce about their first meeting at Fort Bragg.

As Khalid leads his tribe in their separate odyssey, he urges caution to avoid Russian detection.

Russians fire on Rambo, Mousa, and the others. The horses run off, one of them carrying Trautman's litter.

Michelle tries to stop them and gets her arm broken. Rambo launches a grenade at the source of the shooting.[64] The action sets off a snow avalanche. Rambo forces himself onward and suddenly realizes that he is weeping.

Khalid leads his party to Pakistan and safety. Rahim watches the gunships depart and joins with Khalid, riding together.

Just as they are in sight of Pakistan, Rambo hears gunships. Cannons fire. The earth shakes. Akram and his people fire back at the Russians. Between horses, rifles, and knives, Rambo and the Afghans defeat the Soviet contingent. Rambo's life is spared by a sergeant, "Because life is suffering."

Rambo and Trautman make their goodbyes and head into Pakistan and safety.

SIDEBAR

Richard Crenna: The Actor Who Became a Symbol

Although he played scores of memorable roles on television and in motion pictures, many of them cerebral, some comic, and all of them consummately, Richard Crenna will always be remembered for the one least like himself: the über-military Colonel Samuel Trautman in three *Rambo* films.

"I prefer to think of him as a hero," he said of the colonel who "created" Rambo. "He's a man who is obligated to devote his life to the defense of his country. I think he feels himself a good man, a man who's defending, if you will, democracy in the world, and as such, there are some people who will say, 'That attitude is militaristic' and so on and so forth. You always get criticism; any time you put on a uniform, you're going to be criticized by somebody."[65] He then added,

"If you're going to go down for something, that's as good as anything, I guess. It's a lot of fun to be a part of the social phenomenon of *Rambo*. It's a different audience than perhaps I've had in the past. It enables me to reach a constantly growing younger audience."[66]

Crenna, two weeks shy of fifty-seven when he shot *First Blood*, heroically took the role of Rambo's trainer, Colonel Sam Trautman, with precious little time to prepare. Nevertheless, he hit the ground acting and continued to find new facets for the military man through two sequels.

"I'm not one of these actors who has to ride around in a patrol car to play a policeman," he said, "other than a Western, where I will go out and ride horses so I will get my fanny back into shape. But I go into the heart of the character more than the specifics of the character—I always like to leave that in the hands of the director. I have to attribute the character of Trautman to Ted Kotcheff. When I got on the set, I gave my rendition of Trautman. He made the corrections that he wanted in the character, and we worked very well together. I was very comfortable with the person that he put in my uniform." Crenna was not using metaphors referring to his uniform; the six-foot-one actor stuck so far out of five-foot-nine Kirk Douglas's military clothing that costume designer Tom Bronson had to find a trench coat to cover the shortfall.

Born in 1926 in Los Angeles, to Italian-American parents, Crenna served two years in the army just as World War II ended, and after discharge he studied literature at the University of Southern California. He began acting in radio with the comedy series *The Great Gildersleeve* and *Our Miss Brooks*, moving to television when the latter debuted on CBS in 1952. There, he memorably played Walter Denton, Eve Arden's teacher's pet, in three seasons of the sitcom, from 1952 to 1955. He transitioned smoothly from that comedy role into the light dramatic role of Luke McCoy in 225 episodes of the bucolic family series *The Real McCoys*, ending in 1963. Maturing and broadening his image, he made countless guest appearances in just about every dramatic network show being produced for the rest of the century, easily crossing back and forth into feature films such as *The Sand Pebbles* (1966), *Wait Until Dark* (1967), *Red Sky at Morning* (1971), and the respected but short-lived episodic series *Slattery's People* (1964–1965) and *All's Fair* (1976–1977), the miniseries *Centennial* (1978–1979), and many more. His presence was always assured, reliable, and professional.

Over the years he developed, not a method, but a process. He was reluctant to watch himself in dailies lest he keep repeating a particular affectation. He wanted to believe himself as someone else, even if that "someone else" still looked like Richard Crenna. He trusted his directors.

Although Crenna's filmography lists well over a hundred credits, he was still pleased when fans reached back to their first encounter. For years, people looked at him as Walter Denton, then Luke McCoy, but, rather than feel typecast, he was thankful that he made an impression on them. But it's Sam Trautman who had the most profound effect. "I was not surprised at the success of the film," he said. "When I read the script, I thought it was a terrific adventure story. I thought it was a wonderfully constructed motion picture. I thought it had a theme that had not really been dealt with in motion pictures. I felt that the audience was ready for that kind of film. That didn't enter into my decision to do the film; my decision to do the film was that they asked me to. But in reflecting on it, I thought it would be a film that would be . . . successful by the nature of its adventuresome story."[67]

Ever the professional. Crenna had nothing but praise for his costar. "I enjoyed working with Stallone," he announced, as if expecting to surprise people with the admission about the mercurial actor. "I found him to be difficult to those people who were not professional, and not at all difficult to people who were doing their job, and I respected that. First of all, I respected him because of the work he had done in *Rocky* and the attitude and stance he had taken in holding on to that picture until he could play the role and do what he wanted to do."[68]

Crenna was about more than acting. He was national chairman of the hospitalized veterans and was moved by the gratitude he received from men and women in the services for portraying them as outstanding patriots.

This was particularly true when *Rambo II* was released.

"I think it will be controversial," he told an interviewer at the time. "I think there will be a lot of criticism, pro and con. It will open a lot of wounds—a lot of wounds that probably need reopening. We still have, what, 2,485 or something—close to 2,500 vets that are unaccounted for. They are listed as missing in action. We don't know where they are; it's quite possible that they're still in camps, that they're still being held prisoner. No one knows. No one has told us. It opens that door, and I think it opens it in a way that you're going to have fans standing in the aisles and cheering. One of the lines in the picture, in the very opening of the picture, Trautman goes to Rambo who's in prison for what he had done in *Blood One* [sic], and he outlines the prospect of his going back for POWs, and Rambo says to him, 'Do we get to win this time?' I think that's a sense of frustration that so many of the vets felt. And Trautman says to him, 'This time it's up to you.' It's a kind of 'one man against the world,' and we know how people love that. That's the rallying point around which this film develops—that it is one man against the odds of finding these prisoners."[69]

"I think there was a need for a heroic figure," Crenna added about Rambo and the era that produced him. "We

didn't have any heroes. There were smoldering beginnings of
the contributions of the men and women who had fought in
the Vietnam War. I had always held a resentment for the way
we treated those men and women when they returned from
Vietnam. They were, in my opinion, very much mistreated. I
thought this was an opportunity; I was delighted to be in a
film that made the statement that Rambo made. I was pleased
to be a part of it."[70]

Never forsaking his comedy roots, however, he took a
friendly shot at Rambo and Trautman in 1993's satire *Hot
Shots, Part Deux* in which he plays, well, himself—sort of.
"I was one of the few actors who has been able to satirize his
own character," he said. He played Colonel Denton Walters,
an inversion of the character name Walter Denton from *Our
Miss Brooks*. "I called the Rambo people and asked if they'd
mind if I did this thing. They said, 'Of course not, it's a satire, we're thrilled.' So I'm playing the scene opposite Charlie
Sheen and I'm having an out-of-body experience. I'm seeing the scene and I thought, 'What a pompous ass [I am].' I
started to laugh and I couldn't get through the scene. I broke
myself up about ten times, and there's nothing more embarrassing than that. I said to myself, 'You said these words in a
real movie and now you're saying them in a satire.' It was a
lot of fun to do."[71]

David Morrell had many conversations with him in Israel
when he visited the set of *Rambo III* and later when they were
paired on publicity interviews during the press junket for the
movie. "Richard was always good-natured and loved to meet
fans. I remember us stepping out of the elevator at the hotel
where we were staying. A father was in the lobby with his
young son. Although *The Real McCoys* was no longer in production, the boy was a fan of Richard's character in that series.
Somehow the father and son had learned that Richard was in

the hotel and were hanging around the lobby, hoping to see him. Richard was extremely enthusiastic about meeting them and talked with them for quite a while. When he saw that the father had a camera, Richard asked me to take a photo of the three of them." Morrell added, "One real test of an actor is whether he can make an impression in a small role. He's in *Body Heat* for maybe five minutes. But his quietly menacing manner, merely sipping a drink and smoking a cigar, makes William Hurt's character realize he's a lethal adversary who needs to be killed. It's an amazing performance. But then, everything Richard did was amazing."

Crenna died on January 17, 2003, at the age of seventy-six. The cause was heart failure as a consequence of pancreatic cancer. When *Rambo* (2008) was being planned, it was decided not to recast the role of Trautman but to let him reside forever with the memory of the man who embodied him on-screen.

SIDEBAR

Assignment: Stallone

Whether by fate, coincidence, or God's jest, veteran journalist Pat H. Broeske became the go-to interviewer for Sylvester Stallone during his heyday in the mid-1980s, giving her and her readers unusual insight into the triumphs and tolls of superstardom. Writing mostly for the Los Angeles Times, *the Hollywood industry's hometown newspaper, but also freelancing to other outlets, Broeske gained unique insight into her mercurial subject. After meeting him at a couple of table-hopping press junket interviews ("He knows how to work a room," she says), in 1985 she landed an assignment to do an at-home feature for the upcoming* Rambo: First Blood Part II *for the* Washington

Post *and two years later a location piece in Israel for the* Los
Angeles Times *for* Rambo III. *Over the course of several films
and many interviews, she published a portrait of a man who
was trying to reconcile his ambitions with his limitations, and
the conflict played out at the box office. Here is her take, in
hindsight.*[72]

"It's kind of a fun piece," she recalls. "I went to his house
in Pacific Palisades on Amalfi Road—I'll always remember
it—and was there for a couple of hours. He was alone at the
house, just us. He was about to do *Rambo II* (1985), then
Rocky IV (1985), then he referenced *Over the Top* (1987), so he
had his projects down."

But there was also the cop thriller *Cobra* (1986), "and
it's really a nasty film," she says. "I wrote a piece for Sunday
Calendar, which was the must-read in Southern California.
It was an opinion piece, 'When Heart Is Replaced by Muscle,
the Fans Lose,' and it was about all the things that had made
Rocky a great character, and even some parts of Rambo, that
were gone in *Cobra*. He had betrayed his fans and betrayed
his image. So I wrote this piece and I actually got a call from
Stallone. He goes, 'Uh, I read the piece you wrote about me
and I want to talk about that.' He proceeds to tell me that he
has a movie lined up that has a lot of heart, and it's *Over the
Top*, and it's getting back to some of the things he had done in
Rocky. He said that when the film shoots, I should come out
to the set and cover it, come to Vegas."

Over the Top, about a trucker who wins back his young
son's love by entering an arm-wrestling contest, was shot in
Las Vegas in Summer 1986. Broeske made it to the location
but stepped into some drama in which, although Stallone
had invited her, he avoided her once she arrived. Eventually
they sat in his portable dressing room, "and I said I was really
upset: 'I came all the way here and you stiffed me.' He said,

'Well, I was upset about a lot of things.' I said, 'I get upset about things too, but I have a job to do and I show up for it.'"

During their conversation, Stallone confessed that he was in personal transition. "He's always in personal transition," Broeske says. "It's one of his stories. The film was dorky, but he's sincere, as sincere as he can be."

Next came *Rambo III*. But first came Oliver Stone's *Platoon* at the end of 1986, and it sent shocks throughout Hollywood. "*Platoon* changes people's feelings about Vietnam movies," Broeske notes. "It's realistic, it's not gung-ho action the way *Rambo* is, it doesn't have stereotypes. It really shakes up the industry and—I can't believe I somehow did this—I had the idea, let's see what Jane Fonda thinks. Jane Fonda told me she had just seen *Platoon* and she wept during the movie, her feelings on what she'd done.[73] She felt like for the first time she'd seen a real film about Vietnam and what it did to people. She said, 'Look, I was never really anti-American.' She doesn't regret the things she did, but she does see things in a different light. As an aside, she said, 'At least I wasn't sitting out the Vietnam War like Sly Stallone in a Swiss girls school.' I used it parenthetically in the story.

"I get a phone call, I think it was the next week, from Stallone and, if a phone call could have blown out the entire phone system in Times-Mirror Square from the language and sound volume and anger, that phone call would have done it. He was so mad at me for putting in Jane Fonda's comment. He held it against me. He told me I 'shouldn't have done that.' He 'thought we were friends.' I said, 'I'm not your publicist.' He said, 'You should have protected me.' I said, 'Protect you from what, Jane Fonda?' He said he was a bigger star than Jane Fonda and I pointed out that his last film, *Cobra*, hadn't done well. He argued that it had done well in

Europe and that he was a big star in Italy. I said, 'So is Steve Reeves' and he hung up on me. I admit it was a cheap shot."

Platoon's influence was profound in curbing the exaggerated battles in war films (e.g., *Missing in Action, Delta Force, American Ninja*, etc.) and making action more reality based. The shift away from wish-fulfillment was most palpable in *Rambo III* with Stallone's emotionally damaged Special Forces hero dispatched to Afghanistan to rescue the only person who means anything to him, Colonel Trautman. Afghanistan wasn't widely known by Americans at the time, but soon would be.

Despite their *Over the Top* rift, when Stallone was readying *Rambo III* in Israel in 1987, he invited Broeske to join him—at the Dead Sea. Bygones were bygones, and professionalism reigned.

"We got along," Broeske says, sounding a little surprised. "It was fine. It was 120-some degrees, I'm not kidding. It was so hot they had water boys and water girls wandering around the set making you drink water, and they would stand there while you downed a glass of water."

Not all the heat came from the sun, however. "When I arrived," Broeske continues, "Andy Vajna was banned from the set. The director, Russell Mulcahy, had been fired and Peter MacDonald had become the director. The producers were banned from the set. I was on the set for two and a half days. Buzz Feitshans was on the set; he later got banned. It's Stallone that's banning people. I don't know why they got banned, I just know when I got there it was weird." She pauses to consider the situation. "Stallone was always in charge."

And yet, "Stallone was fun, he was jokey, he was again at a personal crossroads—he's always at a personal crossroads—he was divorced from Brigitte Nielsen. Richard Crenna was a really, really nice guy. He was an intellectual; he had stacks and stacks of books. His wife would send them and they would discuss the books on the phone and in letters. He said you really need to ground yourself if you work in show business."

Broeske had also been gaining insight into Rambo, having written the *Los Angeles Times* Sunday Calendar cover story "The Curious Evolution of John Rambo" in 1985. It was a meticulous account of the gestation and development of *First Blood* that untangled the knot by which most films, but particularly that one, reached the screen. It impressed author David Morrell so much that he included it in his 2016 special edition reissue of *Rambo: First Blood Part II*.

Her *Rambo III* piece, the one datelined the Dead Sea, was called "Third Blood" and chronicled that film's hot, dusty, and challenging production.[74] One location escapade that her article did not include stays in both her and Stallone's minds, albeit differently. Proud of the impressive military equipment in the film, Stallone offered to arrange for her to be flown in one of the combat choppers. Afraid of heights, and especially opposed to riding in an open aircraft without side doors, she declined. Stallone insisted. Finally, an executive interceded and said that the company's insurance didn't cover dead journalists. Stallone reluctantly backed off. Years later, however, appearing on the *Late Show with David Letterman*, the actor said he did, in fact, take her for a ride. "When [Pat] got aboard, she weighed, like, 250 pounds—but she came off the copter 'a dwarf.'" "Great story," Broeske countered on her website. "However, there was never any such escapade ... also, for the record, my '80s-era bod was a size 10! (I'm not sayin' nothin' about today . . .)."[75] "[I] groaned when I heard what he said about me (with my full name)! I wasn't thrilled to be mentioned—I mean, aside from the fact that the anecdote didn't happen."[76]

Sly and Pat had no subsequent contact. She is today a busy author and freelance writer, and he is, well, Sylvester Stallone. And what is her lasting assessment of the man who is both Rocky and Rambo and everything in between? "He can go off pretty fast and then he can come back down," she says with a distance of some forty years. Then she adds, somewhat relieved, "I didn't end badly with him."

SIDEBAR

The Song of Rambo

It's hard to pick Jerry Goldsmith's best work. He won the Academy Award for Best Original Score for *The Omen* (1977) and was nominated for seventeen more Oscars, including for *L.A. Confidential* (1998), *Poltergeist* (1983), *Star Trek: The Motion Picture* (1980), *The Wind and the Lion* (1976), *Chinatown* (1975), and *Patton* (1971), out of some two hundred scores.[77]

Film scores are a unique component of cinema. Where directors, producers, and actors feel free to rewrite scripts few dare to alter a composer's work. Some directors even dislike music, feeling that, if they've done their job properly, the film shouldn't need it. On the other hand, some composers, such as the incomparable Max Steiner, used to say that, if the audience is paying attention to the music, he's the one who hasn't done his job right.[78]

At first, Goldsmith resisted joining the *First Blood* team. Mario Kassar recalled, "I tried to convince him. It wasn't easy in the beginning. It took him a little while, but then he agreed, and I think we have to be very thankful to him because he did an amazing score."[79] Adds Andy Vajna, "We had temp-scored it with Jerry Goldsmith music and so it had the same emotional impact. Then when it got the standing ovation [at the preview], I mean he was in heaven."[80]

A temp score is just that: fill-in music from another movie that is used while a film is being edited to give the composer a sense of what the director and producer want. Although widely used during the editing process, these scores pose a creative and diplomatic minefield.

"Sometimes the composer wants you to do a temp of the film he's going to score, but sometimes they don't," explains writer Daniel Schweiger, who specializes in creating temp scores for in-progress films. "I think Jerry grudgingly appreciated the temp tracks at times . . . But it makes the composer compete against himself, and I couldn't imagine ever being in that situation. I've also done temps where the composer specifically asked me to only temp in his music."[81]

"Jerry Goldsmith's creative score helped define John Rambo," writes James Parker on the Jerry Goldsmith website, "his struggles, frustrations, and his identity as an individual. The use of a solo trumpet to introduce the Rambo theme in 'Home Coming' and reprise it several times in the score was a masterful idea. The solo trumpet cries out proclaiming itself as if to say 'I exist' while the melody signifies a combination of feelings. In this wonderful theme one hears loneliness, solitude, sadness, but also pride without regret. Rambo did his duty for his beloved country yet feels betrayed. As this reviewer recalls, we (the troops) were hated by all political persuasions upon our return. Goldsmith, with his talent and genius for understanding characters, aptly represented these complex feelings and issues."[82]

Music historian and writer Jeff Bond observes, "Goldsmith dissects Rambo's psychology through the use of three different, important motifs" that "reflect Rambo's nostalgia for his 'normal life' as a civilian, something he thinks he is returning to as he enters town at the beginning of the film, but which is actually forever lost to the veteran due to the psychological wounds left within him by his wartime experiences, and society's rejection of men like him." Using different orchestrations, Goldsmith makes the theme apply to Rambo's longing, his anger, and his melancholy as his odyssey proceeds.

"The *First Blood* score is mournful and patriotic," Schweiger says, "and yet dark because Rambo's screwed up. He lost the war. So you're not playing this triumphant World War II fighter, you're playing a guy who's lost. Rambo's a product of the 1960s and God knows what he was listening to in Vietnam—rock music. I don't know if this ever crossed Jerry Goldsmith's mind—it probably did not—but you have to remember that the character's wandering around America, so you have a kind of Western lone hero going through rural surroundings. So there's a guitar for that kind of element of this wanderer."

Between the downbeat ending of *First Blood* and the release of *First Blood Part II*, Rambo changed from antihero into superhero. For *Part II*, Goldsmith integrates the Asian setting with Asian musical motifs abetted by an electronic keyboard that imparts a modern sound. He generates tension by mixing electronic with symphonic sounds, expressing the cultural conflict taking place as well as recalling the mixture of nostalgia and nightmare that Rambo feels by returning to the site of his wartime confinement. Goldsmith even sneaks in Russian-sounding themes when Rambo is tormented, not by the Viet Cong, but by their Russian overlords.

The score for *Rambo III* was recorded in producer Andrew Vajna's homeland of Hungary with the Hungarian State Orchestra and Hungarian State Opera Orchestra. It was a cost-cutting move to avoid American musicians' unions, but it also, per Jeff Bond, required modifying the complexity of the music. The composer's Rambo theme insinuates itself in Asian and Middle Eastern styles as the film moves from Bangkok to Afghanistan. He also composed end credit music.

Jerry Goldsmith died from cancer in 2004, but his themes live in *Rambo* (2008) and *Last Blood* (2019) as composer Brian Tyler interpolated them with his own music in the fourth and fifth films. In November 2022, Goldsmith's three complete *Rambo* scores enjoyed a special five-disc collector's vinyl pressing from Quartet Records, produced by Neil S. Bulk with mastering by Chris Malone and an informative, twelve-page liner note booklet written by Jeff Bond.[83] Bond is also the author of a two-volume biography of Goldsmith.

CHAPTER 8

Rambo Rebooted

"**I** didn't like the way the last *Rambo* ended," Sylvester Stallone confessed in a 2011 interview in which he was asked whether he should have dared, in 2008, to make a sequel to 1988's *Rambo III*. "Dare I?" he joked. "Oh my God, how old is Rambo? This guy is coughing dust already. And I thought, it's not about Rambo, just like *Rocky* was not about Rocky—it was about isolation, loneliness, desperation. How do you face the last chapter of your life? *Rambo* was about an ideology of a fellow who was embraced by this country when they needed him and then rejected, so he lives in the jungle like a beast. He just is simmering with all this fury and no place to put it. And then, lo and behold, in comes this group, a Christian group, an enlightened group, someone who has a Pollyanna outlook on the world that we could all be brothers. And, of course, Rambo knows that it's totally different. And I thought, oh boy, that's a movie to make because you're dealing with two philosophies, optimism and pessimism, nihilism, and put it all together. Then it takes it to another level. I didn't try to pull any punches. It was brutal because what is going on in Burma is brutal and I wanted to be real."[1]

This time there could be no Sam Trautman. Richard Crenna, who had played the pragmatic colonel through three films, had died in 2003. Although he would be seen briefly in a flashback from *First Blood* and the new film would be dedicated to him, he was not otherwise involved (his voice would be heard in *Last Blood*, 2019). There were rumors that James

Brolin would replace him in what was being called *Rambo 4* playing an "overseas American operations manager" named "Ed Baumgardner," but Stallone nixed the idea. The cover story was that Trautman died sometime after his Afghani ordeal in 1985.[2]

By then, Carolco Pictures had filed for bankruptcy in 1995 (see the sidebar about Carolco). Studio Canal (Canal+) had bought the rights to market the first three Rambo films, while Harvey and Bob Weinstein's Miramax company acquired the right to make future ones, planning to release them through its Dimension Films genre division.

"In 1997, I received a phone call from an executive at Miramax," David Morrell recalls. "He said that they'd been trying to find a suitable Rambo story but didn't feel they were on the right track. As he described some of the stories they'd been developing, I realized that they'd misinterpreted Rambo as a gun-for-fire, a mercenary. One of the stories they described involved Rambo being with a group of treasure hunters, looking for priceless archaeological artifacts against the background of the first Gulf War. When I told the executive that this approach contradicted the core of the character, that Rambo wasn't a mercenary, that he hated combat, the executive sounded surprised and invited me to New York, where I had a multi-hour meeting with him and several other executives. In the end, they hired me to write two treatments and what's called a bible for the character, explaining his background and characteristics. One of the ideas they suggested involved Rambo infiltrating a group of domestic terrorists who planned to blow up a government building in the Midwest, a situation reminiscent of Timothy McVeigh's Oklahoma City bombing in April 1995.

"I didn't like how that idea turned out and preferred the second treatment I wrote, in which Trautman organized an Outward Bound–type school, in which former special-operations personnel instruct teenagers about the Idaho mountains and the leadership skills necessary to survive in the wilderness. Rambo bonds with a spirited teenage girl, who's partly Hispanic. What Rambo doesn't know is that she's the daughter of a Central American drug lord whose Anglo wife fled from him and is living under an assumed name in the United States. When the drug lord discovers where his daughter is, he orders a team to kidnap her. In an intense action sequence that involves river-rafting, Rambo is unable to stop the abduction. After he learns who's responsible for the kidnapping, he goes to Central America and rescues the girl. The majority of the plot involved their escape through a jungle. She uses the outdoor skills he taught her at the school and becomes a kind of daughter to him. In the climax, she's forced to kill someone to save him, and he kneels before her, weeping about the cost to her. I loved the idea that Rambo might eventually find redemption in that intensely emotional relationship, finally having a sort of family, but nothing came from the work I did for Miramax. Eight years later, in 2005, Miramax licensed the right to make future Rambo films to Millennium Films, where *Rambo IV* and *Rambo V* were developed. I had no discussion with any Millennium executive about the character."

The *Rambo IV* screenplay was eventually credited to Art Monterastelli and Sylvester Stallone,[3] the result (see the sidebar later in this chapter) of a Writers Guild arbitration that says more about the way Hollywood works than a month of watching TMZ. By the time *Rambo* (international title *John Rambo*) was released, "Ed Baumgardner" had become "Arthur Marsh" and his role had shrunk to two pages.

Although Morrell didn't have any conversations with Millennium executives, Stallone did phone him to talk about his goals for the fourth movie. "He had two thoughts about it," Morrell told writer Elaine Bergstrom. "One was that none of the movies captured the anger, so to speak, or the despair of [my] novel. This time around he was going to capture that. The second thing was, he felt that perhaps the second and third films glamorized the violence in a way that he wasn't happy about. And this fourth movie was going to be ultraviolent in a shocking way that would try to replicate what the violence would be like in real life. He would use this in order to show the impact this would have on the character—how this would deaden his soul."[4]

Initially, *First Blood* director Ted Kotcheff and that film's unit publicist, Burton Elias, were asked for story ideas. In 1990, they submitted to Carolco a twelve-page proposal that refigures Rambo as an ecological warrior who goes to South America to protect the rain forest.[5] Apparently that was a nonstarter, for by 1995 a 106-page screenplay had been written by actor Nick Koff and cinematographer/art director Lee Ford Parker. It also went into Rambo limbo.

Then Stallone stunned everybody by announcing that he no longer wanted to make action movies, a decision that may have been a negotiating ploy or an acknowledgment of mortality. Regardless, it soon dissipated.[6] In 2005, Miramax sold the Rambo rights to Avi Lerner's Millennium/NuImage Films, and the road was cleared for *Rambo IV* as soon as Stallone finished directing *Rocky Balboa* from December 2005 to January 2006. All he still needed was a story. At first, he considered Rambo venturing into Mexico to rescue a kidnapped girl. (Whether anyone at Millennium read the kidnapped-girl treatment that Morrell had written for Miramax is unknown.) This idea would eventually become the crux of *Last Blood* in 2019, but in 2006 it lacked what he called the "lost man wandering in the world" DNA that distinguished his three earlier Rambos.

The rescue plot has been a staple of motion pictures. It has numerous resonances from classics like John Ford's *The Searchers* (1956) to *Trackdown* (Richard T. Heffron, 1976) to *Hardcore* (Paul Schrader, 1979) to *Homefront* (2013), scripted by Stallone for director Gary Fleder.[7]

Forsaking earlier ideas, *Rambo* started fresh. Even though Stallone had recently exhausted himself directing *Rocky Balboa*, the star, then in his sixties, committed to directing *Rambo IV* as well, vowing to make the movie look as though Rambo himself had directed it. First, writer Monterastelli (later rewritten by Stallone) and Stallone settled on the plight of the Karen people who were at the mercy of the military junta in civil war–torn Burma (Myanmar). The project was called *Rambo IV: In the Serpent's Eye*.[8]

Burma, in Southeast Asia, has been known as Myanmar since 1989. It is one of the most politically repressive and unstable regions in the world, having been in civil war since 1948. Fighting between the government and local armed ethnic groups has been ongoing. There seemed to be hope in 1990 with the election of the National League for Democracy's Aung San Suu Kyi, but the election deniers of the military refused to accept her, and the country remains highly volatile.[9] It was Stallone's call to set *Rambo* there to bring attention to the nation's crisis as well as to present a different landscape than his previous missions. Unable to actually film there (Myanmar is on the US State Department's Travel Advisory List),[10] the company settled on Thailand and Mexico.

The $50 million[11] production began shooting on January 22, 2007,[12] in Chiang Mai, Thailand, not far from the border of Burma (now called Myanmar). Burma shot back. Stallone and his crew were filming on the Salween River, the only clear path to Myanmar from Thailand as land paths are heavily mined. Myanmar had been cracking down on pro-democracy demonstrations and, for some reason, Burmese troops fired at the *Rambo IV* production. According to Stallone, "We were told we could get seriously hurt if we went on. I witnessed survivors with legs cut off and all kinds of land mine injuries, maggot-infested wounds and ears cut off. We hear about Vietnam and Cambodia, but the results of this conflict are more horrific. This is a hellhole beyond your wildest dreams."[13] Thinly veiled threats were also made by representatives of the Myanmar government who were concerned with how they were portrayed, not caring that their threats further tarnished their image.

Shooting an antiwar movie in a war zone was cause for self-examination. "*Rocky* represents the optimistic side of life, and *Rambo* represents purgatory," Stallone told *Time*'s Joel Stein, explaining that he decided to make an antiwar film that wasn't about the Middle East. This was at a time when Americans had been told that Saddam Hussein was behind the 9/11 attacks and were pointing their fingers at Iraq. Stallone went out of his way to hire Burmese extras for the film, particularly those from the Karen Party, even though some of them feared reprisals from the ruling military.

Like Rambo, Stallone was done with war. He said that, in 2004, he had abandoned the Republican Party by voting against George W. Bush, whom he called obstinate and arrogant. "Go out there and ride in a Humvee ten times, and then I'll listen to you. Take the ride. Have your bowels go into a square knot. Then I'll respect you."[14]

In the film, Rambo lives under a shadow of cynicism and disillusionment, every molecule of it justified by experience every fan knows from the previous films. Rambo earns money by collecting snakes for the tourist trade, so the Mae

Sa snake farm was leased along with its ophidian inhabitants. Stallone made his slithery scene partners look good.

He is called "Boatman" by the missionaries whom he reluctantly takes upstream like Charon navigating the River Styx into Hades in Greek mythology. He is sullen and withdrawn. He makes his case to Sarah, the only woman among the church people, that nothing they do is going to change a thing in war-torn Burma, a conclusion he reached after earlier soul-destroying journeys through death, destruction, and disenfranchisement. "What I was trying to say is that nothing changes," Stallone held. "The world will never come together and say we are one. Rambo thought he would have accomplished something with all he has given. I think about the lifelong police officer who retired after fifty years, and crime is up. He's gotten hurt, he's lost his wife, and what has he accomplished? Crime is up."[15]

And yet, even though Rambo would deny it, he holds a glimmer of hope, the kind of hope that the missionaries express in their guileless, faith-based optimism. It remains his secret why he consents to ferry the group (sacrifice? affection for Sarah? hope for redemption?), but he does, and like so many wounded heroes who try to escape life, life summons him back. (This theme will repeat in *Last Blood*, albeit for more personal reasons.)

The film raises a number of significant questions, rare for an action movie. First, the missionaries are not only bringing medical help to the people, but they are also spreading Christianity. Fortunately for the plot, the Karens are already a Christian people,[16] but it prompts the moral question around proselytizing—not just Christianity but Islam and other faiths—given the tragic history of what happens when one civilization imposes its spiritual beliefs upon another. There is also the hypocrisy of the character of Arthur Marsh, a church leader who hires mercenaries to rescue the missionaries who shouldn't have been there in the first place. (Recall that, in an early draft, Marsh was "Ed Baumgardner," a CIA operative.)

Rambo is a violent film, in some ways more violent than the Saffron Rebellion itself. By actual count of Jeremy Urquhart in Collider, 247 people are, he writes, "mowed down and killed in often horrific ways. It could be described as being a bit much, but those who like their action movies gruff, tough, and no-nonsense might find something to like here."[17] There is a pragmatic reason for this; according to what Stallone told the Associated Press, it was cheaper to stage graphic violence using computer-generated imagery than to do it the usual way with explosive squib and traditional physical pyrotechnic effects. "We were all sitting around looking at the small production budget," he recounted. "Then I said 'Hey, fake blood is cheap, let's make it all-out bloody.'"[18] The result is an operatic succession of death and dismemberment with flying body parts, spurting blood, people atomized by land mines, gutted, punctured, and otherwise rubbed off the face of the earth.

The protracted violence was influenced by Stallone's admiration for director Sam Peckinpah, especially Peckinpah's milestone 1969 Western, The Wild Bunch. At the time of its release, some critics chastised The Wild Bunch for the intensity of its violence, much of it shown in slow motion. Other critics praised its genre-changing innovations. The movie is set during the Mexican Revolution of the 1910s (the Americans-in-a-foreign-country theme led some critics to think of it as a Vietnam parable). In it, William Holden leads a team of bandits who, in the climax, slaughter a Mexican garrison, sacrificing themselves for a personal code of honor and avenging one of their comrades. Says Morrell,

"It's ironic that Peckinpah and *The Wild Bunch* are two of the biggest influences on my novel *First Blood*, and then, in a phone call, Sly told me he wanted to present a Rambo movie that deglamorized the violence and made it a Sam Peckinpah Rambo movie. In *Rambo IV*, there are visual allusions to the prior film, especially at the end where Rambo is wounded and slumps across the huge gun. Compare that with William Holden slumping over the water-cooled machine gun at the end of *The Wild Bunch*."[19]

Filming wrapped on May 4, 2007, with an extraordinarily long (nine-month) post-production allowance for a January 22, 2008, release. This was necessitated by the film's huge demands for computer-generated imagery; upward of one hundred visual effects artists (many of them from Eastern Europe) were tasked with complementing the work of the nearly forty mechanical effects technicians who created the physical effects in front of the camera. Among the more astonishing effects is that a single bullet can be seen going through two and three people. This is an accurate, observed battlefield phenomenon, but it may be the first time it ever appeared on-screen.

While this was going on, somebody got the idea to change the film's title—or, rather, to settle on one. In addition to being called *Rambo 4*, it had been known as *Pearl of the Cobra* (after one of Stallone's screenplays), which was enigmatic to the point of obscurity. As if the other variation of earlier franchise titles (*First Blood, Rambo: First Blood Part II, Rambo III*) weren't confusing enough, on October 12, 2007, Lionsgate, which was distributing the film, changed the name to *Rambo: To Hell and Back*.[20] This name change caused confusion among fans so that, to quell the rebellion, Stallone called *Ain't It Cool News* guru Harry Knowles, insisting, "You know Lionsgate jumped the gun on this. I just was thinking that the title *John Rambo* was derivative of *Rocky Balboa* and might give people the idea that this is the last Rambo film, and I don't necessarily feel that it will be. He's not an athlete. There's no reason he can't continue onto another adventure. Like John Wayne with *The Searchers*."[21]

Under the title *Rambo* (in America and Canada) and *John Rambo* (internationally), the film was released in January 2008. When the expanded director's cut was released on home video, the title of that version became *John Rambo*.[22]

By whatever title, the film did not play in theaters everywhere. For obvious reasons, it wasn't shown in Myanmar. But Britain's leading cinema chain, Odeon, also refused to show it (London's opening was February 12, 2008), claiming "commercial reasons," a strange explanation to avoid booking a presumably guaranteed hit. Rival exhibitors said it was probably a disagreement with international distributor Sony over financial terms.[23] But perhaps it was a reaction to advance reviews, most of which did to the film what Rambo does to the Burmese army.

Nevertheless, the film is beautifully made. Each camera angle is chosen not just to record what is going on but to give it an impact. The cinematography by Glen MacPherson is rich and sensual and sets off the lush locations; one can almost feel the heat and humidity. Stallone's directing is competent in the best meaning of the word; he tells his story in a straightforward manner, and his dramatic scenes transition perfectly into the stunt sequences. The camera doesn't perform aerobatics, all the better to know exactly what is going on at any time.

The battles, of course, dominate the last act. They are choreographed by stunt coordinators Kawee Sirikhanaerut, Sermsin Koonsanchotsin, Supoj Khaowwong, Noon Orsatti, Chad Stahelski and some ninety stunt performers.

An uncredited Stanimir Stamatov doubles for Stallone. They all meet their CGI fates with gruesome efficiency. While the endless slaughter at times takes on the numbing depersonalization of a video game, there are enough reaction shots and a perfectly executed climactic kill to tie everything together— and then do it even better in the expanded director's cut.

Stallone wasn't finished with Burma once *Rambo* was in release. Perhaps channeling his on-screen persona, he offered, during a Madrid promotional photo session, to go to Myanmar and face down the military junta who had denounced the veracity of his film. "Let me take a tour of your country without someone pointing a gun at my head and we'll show you where all the bodies are buried," he challenged. "Or let's go debate in Washington in front of a congressional hearing . . . but I doubt that's going to happen. I'm only hoping that the Burmese military, because they take such incredible offense to this, would call it lies and scurrilous propaganda. Why don't you invite me over?"

Stallone's bravado was justified by the fact that the film had been officially banned[24] in Myanmar. Yet it was being bootlegged there and circulated among dissidents and others who opposed the country's ruling junta from within.

"These incredibly brave people have found kind of a voice, in a very odd way, in American cinema," Stallone added. "That, to me, is one of the proudest moments I've ever had in film."[25]

Rambo opened first in the Philippines on January 23, 2009, and on January 25 on 2,751 US screens to amass a worldwide gross of $113,244,290, over 60 percent of which came from the international release.[26] The surprising ratio of domestic revenue to international is significant. Traditionally, American-made films generate two-thirds of their income from the United States and the final third from the rest of the world. In 1997, for the first time, aggregated international grosses for American films exceeded domestic grosses.[27] This caused the financial backers of US movies to demand that future films appeal primarily to other countries, particularly Asia, whose moviegoing audience is vast. *Rambo* was a further sign that the globalization of Hollywood had begun.

SIDEBAR

Synopsis of the Film *Rambo*

Burma[28] is ravaged by sixty years of genocidal civil wars. Now in the Saffron Revolution, government SPDC (State Police and Development Council) Major Pa Tee Tint (Maung Maung Khin) leads his troops from village to village, impressing young men into the army and threatening their families with destruction should they complain to the Karen rebels. Under Major Tint, the Burmese Army also enjoys forcing their captives to flee across rice paddies which they have larded with hidden mines, shooting at the terrified villagers and watching them get blown up for sport.

In a backwater settlement in neighboring Thailand, John Rambo (Sylvester Stallone), some twenty years after his rescue of Colonel Trautman from Afghanistan, has become the captain of a small charter boat, harvesting snakes for a local reptile fighting club that caters to tourists. While working in his home foundry, he is approached by a group of Christian missionaries who want to hire him to guide them up the Salween River into forbidden Burma, carrying medical supplies and Bibles. At first, he rejects the charter when it is proposed by the group's ineffectual leader Michael Burnett (Paul Schulze), and cynically explains that people will never change and that saving the world is a lost cause. Burnett gives up, but the sole woman among them, Sarah Miller (Julie Benz), refuses to accept Rambo's cynicism.

For reasons of his own (although in footage included in the director's cut it's because he admires Miller's decency), Rambo changes his mind and agrees to help. The group heads upriver. En route, Rambo reveals that his name is John, that he comes from Bowie, Arizona, and that he was drafted to go to 'Nam. When Burmese pirates attack them and attempt to kidnap the blond Sarah, Rambo whips out a handgun and shoots six of them. When he shoots one of them a second time to finish him, Burnett chastises him, "Who are you [to play with people's lives]?" Rambo turns the boat around, but Sarah exhorts them to continue, "because the people up there are being killed like this every day." Rambo reminds her of his warning that their mission will not change anything.

Rambo deposits the missionaries at the shore of Klaw Kbe Lo village. On the way back down the river, he passes the pirate boat with the bodies of the dead pirates and sets fire to it.[29] Meanwhile, the missionaries give the Karen people medical attention, food, and Bibles. Suddenly the village is attacked by the SPDC, who shoot some young men, round others up for military service, take the women to rape, and capture the missionaries. Major Tint keeps Sarah for himself.

During a violent storm, both weather-based and emotional, Rambo, in his shack, flashes back to his Special Forces service, his relationship with Trautman, and his rampage in Hope.[30] His nightmarish reverie is interrupted by the arrival of Father Arthur Marsh (Ken Howard) of the missionaries' church, who asks Rambo to go back up the river, this time with a team of mercenaries to extract the missionaries, inasmuch as the embassy has declined to help the Church because of strained US relations with Burma. Rambo resolutely heads to his personal foundry and fashions a crude but terrifying machete-like weapon that puts his earlier Rambo knives to shame. Gleaming from the heat, he laments, "War is in your blood. Don't fight it. You didn't kill for your country, you killed for yourself. The gods are never going to make that go away. When you're pushed, killing is as easy as breathing."[31] This remarkable speech is both expiation for himself and an explanation to his critics (few of whom, if any, commented on it).

The mercenaries arrive, led by braggart Lewis (Graham McTavish), who taunts the stoic Rambo, not knowing his background, to hurry so they can finish their job. Only the team's armament expert Schoolboy (Matthew Marsden) has any sense that Rambo is more than what he reveals.

At the SPDC Light Infantry Battalion 360, the army uses beatings to train the kidnapped kids into becoming soldiers while the missionaries are held hostage. When the mercenaries arrive, Rambo wants to go with them, but Lewis, still unaware that Rambo is Rambo, tells him condescendingly to wait for them at the boat. The mercenaries discover that the village is destroyed and abandoned. They track the soldiers and realize, to their surprise, that the enemy are hundreds strong. Lewis wants to give up and go back to the boat, but Rambo shows up and pulls out his compound bow and aims it at Lewis's eye. The other mercenaries pull guns on Rambo, and it's a standoff until Lewis blinks and the group proceeds. "This is who we are," Rambo says, "live for nothing or die for something."

Meanwhile, the SPDC continues tossing mines into the rice paddies and forcing prisoners to scramble across, shooting them on the other side if they are lucky enough to survive. Rambo takes charge of the mercenaries. They shoot the soldiers and commandeer their troop truck. At night, they drive the truck into the SPDC compound, deploying some of the mercenaries along the way. While the Burmese soldiers are distracted in the mess hall, where they force captive women to take off their clothes, Rambo dispatches Sarah's captor by ripping out his throat. Schoolboy stays with Sarah and Rambo as they head for the boat. The other mercenaries also run for the boat.

Come daylight, the SPDC army discovers the carnage and goes on alert, using dogs to track the escapees. Lewis steps on a mine and loses his foot. The others on his team fashion a litter to carry him. Their local guide abandons them. Now there are two sets of people: Rambo, Sarah, and Schoolboy, and the mercenaries with the missionaries. Rambo tears off a piece of Sarah's skirt and wraps it around his shoe, using her scent to lead the tracking dogs away from her and Schoolboy as they head for the boat without him.

Knowing he is being followed, Rambo sets a Tallboy bomb primed with a Claymore mine and a trip wire, then runs. When the soldiers trigger the device, the explosion sends shock waves for hundreds of yards, flattening everything, attracting the attention of a Burmese army gunboat.

At the shore, Rambo commandeers a machine gun atop an armored vehicle and shoots hundreds of the enemy. Many of the shots penetrate multiple people. Then the mercenaries join in. Even Burnett "smites" one of the enemy with a stone in the biblical fashion. Finally, a contingent of Karen rebels shows up and confronts the army. Rambo chases the major and disembowels him with his homemade weapon. While the missionaries tend to the survivors, Rambo walks away from war.

Back in America, he arrives in Bowie, Arizona, to reconcile with his father on the family's horse farm.

Alternate version:

For the Blu-ray release, Stallone added nine minutes to what was called a "Director's Cut." The title was changed to *John Rambo* and the logo for The Weinstein Company was removed.

This recut opens, after a newsreel summary of the Burmese conflict, on pastoral images of Rambo trapping cobras (he now wrangles a second snake, and it truly appears to be Stallone doing it) before being approached by the missionaries. The scene in which Sarah returns in the rain to try once more to persuade Rambo to take them is extended, allowing Rambo to editorialize about the futility of war: "It's in the blood. It's natural. Peace, that's an accident. It's what is. When you're pushed, killing is as easy as breathing. The killing stops in one place and it starts in another. But that's OK 'cause you're killing for your country. But it ain't your country who's asking, it's a few men at the top who want it. Old men start it, young men fight it. Nobody wins. Everybody in the middle dies, and nobody tells the truth."[32]

There are a few shots added to Rambo's burning of the pirate boat, and a moving moment when, after dropping off the missionaries, Rambo strokes the cross amulet that Sarah gave him and imagines her presence with him on his boat. Rambo suffers more battle flashbacks (culled from the first three films) and is seen brooding more profoundly so that when Arthur Marsh shows up to ask him to save the missionaries, his assent is more plausible, and Marsh's prayer of peace, intercut with Rambo's preparation for war, becomes ironic.

Some other scenes are rearranged, but the major change is to make the film more emotionally involving, particularly in the farewell between Rambo and Sarah. The theatrical cut had Sarah and Burnett ministering to the wounded while

Rambo, standing above them on a hill, gazes out at the carnage of battle, then walks off with barely a return stare at the two people who drew him into the conflict. In Stallone's recut, Rambo makes distant eye contact with Sarah and Burnett, and the cutaways to the carnage are eliminated. This technique of "double cutting"—that is, going back and forth several times between two people looking at each other—triggers audience sympathy and makes Rambo's wordless decision to leave more moving. He next shows up at the Rambo homestead in Bowie, looking almost exactly as he did at the start of *First Blood*. This suggests an optimistic "new beginning" which will sadly be undone in 2019's *Last Blood*.

SIDEBAR

Write On, Rambo

When a motion picture is produced under the Writers Guild of America minimum basic agreement (MBA), the writing credits are subject to arbitration if anybody who wrote for the film seeks screen credit. The rules are complicated and controversial (if not incomprehensible), but inasmuch as credits are a screenwriter's curriculum vitae, proper allocation is essential.

Although *Rambo* (aka *John Rambo*, *Rambo 4*, *Rambo IV*, and *Rambo: The Fight Continues*) carries the screenplay credit of Art Monterastelli and Sylvester Stallone based on characters created by David Morrell, fifteen additional writers are known to have contributed to the project during the course of its creation. On November 15, 2007, they were informed in writing by Sally Burmester, WGA senior credits administrator, of an arbitration scheduled before the end of the year. They were shown a list of the arbiters and were told they could delete anyone they did not wish to take part in the arbitration. The process had to be completed efficiently to be able to create accurate screen credits on the release prints that would hit the world's screens on January 23, 2008.

Arbitration is not a casual affair. Volunteers must read every page that everyone wrote and determine how much of what's on them wound up in the finished film. Below is an inventory of what the arbiters had to examine. It shows how many people worked on the film. They will never be able to claim credit, even though they may have been paid for it, because their words or ideas were not used, or not enough of them were used.

As noted in the Writers Guild manual, the word *and* signifies additional writers added in that order, while the ampersand (&) signifies a writing team established from the beginning. A treatment is a written plot synopsis in prose rather than dialogue. Revisions are changes made by writers to their earlier work. Also evident are people who wrote entire screenplays from their treatments that were ultimately rejected. This list shows that, early on, Ted Kotcheff, who directed *First Blood*, was invited to submit a story idea for *Rambo 4* that was not used. Also shown is a screenplay by Dan Gordon that wasn't used, although Gordon would make contributions to *Last Blood* in 2019 that were apparently arbitrated to story credit.

Here is the literary body count from what is rightly called "development hell":

1. *First Blood* DVD of 1982 film, source material for character reference

2. *Rambo: First Blood Part II*, DVD of 1985 film, source material for character reference

3. *Rambo III*, DVD of 1988 film, source material for character reference

4. Treatment by Burton Elias & Ted Kotcheff, 1990, 12 pp.

5. Screenplay by Nick Koff & Lee Ford Parker, 1995, 106 pp.

6. Screenplay by Dan Gordon, 3/28/05, 117 pp.

7. Screenplay by Sylvester Stallone, 7/14/05, 108 pp.

8. Treatment by Kevin Bernhardt, 9/23/05, 2 pp.

9. Revisions by Kevin Bernhardt, 10/26/05, 6 pp.

10. Treatment by Andy Hurst, 11/20/05, 6 pp.

11. Screenplay by Andy Hurst, 12/21/05, 101 pp.

12. Screenplay by Kevin Bernhardt, 1/20/06, 114 pp.

13. Screenplay by Kevin Lund & T. J. Scott, 1/27/06, 100 pp.

14. Revisions by Kevin Bernhardt, 3/29/06, 26 pp.

15. Revisions by Art Monterastelli, 7/19/06, 12 pp.

16. Screenplay by Art Monterastelli, 10/15/06, 102 pp.

17. Scene by Sylvester Stallone, 10/19/06, 3 pp.

18. Screenplay by Sylvester Stallone, 11/6/06, 109 pp.

19. Screenplay by Sylvester Stallone, 2/9/07, 100 pp.

20. Screenplay by Sylvester Stallone, 2/25/07, 100 pp.

21. Screenplay by Sylvester Stallone, 3/7/07, 100 pp.

22. Revisions by Sylvester Stallone, 3/12/07, 2 pp.

23. Screenplay by Sylvester Stallone, 3/21/07, 100 pp.

24. Revisions by Sylvester Stallone, 4/1/07, 33 pp.

25. Screenplay by Sylvester Stallone, 4/1/07, 100 pp.

26. Final Shooting Script by Sylvester Stallone, 4/16/07, 100 pp.

As the final screen credits show, the arbitration was resolved to shared credit between Art Monterastelli and Sylvester Stallone.

CHAPTER 9

Too Long at the Fair: *Rambo: Last Blood*

Old soldiers never die," said General Douglas MacArthur in 1951, quoting a famous military hymn in his farewell address to Congress, "they just fade away."[1] As John Rambo was to learn to his detriment in *Rambo: Last Blood*, not every old soldier can follow this self-aggrandizing advice. Instead, like Michael Corleone in the third *Godfather* film, just when he thought he was out, they pull him back in. The highly controversial result was a film that attempts to mythologize the Rambo legend but, for many people, savaged it. Those perceptions are worth exploring.

Last Blood was designed to cap the Rambo saga. Whether it was called part of a franchise, a series, a sequel, or a continuation, in this one both the character and the performer seemed ready to leave. By the time Sylvester Stallone filmed it, he had revisited *The Expendables* (2010) twice, in 2012 and 2014, and probably held some kind of record for *Rocky* (1976) with seven sequels or spin-offs, in 1979 (*Rocky II*), 1982 (*Rocky III*), 1985 (*Rocky IV*), 1990 (*Rocky V*), 2006 (*Rocky Balboa*), 2015 (*Creed*), and 2018 (*Creed 2*). Although some filmmakers try to dodge criticism for sequels by saying the concept of continuations is no different than episodes in a popular television series, in movies the main characters are supposed to undergo significant change in the course of their journey, whereas TV series characters usually do not change at the risk of losing their faithful audience.

Stallone was nearly sixty-two in 2008 when he announced,

on February 2, that he would make a *Rambo V* (provided that *Rambo IV*, which had been released a week earlier on January 25, was a success).[2] Given Hollywood's economic formula, which states roughly that a film must gross three times its budget just to break even, *Rambo IV* finished in the red.[3] Despite this, a month later, Stallone told the website Moviehole.net that he was halfway finished with the script for *Rambo V* and would shoot it in Bulgaria, but that he wasn't sure whether it would involve Rambo going off to another war or addressing a domestic threat.[4] It would turn out to be shades of both.

In 2008, Miramax (which had acquired the Rambo film rights from bankrupt Carolco Pictures) had licensed those rights to Millennium Films. Millennium then commissioned a script that had Rambo fighting drug lords and sex traffickers on the Mexican border.[5] An entirely different approach involved Rambo leading a special forces team to hunt and destroy a secret government program in the American Northeast that was genetically modifying elite troops to optimize their killing skills. As much as this sounds like *Captain America* meets *Predator*, it was based on a 1999 science fiction book titled *Hunter* by James Byron Huggins, about Nathaniel Hunter, the world's greatest tracker.[6] The working title was announced as *Rambo V: The Savage Hunt*.[7] There were also rumors that Rambo's backstory would involve him becoming a horse trainer. By the end of the year, Rambo and Stallone had fallen back on the Mexican cartel kidnapping concept.[8]

The Hollywood term *development hell* was coined to describe how everybody says they want to make a particular movie, but nobody has the clout or courage to actually do it. Even with a proven box office element like Sylvester Stallone—or perhaps because of the costs associated with a proven box office element like Sylvester Stallone—the stakes become so high that nobody wants to make a commitment lest they be held responsible if the worst happens. When William Goldman famously wrote "nobody knows anything," he didn't mean that filmmakers were stupid, he meant that there are no certainties.

Perhaps this is why, in May 2010, Stallone insisted that he was "done" with Rambo, telling Josh Wigler of CBR. com, "I don't think there'll be any more. I'm about 99% sure I was going to do it . . . but I feel that, with Rocky Balboa, that character came complete circle. He went home. But for Rambo to go on another adventure might be, I think, misinterpreted as a mercenary gesture and not necessary. I don't want that to happen."[9]

When Millennium/NuImage announced *Rambo V* at Cannes that spring, therefore, Stallone disavowed any involvement and disclosed to Harry Knowles of *Ain't It Cool News* that he had been informed that if he didn't want to play Rambo, somebody else would. "Stallone told me in no uncertain terms," Knowles reported, "at the end of *John Rambo* [international title of *Rambo*], when he sees his home, those horses and he looks back at that road . . . for Sly, that was a road he is never walking down again."[10]

In 2011, Sean Hood, who would later write the *Conan the Barbarian* remake, had been hired to write *Rambo: Last Stand*.[11] It was put on hold the next year.[12] In 2013 Stallone announced, in association with NuImage and Entertainment One (a derivative of Hasbro toys), that he would be involved in a Rambo TV series.[13] Not that *Rambo V* was entirely dead; in June 2014 Splendid Films of Germany said that Stallone was writing the script for *Rambo V*,[14] which, by the end of the year, would be called *Rambo: Last Blood*, with Stallone directing. Avi Lerner and Millennium Films would produce.[15]

Many factors figure into why people and companies choose to make a given film: Do they want to visit a particular location? Do they want to work with a given actor or director? Do they owe alimony or taxes? Does the project speak to a personal concern? Some of these can be overcome by money. If the star is secure enough, the last factor—a personal concern—weighs in.

On July 13, 2012, Sage Moonblood Stallone, Sylvester Stallone's eldest child, died at the age of thirty-six from the effects of coronary artery disease. No substances were involved. Although Stallone has never publicly said so, it is possible that the tragic loss of his son had a hand in why he chose to make *Last Blood*. The film's plot device—Rambo seeks the men who kidnapped and killed his surrogate daughter—speaks to the horror and grief of a parent whose child predeceases him. From this point of view, Rambo has more to do with Stallone as a man than Stallone has to do with Rambo as a character. (As he noted several times in *Sly*, the 2023 Netflix documentary about him, Stallone looks for ways to use major incidents and emotions in his life as subtexts in the movies he makes.)

Then, in early 2016, Stallone announced that all bets were off. There would be no *Rambo V*.[16] There were whispers of a prequel that would be about Rambo's original tour of Vietnam (which of course would require a younger actor in the role), but nothing came of it—at the time.

"You know when you realize there's nothing more to pull out?" Stallone told Ramin Setoodeh. "As an action film, I was very satisfied that [*Rambo*] dealt with the Burmese situation. It had one foot in a current event, the longest civil war in history, sixty-five years at that time. It was so brutal, which civil war is. I was shocked they even gave me an A-rating [British].[17] I didn't want to compromise. I said, 'This is probably going to be the last decent film of this genre that I'm going to do as a solo act.' When that was accomplished, I never felt the same willingness to do it again. There's nothing left. When

they asked me to do another *Rambo*, I said, 'If I can't do better than I did last time, and I can't, then why'?"[18]

And yet something was in the air that would rekindle his
interest in *Last Blood*. On June 16, 2015, New York businessman Donald Trump announced his candidacy for the pres-
idency of the United States. He used the speech to promise
many things, including a crackdown on immigration, particularly (in fact, primarily) from Mexico. "When Mexico
sends its people," he insisted to a largely Hispanic audience,
"they're not sending their best. They're sending people that
have lots of problems, and they're bringing those problems
with us [sic]. They're bringing drugs. They're bringing crime.
They're rapists." Then he added, "And some, I assume, are
good people." Suddenly the idea of sending Rambo into Mexico to rescue a kidnapped girl from Mexican sex traffickers
seemed extremely timely and commercial.

Rambo: Last Blood traveled a great distance between
script and screen. To see what happened along the way, it is
useful to consider the original screenplay by Matt Cirulnick
dated May 7, 2018. Cirulnick was commissioned to write the
first draft that was later rewritten with Stallone incorporating
ideas from Dan Gordon. (Final credits are determined by the
Writers Guild.) It provides important narrative backstory to
what *Last Blood* finally became.[19] Not only that, *Last Blood*
exists in two versions.

SIDEBAR

Synopsis of the Film *Rambo: Last Blood*

Two versions of *Rambo: Last Blood* were released: one in
the US that runs approximately 90 minutes and one for the
international market at approximately 100 minutes (at this

writing, this longer version is available in the US only on Amazon Prime). The international version includes scenes that add significant resonances to the story.[20]

Synopsis of US Release

John Rambo (Sylvester Stallone) is finally at peace, but only in appearances. Every morning, he needs medication to control his mood[21] and works off his ennui in his home forging knives and repairing machines for the locals. He has taken over his deceased father's horse ranch in Bowie, Arizona, sharing it with his father's housekeeper, Maria Beltran (Adriana Barraza), and her granddaughter, Gabriella (Yvette Monrial). Gabri's father, Manuel (Marco de la O), abandoned Gabri and her mother ten years earlier, and after Gabri's mother died of cancer, the girl came to live with her grandmother Maria at the Rambo ranch.

Beneath the ranch, as within Rambo, there is turmoil. Over the eleven years since returning from Burma, he has dug a web of tunnels under his property for reasons he has never expressed, even to Gabri, to whom he has become a surrogate father.[22]

Gabri compliments "Uncle John" for getting over his past, but he clearly has not. As Rambo responds to her comment about healing, he says, "I haven't changed, I just try to keep a lid on it every day." He is full of regrets and wishes that somebody had stopped him from joining the army when he was seventeen. Gabri and Rambo are close. As a college gift, he forges a letter opener for her to take with her, but she informs him that nobody writes letters anymore, underscoring that he is mired in another time. When she says she's going to a party that her friend Antonia is throwing, Rambo invites her to have the party in his tunnels instead—a rare entrée into his privacy.[23] At the party, a boy hits on her but she rebuffs him. Rambo watches from the distant ranch house porch, sitting in the rocking chair, which his father built and in which he died.[24]

During the party, Gabri gets a call from her friend Gizelle, who now lives in Mexico, saying that she has found Gabri's birth father, Manuel. Her grandmother and Rambo caution her not to go and she agrees to obey them. Despite her promise, she does, driving to Mexico, where Gizelle leads her to her father's apartment. There she is stunned when he tells her that he never liked either her or her mother, and that's why he left them. Gabri is shattered. To lighten her mood, Gizelle takes her to a bar where she can have some drinks and cut loose. At the bar, a man puts drugs into her cocktail.

Next morning Maria tells Rambo that Gabri has not returned. She hands him the addresses Gabri left behind of both Gizelle and her father. Rambo goes to find her.

Gabrielle awakens in the brothel run by Victor Martinez, who, as an example to all the girls he has confined, brutally beats another girl who has tried to run away. They are all marked for the sex trade.

In Mexico, Rambo confronts Manuel, who truthfully has no idea where Gabri is. Rambo tells him he should have broken his neck ten years ago when he deserted the family. Next Rambo visits Gizelle, who gives him a song and dance about losing track of Gabri at the bar. When he sees that she is wearing a bracelet that was given to Gabri by Gabri's mother, he knows Gizelle set Gabri up. Whipping out his Rambo knife, he orders her to take him to the club where it happened. There she identifies the recruiter, El Flaco (Pascacio López). While he looks at El Flaco, Rambo is watched by a dark-haired young woman sitting across the room.

El Flaco leaves the bar with a girl. Rambo follows him into the club's parking lot, grabs him, and tells the girl to leave. He shows El Flaco a photo of Gabri and asks where she is. When El Flaco hesitates, Rambo breaks his collarbone, stabs him in the thigh, and starts to rip off his arm. He talks, and Rambo and Flaco drive away as the dark-haired woman from the bar, Carmen, follows in her car.

Rambo studies the building where Flaco tells him the girls are held whom he drugged and delivered. A Martinez sentry notices him. In fact, half the tough guys in Mexico notice him and follow him to a rooftop where they beat him severely and take his ID. Seeing a photo of Gabri that Rambo keeps in his wallet, Hugo Martinez promises to treat her more harshly now that he knows someone is concerned about her. He scars Rambo with Rambo's own knife. Rather than dump him in acid, he wants him to live and suffer for what his inquiry has done to Gabri. Abandoned and bloody, Rambo is rescued by Carmen.

Vincent Martinez asks his brother Hugo for "the girl," Gabri, and takes a syringe to render her unconscious while he disfigures her face.

Montage of waiting: Maria, Carmen, Vincent, Hugo. Gabri becoming addicted. A doctor patches up Rambo at the dark-haired woman's house. When Rambo finally recovers enough to talk, Carmen reveals that he has been unconscious for four days. She says she is an independent journalist following Flaco and that's how she saw what Rambo did to him. She tells him that it was the Martinez brothers who also kidnapped her sister and overdosed her three years ago. He asks for her help finding them.

Rambo drives to the brothel where he kills three guards and three johns with a hammer, takes Gabri, and drives off with her. Victor Martinez uses Hugo's refusal to kill Rambo as a chance to take over the business from his brother. But

Hugo has Rambo's Arizona driver's license and now knows where to find him.[25]

Gabri dies on the way home. "Why not me?" broods Rambo.[26] Easily dodging US-Mexico Customs into the States, he drives through a flimsy barbed-wire fence and heads back to Bowie. There he tells Maria that Gabri is dead. They bury Gabri on the ranch, and Maria, having no reason to remain among the memories, leaves to live with her sister. Similarly, Rambo says, "I'm just going to move around. Like always."

But first, Rambo makes plans for the expected Martinez assault. He booby-traps his tunnel and the grounds, waiting for them. Then he drives back into Mexico to ask Carmen to help him locate Vincent. When Carmen protests that nobody can make a difference and to move on, Rambo asks her "How is it ever done? I want them to know that death is coming and there's nothing they can do to stop it."

Rambo breaks into Vincent Martinez's house, stabs several guards, and leaves Vincent tied and decapitated on his bed. Police, Hugo, and reporters cover the aftermath. Hugo finds Rambo's calling card—Gabri's photo—stabbed into Vincent's chest and takes the bait, assembling an army. In Bowie, Rambo frees his horses, meditates at the foot of Gabri's grave, and girds for the impending assault.

As expected, Hugo's men arrive in an SUV convoy and spread out across the ranch. Several of their vehicles blow up on land mines. A group of men is set ablaze, and others are shot. Once the pursuers descend into the tunnels, Rambo mangles them in groups of ones, twos, and threes by impaling, magnesium shotgun shells, Claymore mines, beheading, and an array of poles, knives, hatchets, machetes, and spikes, as his subterranean loudspeakers blast the Doors' "Five to One."

Rambo himself is wounded in his side but perseveres. He calls out "here" to lure Hugo after him. Hugo shoots him in the shoulder. Knowing Hugo is the last survivor, Rambo sets off a series of charges in a sequence designed to drive Hugo out of the tunnels and onto the surface, where Rambo tells him, "I wanted you last." He promises to rip out his heart "as you did mine."

Hugo ends his pursuit in the stables where Rambo crucifies him to the wall with arrows and then does, indeed, cut out his heart.

Finally, completely spent, Rambo walks slowly, painfully to his front porch and sits in his father's rocking chair. He is still alive as we pull back and dissolve to a montage of shots from the four previous Rambo movies. The last image—and it may be a flashback, a dream, or a spiritual ascent—shows Rambo riding off on his horse toward the mountains.

Differences Between the Domestic and International Versions

The international version begins with a torrential rainstorm. Rambo has become the go-to person in Bowie and offers his rescue services when three hikers become lost in the monsoon. The first hiker that he finds is a woman (unbilled) who has drowned, wrapped in her hiking gear. He searches for the other two, a man (Nick Wittman) and a woman (unbilled), as floodwaters rip through the mountain. He saves the woman by tying her to him against a rock, but the man flees when Rambo tells him that his wife is dead. Later Rambo learns that the man has also died. This rekindles his survivor's guilt. The sheriff (Lewis Mandylor) and chief (Aaron Cohen) thank him, as does the woman he saved, but he remains sullen. The truth is that Rambo is part of, and apart from, his old hometown. Unlike in Hope, which he destroyed in *First Blood*, in *Last Blood* he is now driven to contribute to his town within the limits of his post-traumatic stress.

A few moments are added to the international release version that were not in the US version, such as Rambo mulling to his housekeeper, Maria, that he lost the two hikers: "Couldn't save them. Couldn't save my brothers in the war, either." He now takes heavy medication and has come to accept the existential fact that nothing any single man can do has any real effect on the evil[27] that exists in the world, yet he maintains a spark of optimism that it might still be possible. He goes to bed after the storm, not in the house, but in a closed-off room in a network of tunnels he has dug under the ranch, where he plays Doors music and pushes his fists into his eyes. From here the differences between the domestic and international versions of *Last Blood* are small but telling.

The flood rescue sequence that leads the international edition serves to establish Rambo as someone who is known around the community as a helper, a concerned citizen. It also reminds him that he cannot save everybody, a harsh reality that will play out with the death of his adoptive daughter. But the sequence is ultimately incongruous and unnecessary because it is tonally different from the rest of the film. The color scheme and terrain are inconsistent with the rest of the movie. The sequence does, however, show Rambo as a man who will work against all odds if he is motivated to perform a mission, even a fruitless one, much as he chastised the missionaries in *Rambo* for their impractical idea of making a difference in Burma. In their case, they were fighting humans; here Rambo is fighting nature, a reversal from when he was fighting a war.

The international edit puts more attention on the Martinez brothers, showing off both their ambitions (they want to join an international slavery cartel) and their competitive fraternal differences. Their characters are drawn more fully with the addition of just a few minutes of footage, but only to the extent of adding justification for their deaths. It does, however, give the actors more screen time for international sales purposes. In the international version there is a scene of Mexican police in league with the traffickers, who invite them into the brothel to take their pleasure with the girls.

Lastly, the running times of both versions are deceptive. Although the domestic cut runs 1:29:28 and the international cut goes 1:41:34, the last ten minutes of each is consumed with a flashback montage and elaborate end credits (including many CGI artists and retake crews). This means that the actual storytelling goes seventy-nine and ninety-one minutes respectively, making the first version unusually short for an American feature-length film.

Matt Cirulnick's script, which was changed significantly, is a smartly written work that begins not with Rambo or a storm sequence but with the kidnapping of eight-year-old Melissa Delgado, Carmen's sister, that ends with her death from trauma as she escapes her captor's speeding car and dies in the Mexican street in Carmen's arms. This is the event to which Carmen refers in the film as Rambo is healing on her sofa, identifying herself as an independent journalist, a swipe at how the local papers ignore human trafficking.

But a Rambo film must begin with Rambo. Here he is personally invested as a man, not as a soldier. In the script, he is still a coiled spring who has flashbacks to Vietnam, dives for the ground when a car backfires, lunges into road rage, and drinks himself to sleep every night in a bar listening to the Rolling Stones (not the Doors) on the jukebox, pausing on one occasion to attack three mixed martial arts jerks who dare to unplug it. There are no subterranean tunnels and no altruistic rescue missions. This is a somber, defeated, haunted Rambo waiting for the release of death. Here his adoptive daughter Gabrielle is drugged and kidnapped from a bar in Arizona, not Mexico. In this way she is entirely a victim, rather than in the film, where she foolishly places herself in danger by driving to Mexico against her promise to her grandmother and Rambo to remain stateside. The latter version makes her action in the film the same creaky plot contrivance used in movies in which the naïve woman goes into the attic where everybody in the audience knows the killer is waiting. Worse, this outdated convention subtly implies that the victimized woman "deserves it."

Much of the film plays as in the original concept, but the differences stand out. The chief change is that Carmen reveals that she served in the army for three years. This is significant when she joins Rambo in wreaking havoc on the Martinez gang. Giving Rambo a partner, and a female one at that, must have sounded too much like Julia Nickson's "Co" character in *First Blood Part II*. It is certainly antithetical to the concept of a loner working his way through PTSD. Although Rambo is driven by desire to save Gabri, he is also suicidal. Because of this, when he is surrounded by Martinez's minions for his rooftop beating, he "looks around, satisfied with the prospect of death in combat."[28]

Carmen finds him after the pummeling and drives him to his Bowie ranch, where he takes three weeks, not four days, to recover, and there is no Mexican doctor to help. Rambo and Carmen return to Mexico to torture a business associate of the Martinezes, Robert Siedel, into giving them a laptop computer containing contacts and victims. Rambo renews Carmen's desire to seek revenge for her sister but adds a dose of moral ambiguity:

> RAMBO: In the real world, the bad guys usually win.
>
> CARMEN: What does that make you?

RAMBO: I never said I'm a good guy.

Rambo and Carmen team up to attack Victor Martinez's compound, killing as many henchmen and johns as
possible. Rambo rescues Gabri, who is about to be shipped
off on a submarine, but she dies of blood loss, not an over-
dose. Returning to the Bowie horse farm, he unearths a buried arsenal, and when Hugo Martinez's army arrives in force
to kill him (slaughtering the town constabulary along the
way), he picks them off one by one with a variety of means,
becoming wounded himself until only he and Hugo are left,
man-to-man, unarmed. With the last of his strength, Rambo
breaks Hugo's neck, then hobbles to his porch and rocking
chair. "His arm dangles at his side," the script says, "whether
from exhaustion or death, we cannot tell."

The original script appropriately, even tragically, presents
Rambo as a man who is ready to die but feels he must do so
for a worthy cause, and if it can't be for country, then it will
be for family. The rewrite used by director Adrian Grunberg
eliminates Carmen as a revenge partner and leaves Rambo
mortally wounded but presumably still alive in his rocker.

The movie began shooting on October 2, 2018, in Bulgaria, which had been selected as a photographic double for
Bowie, Arizona[29] and wrapped efficiently on December 4[30]
with pickups and reshoots taking place at the end of May
2019.[31] It was released on September 20, 2019.

Grunberg, formerly a second unit director (second unit
handles action), worked with a nearly seventy-member stunt
crew, most of whom were Slavic men posing as Hispanics.
Much of the action was shot by cinematographer Brendan
Galvin in a constructed tunnel set in near darkness. The darkness is appropriate for tension, but sometimes it's too dark to
see who is trying to kill whom, and this confusion is abetted

by the rapid cutting of editors Carsten Kurpanek and Todd E. Miller. The result is that the violence is portrayed incoherently. Possibly this was done to dodge an NC-17 rating for the theatrical release, but it should not have mattered for home video and the footage would have best been restored. Consequently, Rambo's revenge—and the film—lacks the necessary catharsis.

In promoting the film, Stallone spoke thoughtfully of the character he had been playing, identifying with, and being identified with, over the course of four decades. "The warrior can never find peace," he told Rebecca Davis of *Variety*. "He just can't." He said that he had written the film's theme on a Post-it—"He came home, but he never arrived"—and it guided him from the end of *Rambo* in 2008 to the start of *Last Blood* in 2018. "It's not PTSD, but a hunger. This Latino girl and family" were his motivation, "and she's the only anchor he has left that touches his heart because everything else he has touched has died." He also expressed disdain for what modern action films had become. "These films now are scientific. They're made by techno-wizards, whereas, with the earlier action films, you actually saw this guy thinking. With this *Rambo* I'm looking at something much more simplified: Like man-on-man, in a cave. It's pretty simple. Really basic, no CGI."[32]

He also spoke of his vulnerability. In the film, the villains refer to him as an "old man" and even his adoptive daughter chides him for giving her a letter opener when "nobody writes letters anymore." "Rambo, he's always getting hurt," Stallone said, "but now he's getting older, so he's getting hurt even more. He knows he's not as fast. I'm not a great fighter anymore, but I fight great fighters and get hurt. I've always approached it from that angle because, that way, the audience goes, 'Oh, good. So he's not the best. He can die.'"[33]

The time-honored convention in action films is that the hero appears to be beaten in the third act just before he recovers and bashes the villain to bits. In *Last Blood*, however, Stallone bravely allows himself to be trashed in his first encounter with the cartel toughs, a powerful beating that occurs halfway through the film and sidelines him for a considerable amount of time before he comes back to finish them off. This formula can also be found in *First Blood Part II* with his capture by the Russians. In a genre where heroes don't even get a black eye, John Rambo needs minor surgery. It humanizes him and creates sympathy on top of Stallone's brooding performances.

Produced on a comparatively frugal budget of $50 million (frugal for 2018, that is), *Last Blood* accrued a worldwide theatrical gross of $91.5 million[34] followed by home video sales of $26.6 million in the US.[35] As with *Rambo* in 2008, the figures suggest that the film likely lost money (based on a conventional ratio of three-to-one in terms of box office returns compared to the budget). It also showed that Rambo could defeat anybody but the critics. As with previous entries, the film was attacked for its negative portrayal of "the other," in this case Mexicans. Intentionally or not, it exploited a rising xenophobia that was sweeping America. *Last Blood* was also criticized for extreme violence. Unlike previous *Rambo*s, where violence was clearly required to survive in the woods, to free prisoners, or to repel pursuing armies, this time it was all about revenge. It was designed to be cathartic; whether it succeeded was another matter.

According to the critics, it didn't. On his website, writer Christian Toto ran a compendium of the film's many negative reviews by liberal critics, to which he reacted, "Today's woke film critics, and they are legion, won't let screenwriters depict people of color as the bad guys. If you do, your film will get labeled as racist as quickly as possible."[36] Toto noted that these critics wanted the film's villains to be rendered more sympathetically and, by extension, that the filmmakers were implying that all brown people are like the criminals in the film.

Toto is keenly aware that, the more rounded the portrait of movie villains, the more sympathy they receive and the less effectively the sides can be drawn. "You can have cartoon characters, you can have one-dimensional characters," he says, "but I don't think that's the case with that particular Rambo film. I think there's something happening in either the cultural class or the critical class or the journalistic class, for lack of a better phrase, where they're seeking out these tropes, these narratives, these themes, and, even if they're not quite there, they will point them out and call them out. I think, in this case, it was unfair."[37]

The Latino press took a more personal view. In a survey on the website Remezda.com, their critics saw *Last Blood*'s villains not as governmental combatants as in previous Rambo films but as a cartel defined solely by its ethnicity. Claudia Puig noted, "In this wrongheaded film, all the legions of characters that live in Mexico—save one journalist—are depicted as avaricious, uber-violent and heartless. ... The methods used to torture legions of dark-skinned men in a series of tunnels under Rambo's farmhouse are engineered to elicit laughter, cheers, and applause from the audiences."[38] She was not alone.

Last Blood is something of a swan song for both the actor and the character whom he had, by then, been playing for thirty-seven years. David Morrell recalls a text Stallone sent him. "Sly said that he still saw Rambo in enormous anguish because of everything that had happened to him. Through his love for a substitute daughter, the character found a form of redemption, only to have it taken away from him. Sly went on to say that he imagined the character asking why God had forsaken him after everything he'd been through and that after the film's climax of revenge, the character was in a hell from which there wasn't an exit. That statement marks an interesting contrast with what Sly said long ago about the change to the end of my novel so that in the movie of *First Blood* there was a positive outcome, a message of hope.

"I admire *Last Blood*'s intentions. The original draft sounds fascinating and complicated. But I wonder, would a man who had a violent breakdown because of flashbacks to being tortured in a pit in Vietnam subject himself to digging tunnels under his home? We can say that the tunnels might be intended as a physical version of his tortured subconscious, or else we can say that he's testing himself, but I still can't believe that someone who (in the first story) not only suffered through the pit in Vietnam but was also tortured in a basement jail cell and then endured the horrors of the rat cave (in my novel it's a bat cave) would want to be enclosed again. Also, I don't believe that he would allow young people to have a party in the tunnel, with all those weapons in reach. And I have trouble believing that Rambo, a white man bulked up like the Incredible Hulk, could slip unnoticed into the Mexican bar where Gabri was drugged and, again unnoticed, confront one of the men responsible for it. In *Rambo II*, the character insists that the mind is the best weapon, but here, the master of tactics simply walks up to what appear to be two hundred guys, confronts their leader, and insists on the return of the girl. Why is he surprised when they beat the hell out of him? What else did he expect? For these reasons, I tend to think that this is a Rambo movie only in name.

Character traits that were established in the earlier films are contradicted."[39]

But it might be said that, after thirty-seven years from *First Blood* to *Last Blood*, Rambo freed himself from the page and entered the realm of movie legend where rules are made and broken as befits the swing of audience taste. Rambo and America traveled a long and winding road together between 1972, when the novel *First Blood* was published, and 2019, when the last (so far) Rambo movie was released. It began with a serious drama about an alienated Vietnam veteran and ended with what feels like an exploitation film from the 1970s, one of which, *Trackdown* (1976), has a similar plot. Although Sylvester Stallone and his succession of writers, producers, and directors say they are not making political statements, interpreting the films as a reflection of the politics of their times is unavoidable. The films appear to have been financially successful—$819 million from ticket sales is impressive, plus an unknown amount of ancillary income from video, TV sales, and merchandising—yet the third, fourth, and fifth films likely ended up in the red. In Hollywood, of course, it's possible, even normal, for a film to make money without showing a profit. The industry term for this conundrum is "rolling breaks," in which people who receive a percentage of the gross income are paid first, leaving little or nothing for those who get paid down the line out of net profits (or, as cynics refer to them, "nyet profits"). Hollywood wisdom holds that eight out of ten films lose money; the system would collapse if the studios had to wait for money to hit the bottom line.

For the public, though, Rambo lives and belongs to them. His influence is strong and powerful. Confides Morrell, "I was part of the first USO tour to a war zone. It was in 2010 and I went with four other writers to Iraq while the war was on. We slept in a shipping container that had a bomb shelter in a corner in case we were attacked. Before we went, we visited two military hospitals in the Washington, DC, area, where there were veterans who had lost one arm, two arms, one leg, two legs, or all of them. I talked with these seriously wounded veterans. The only reason I could do it was that I'd been in a children's cancer ward for months with my son and my granddaughter, both of whom died from bone cancer. I held my granddaughter's feet when she was taken off her life-support machines. So, I'd been down this road somewhat, although I could never imagine what all these young men had experienced.

"In addition to the hospital bed, in a corner of the room, there was a recliner chair that could be turned into another bed. There was always a woman—a mother, a wife, or a serious girlfriend, who'd been there for months. Many of them said to me, 'He's in this hospital because he had to be a hero.' They looked like they were going to weep. Only one of these young men wouldn't talk to me. He'd lost his arms and legs, and he kept staring toward the wall at the bottom of his bed. When the others learned that I'd created Rambo, they told me about stepping on a mine and getting their feet blown off or being maimed by some other type of explosion. What they described was horrifying. Nearly all of them said they'd joined the military because of the second and third Rambo films. I said, 'Well, I guess, even though I didn't write those films, in some ways I'm responsible for you being here.' And they said, 'Oh, no, no, don't even think about it. If I could, I'd go back and do it again.'"

This is Rambo, and these are the men who were shaped by him. He is more than a phenomenon; he has become an institution. Over the course of four decades, audiences have grown up with him and America has followed. Across this span, he has gone from being a metaphor for a lost generation of warriors to becoming a standard-bearer for a dream that persists in those who fought wars and those who support and honor them.

CHAPTER 10

A Piece of the Action

That movies influence culture is not a new or unique observation; the question is how much they do it. Setting aside for now whether screen violence inspires, reflects, or ignores it in real life, there is a less scholarly, more friendly relationship: the desire of fans to extend the experience of seeing their favorite movie by buying a product associated with it, or showing loyalty to a beloved star by emulating their manner of dress.

The bond between star and fan is akin to love. Costumes that Gloria Swanson wore in her films for Cecil B. DeMille in the 1920s quickly showed up on local dress shop racks. When Clark Gable bared his chest in *It Happened One Night* (1934), undershirt sales supposedly took a tumble. And when Veronica Lake trimmed her "peekaboo" hairstyle into the "Victory Roll" in World War II so that women could work more safely in factories, it showed the power of a star's influence. Marlene Dietrich made ladies' slacks acceptable in the thirties, and Audrey Hepburn made Hubert de Givenchy a household name when she exclusively wore his designs. In more modern times, Theodora van Runkle started a retro fashion trend with her costumes for *Bonnie and Clyde* (1967), as did Diane Keaton with Ruth Morley's distinctive designs for *Annie Hall* (1977). Similarly, men were influenced by Jean Ann Black and Rebecca Deleo's frizzled haircut for Brad Pitt in *Fight Club* (1999), Richard Gere's Giorgio Armani tailoring in *American*

Gigolo (1980), and the deadly black suits, white shirts, and narrow ties in Quentin Tarantino's *Reservoir Dogs* (1992).[1]

Merchandising is more pervasive and more financially rewarding. Among the most notable movie/merch alignments are the Ingersoll watch company's production of Mickey Mouse watches in 1933,[2] Disney's Davy Crockett coonskin caps of 1954, and Kenner's profitable (if tardy) *Star Wars* merchandising in 1978 the year after the movie.[3]

In the 1970s and '80s, television networks and toy manufacturers drew heavy criticism for creating cartoon shows such as *Transformers, He-Man, Ninjago*, etc., for the sole purpose of selling toys to children. The practice remains controversial for companies that made Roy Rogers cap pistols and others that, more recently, produced kid-sized grenade launchers and assault rifle war toys. Taste and decency are important commercial considerations. No movie company in its right mind is going to put out, for example, a *Basic Instinct* ice pick or, worse, *Schindler's List* action figures.

This placed Rambo in a curious position. As constructed, his primary appeal was revenge, not adventure. The very notion of "Rambo: The Home Game" for kids was repulsive. Yet, with so many people yearning to replicate the Rambo experience in their own lives, short of donning a canvas serape and picking people off with an arsenal, how could fans emulate their hero?

The obvious place to start was T-shirts (even though Rambo wore a canvas tank top in *First Blood*). The most perceptive of these read, "All he wanted was something to eat," a reference from the book that didn't make it into the film, about Rambo simply wanting to buy a hamburger at a town diner. The collection from an assortment of sellers, licensed and not, includes men's socks, wall clocks, army-style field jackets, slogan stickers, coffee mugs, sweatshirts, posters, and a twelve-inch figure of Sylvester Stallone complete with an itty-bitty rifle, bandolero, fighting stick, knife, and removable, articulated hands designed to hold each of them ($192.97 from Amazon). There's also a seven-inch Rambo action figure from *Rambo: First Blood Part II* for $199.99, and another seven-inch figure, topless, wearing bright red trousers (just the thing to not stand out in a jungle) and carrying a compound bow. For the ladies there's a "feng shui handmade happy Buddha necklace" just like Co Phuong Bao wore in *Rambo: First Blood Part II.* And wait! It turns out that there *is* a home game. For $99.99 one to four players ages fourteen and up can play with fifty-two "highly detailed minis," two choppers, over one hundred "gear and tactics cards," and ten epic heroes to carry out up to twenty campaigns.

The subject of merchandising was a thorny one for the man who plays Rambo. Speaking to the *Chicago Tribune* while publicizing *Cobra* in 1986, Stallone said that he had no control over the merchandise for *Rambo* even though he derived a percentage of the profit. He was not happy with what was being done. "It's not for kids," he complained. "The movie was not supposed to be for little kids, and I wouldn't let my own children play with those toys." He was also upset about the cartoon series but said that, even though the animated hero looked like him, the producers insisted that it wasn't him, it was only a *likeness* of the character that he didn't own.[4] He was, however, flattered by the likeness of the action figures and was even more flattered by their sculpted physique.

It was unusual for any R-rated film to throw off merchandising, but producer Andrew Vajna insisted that those they permitted were sensitive to the violence issue. "The toys were very safe," he says. "The toys were a lot of fun and the Saturday morning cartoon that we created actually had some really interesting messages in it that were nonviolent messages [such as respecting the environment]. And if you looked at the [first] movie itself, he was never acting out of malice, he was always acting out of self-defense. So we felt justified that that was good enough. I don't think you need to have the plastic gun in order to pretend to shoot somebody as a kid. I think you can use a broomstick, you know, like I did when I was young in Hungary. You can create your own imaginary weapons, so I don't think the actual physicality of that gun makes any difference at all."[5]

He spoke the truth, or at least the reality. "*Rambo* is also America's newest licensing phenomenon," barked the *Los Angeles Herald-Examiner* just after *Rambo: First Blood Part II* went into release.[6] That same week the *Washington Post* noted that DC area weapon and hunting supply stores were selling ten-inch survival knives similar to those that Jimmy Lile (more about him soon) had produced for the sequel, with one merchant saying that his orders had multiplied fiftyfold.[7]

According to the New York–based trade magazine the *Licensing Scope*, Rambo was chosen as the most profitable new license of the year 2008 by 2,500 buyers. Licensing and merchandising writer Marie Moneysmith reported that some forty firms agreed to produce Rambo wares and noted that it was unusual for a live-action character to be so successful inasmuch as most deals are for cartoons. "The American people are looking for a hero," Barbara McClorey, managing editor of the *Licensing Scope*, told Moneysmith. By contrast, she quotes Dianne Mandell, vice president of merchandising and licensing at Stephen J. Cannell Productions, that *First Blood* was not as attractive for licensing as were its sequels because "it was a very different film and it came out at a different time. The United States wasn't quite so pro-military then."[8]

Nevertheless, Ramboiana was a lucrative market. In a world where it took sales of 50,000 posters to break even on a press run, the muscular Stallone Rambo pinup topped 600,000 copies.[9]

Stephen J. Cannell Productions, the producer of hit TV shows such as *The Rockford Files*, *The A-Team*, *Wiseguy*, and many others, landed the merchandising rights.[10] Sixteen months later, Cannell sued Carolco for breach of contract seeking $65 million in damages.[11] Cannell charged that Carolco had attempted to lower or eliminate Cannell's 20 percent sales fee from the merchandising and publication grosses under a February 1985 oral agreement.[12]

As if to disarm Rambo and reach the untapped youth audience, in 1986 Carolco-affiliated Worldvision Enterprises distributed, and Ruby-Spears Productions created, the *Rambo* animated television series, *Rambo: The Force of Freedom*. With Jerry Goldsmith's music during the opening and closing credits, it starred the voices of Neil Ross as Rambo; Alan Oppenheimer as Trautman; Mona Marshall as Katherine Anne "Kat" Taylor, a master of disguises; James Avery as mechanical engineer Edward "Turbo" Hayes; and Michael Ansara as the shady General Warhawk. The series was narrated by Don "In a world where . . ." LaFontaine. It debuted on ABC-TV and lasted sixty-five weekly, sometimes daily, half-hour episodes between April 14, 1986, and December 18, 1986, then hit home video. It did not go unnoticed. For starters, the very idea of turning an R-rated film franchise into a kids' cartoon not only annoyed Sylvester Stallone,[13] it also generated accusations that the producers had hired child psychologists who advised them not to mention Vietnam or POWs in an animated series derived from a film about Vietnam and POWs. Moreover, how could its intended young audience possibly have any idea who Rambo was when they weren't supposed to have been allowed to see his R-rated movies in the first place?

The origin story of the cartoon series was simple: Toy-maker Coleco[14] handed their Rambo action figures to head writer Michael Chain with instructions to do whatever he needed to do, just get a show on the air.[15] At the same time, they were mindful of content restrictions influenced by Action for Children's Television, the Massachusetts-based watchdog group headed by Peggy Charren that was, with congressional support, removing exploitation from what *Variety* liked to call "kidvid." As a result, house rules were that, in the animated episodes, gunshots and lasers, whenever they were fired, never hit anybody, planes could be shot down but the crew had to be shown parachuting to safety, and Rambo had apparently been cured of PTSD. He also ran around entirely topless regardless of the weather.

The series debuted as a five-parter titled *Rambo: The Force of Freedom* before settling into weekly episodes. The ongoing plotline followed Rambo, acting on a "request" from Colonel Trautman, leading his team to seek and destroy the terrorist organization S.A.V.A.G.E. (Specialist Administrators of Vengeance, Anarchy, and Global Extortion) headed by General Warhawk. Rambo, when not leading the Force of Freedom against world enemies, spent his time helping children, animals, and protecting the environment.

According to the pop culture website Topless Robot and reported by Dan Larson on Toy Galaxy,[16] *Rambo* did so well on ABC that it drew the ire of ACT. Arguing the incompatibility of medium and message, ACT scared the network into pulling the show out of their children's viewing time slot and relegating it to 4:00 a.m. playoff until its must-run contract ran out.

Kids could still enjoy Rambo in print, however. Blackthorne Publishing in 1989 issued a comic book series, and in 2022 none other than Sylvester Stallone himself and Chuck

Dixon wrote *First Kill*, a graphic novel showing Rambo's first tour of duty in Vietnam. It was financed by an Indiegogo campaign, instantly topped its funding goals, and was to be published by Splatto comics in 2022.[17]

And, of course, there were the inevitable home video game units that encouraged player or players to experience what Rambo had endured, presumably minus the psychological trauma:

- *Rambo* (1985, Commodore), recreating *Rambo: First Blood Part II* (David Collier and Tony Pomfret, designers);

- *Rambo: First Blood Part II* (1986, SEGA);

- *Rambo*, based on *Rambo: First Blood Part* II (Nintendo, 1987);

- *Rambo III* (SEGA, 1989);

- *Rambo*, based on *Rambo: First Blood Part II* and *Rambo III* (SEGA, 1989);

- *Rambo: The Video Game*, based on *First Blood*, *Rambo: First Blood Part II*, and *Rambo III* (2014, Reef Entertainment).

The most valued merchandise thrown off by the films, however, was not the result of a multimillion-dollar licensing deal or a plastic memento, but the work of a genuine craftsman: the Rambo knife. Created especially for the first two films by Arkansas knifesmith Jimmy Lile, the distinctive, thoughtful, limited-edition all-purpose weapons are prized to this day by collectors.

In the film *First Blood* (it doesn't appear in the novel), Rambo's mere possession of the knife kicks Chief Teasle into arrest mode. The knife has a double saw-edge on the back of the blade, flathead and Phillips screwdriver heads on the guard, and a hollow grip that contains a compass, matches, a fishhook, a suture needle, thread, and other helpful items. The handle is tightly wrapped with a stout cord that can be used for fishing or to fasten to a branch to make a spear. The sheath contains a sharpening tool. For *Rambo: First Blood Part II*, Lile made a somewhat larger knife. He omitted the compass but finished the steel blade with a black coating so it wouldn't reflect at night. After he made the prototypes for Stallone to use on-screen, Lile handmade one hundred numbered copies to sell at $1,000 apiece. They were gone almost as soon as they were offered. For both films, United Cutlery released mass-produced versions of the knives that remain highly sought-after.

Jimmy Lile, born in 1933 in Russellville, Arkansas, was a schoolteacher and construction contractor but always had an interest in knives, having carved a wooden one when he was eight and grinding a nail file into a blade when he was eleven. In 1970, having tired of teaching and construction, he decided to go into knifemaking full-time. In addition to the Rambo knives, he recreated the one made famous by Jim Bowie (remember the Alamo?) and gained a reputation as a consummate craftsman. He died in 1991; he and his wife Marilyn had no children, but his business, Lile Knives, LLC, is now owned by John Henry Hill, Jr., who was Lile's friend for the last twenty years of his life.[18] The original, numbered Lile Rambo knives now sell for as much as $30,000.[19]

For *Rambo III*, Stallone chose another knifemaker, one whose knives he had collected just as he had collected Lile's: Gil Hibben. Hibben was inspired to become a knifemaker because of the now-classic knife that Warner Bros. created for *The Iron Mistress* (1952), a romanticized version of Jim Bowie's life. (Interestingly, both Hibben and Lile were inspired by the Bowie knife.) Hibben grew up in Wyoming and began making knives after his discharge from the navy in 1956. After that, he worked for Boeing Aircraft, where he learned about metals and began making knives from the then relatively new 440C steel. He worked as an Alaskan hunting guide and is a martial arts instructor (Kenpo Karate). He now resides in Kentucky. Hibben made knives for the first three *Expendables* movies and the Klingon bladed weapons in various *Star Trek* movies. But it is for his *Rambo III* and *Rambo IV* knives that he is best known. For *Rambo III*, he designed a distinctive Afghan Bowie-style blade as well as a "mystery" rescue knife that appears only once, when Rambo probes the sand for mines outside the Soviet fort. For the fourth Rambo film, he designed a machete-style blade, which also appears prominently in *Rambo: Last Blood*, although Hibben received no credit in that fifth film. As with Lile's Rambo knives, Hibben released limited-edition numbered copies of his Rambo blades, which are prized by collectors and valued at many thousands of dollars.[20]

The other weapon that fascinated viewers was Rambo's compound bow from which he shot arrows, both traditionally barbed and carrying explosive heads, with unerring accuracy. Created by Hoyt-Easton Archery of Sepulveda, California, the compound bow (described by Morrell in his novelization of *Rambo: First Blood Part II*) is assembled from three parts that fit into a quiver. Unlike a traditional single-string bow, the compound bow has a pulley assembly that reduces the energy needed to draw the bowstring while maintaining the thrust for the arrow, rather than having it dissipate within seconds after it is released, as is typically the case. The arrows, produced by Pony Express Sport Shop, also of Sepulveda, are designed in two sections that can be easily carried and quickly assembled. A screw-on barbed tip allows the traditional arrowhead to be replaced by an incendiary tip. Robin Hood never had it so good.

Social media have spawned a number of Rambo worship sites including collections, fan fiction, slash fiction, tributes, and news. Many celebrate the character and the adventures of Rambo, while others place him in combination with other characters in wildly spun-off situations. These cannot be acknowledged or endorsed here, but suffice it to say that five films, three novels, and the private and public lives of the many people associated with the productions over the years have provided enough backstory to inspire an astonishing range of privately created fiction.

But what of Rambo himself? Surely there are enough wars going on around the world, many with American involvement, whether overt or covert, where Rambo could lend a hand, knife, bow, or gun. The dream has persisted for over a decade that Rambo could become a live-action television series. Even the critical and box office disappointment of 2019's *Rambo: Last Blood* didn't kill such a prospect. Indeed, talks to that effect had surfaced as early as 2013, when Entertainment One and NuImage announced plans for a *Rambo: New Blood* series. Sylvester Stallone, Millennium Productions' Avi Lerner, and writer Jeb Stuart would executive produce for Fox television, although there was some vague messaging as to whether Stallone would appear.[21] The pitch was that Rambo's son, J.R., an ex–Navy SEAL, would go off on missions, but whether his father would send him there or take part himself was unclear. Stallone nixed the idea[22] but talks were still in progress in 2015 while *Rambo: Last Blood* was being put together[23] Stallone issued the final word in 2016 when he told *Variety*, "The heart's willing but the body says, 'Stay home.'" He added, "I don't want to cast aspersions, but it's delicate to try to replace a character with his son. I've seen the son of Flicka, the son of Tarzan, the son of King Kong, the son of Godzilla. It's a very difficult premise."[24]

Yet as with all great hero myths, belief persists that there can be, if not a TV series, then perhaps a *Rambo VI*, with allowances made for Stallone's age (he was born in 1946). After all, wasn't there a *Creed II* in 2018 (when he was seventy-two), an *Expendables 4* in 2023 (when he hit seventy-seven), and a possible *Cliffhanger* reboot (when he became ageless)? And didn't he star in *Tulsa King* and *The Family Stallone*, both for Paramount+, as this was being written?

Even Quentin Tarantino expressed interest in doing a Rambo reboot. "If I just wanted to make a good movie that I knew would be good," he told Movieweb's Ryan Scott, "I would take David Morrell's novel for *First Blood* and do the novel. Not the movie that was made out of *First Blood*. I would do the novel. And Kurt Russell would play the sheriff, and [Adam Driver] would play Rambo. Every time I read it, the dialogue is so fantastic in the David Morrell novel that you're reading it out loud. It would be so good. But now I want to do more than that. But if it was just about to make a good movie, that's out there."[25] With Tarantino planning on retiring after his tenth film, his *Rambo* seems wishful thinking.

There is, however, a *Rambo* film without Rambo. It's *called Son of Rambow* (2007) and is both a coming-of-age comedy and a loving homage to the Stallone portrayal. Set in 1982 in England, it's about the unlikely friendship between two societal outcasts who make a tribute movie to their favorite action hero. Will Poulter is Lee, a troubled adolescent with a tough home life who pirates a copy of *First Blood* from a cinema with his home-video camera. Bill Milner is Will, a sheltered boy whose religious fundamentalist parents won't allow him to see movies, even the educational films shown in class. The two boys join forces to make a short video called

"Son of Rambow," which, in the course of their collaboration, allows them both to become more open to life as well as
to free themselves from the constraints of their home situations. Written and directed by Garth Jennings and approved
by Sylvester Stallone himself (according to Jennings's video
commentary), the movie shifts in tone between bizarre stunts
and actual jeopardy and becomes that rare film that takes its
subject seriously but not itself.

Quite another enterprise is *Flooding with Love for the
Kid*, a one-person play by Zachary Oberzan, whose title is
adapted from one of the last lines of Morrell's novel. The
idea is that people in the audience are Oberzan's friends in
his confined 220-square-foot New York City studio apartment while he explains the differences between the book
and the movie, pretends that his sofa is a cliff, and barks
like Orval Kellerman's dogs. In 2007, the actor recorded the
play in a brilliantly produced video. Reviews in the *Village
Voice*, the *Guardian*, and *MovieMaker* magazine legitimized
the effort, and it was made publicly available in 2018.[26] Far
from *Son of Rambow*, *Flooding with Love for the Kid* is not
a comedy, but a harrowing exploration of the themes in
First Blood (both the novel and the movie) and—not incon-
sequentially—of Oberzan himself, whose personal passion
matches the intensity of the story. This is not a gimmick; it is
a frequently naked (in both meanings of the word) descent
into the psyche of the Rambo character and a suggestion of
what (without saying so) Sylvester Stallone must have gone
through to play him.

That Rambo lives in so many forms is as much a tribute to
David Morrell, a Canadian who created a memorable American archetype in response to forgotten American soldiers, as
it is to Sylvester Stallone, who personified him. Rambo has
become a catalyst as well as a symbol. He represents America's

strengths as well as its weaknesses, its glories as well as its faults. The two cannot be separated. Understanding how they feed each other is crucial to addressing America's survival in a world where the flesh is all too willing but the spirit is not always able.

CHAPTER 11

When Johnny Came Marching Home

War is hell. William Tecumseh Sherman said so in 1880 when he told a group of cadets, "Some of you young men think that war is all glamour and glory, but let me tell you, boys, it is all hell!" What the Civil War general didn't say, however, is that postwar is also hell, particularly for the people who did the fighting. It has likely been thus throughout history; no doubt centurions returning to Rome had nightmares about fighting the barbarians. The euphoria of independence following the Revolutionary War was surely diminished by war-weary Minutemen returning to farm and family. World War I wiped an entire generation of men off Europe's scorched earth, and those who returned from battle can be said to have burned themselves out during the Jazz Age. Other than the influenza epidemic, what other malady followed the boys home? Not until the February 1915 issue of the medical journal *The Lancet* were their symptoms defined: "loss of memory, vision, smell, and taste" with an overlay of hysteria labeled "shell shock."[1] Eager to quell a panic that might cut enlistment, the government tempered the term to "battle fatigue." Its current name is PTSD—post-traumatic stress disorder. And it flourishes.

The plight of returning veterans and the drama of their reentry into a world that moved on without them have been the subject of several films. Many of these use war as a simple plot motivation ("they taught him to kill," etc.), but some make a serious attempt to show the effects of war and the difficulties of readjustment. It's a broad subject that deserves its own book, just as the 33,000-plus homeless vets now living on America's streets deserve attention and action.[2]

Much is made in *First Blood*, both the book and movie, about prior war service. John Rambo's Green Beret training gives him the skills to do what he does to Hope. He is a coiled spring about to let go, and it takes learning about the death of Delmar to loosen the restraints. But the trigger itself is his treatment at the hands of Sheriff Teasle. Although Teasle, in the novel, is a Korean War veteran and is going through a marital separation, those elements are missing from the film, so all that exists on-screen is the sheriff's disgust at Rambo's ragtag appearance. At their first meeting, Teasle doesn't even know that Rambo is a Vietnam vet, and Rambo has no idea that Teasle is a Korean War vet.

None of this is Rambo's concern. He just wants to be left alone, especially after learning that Delmar is dead.

Vets dealt with PTSD in many ways. When *The Deerhunter* opened in 1978, stories began circulating from theater personnel that men who appeared to be veterans would buy a ticket for the 10:00 a.m. show and stay until the house was cleared at midnight. They weren't necessarily doing it out of artistic appreciation; watching that film over and over was their exorcism, their only way of ridding themselves of feelings and experiences that they could never, ever tell their families or anyone who hadn't been there.[3] The Veterans Administration is aware of such instances. "Responses [to war films] vary person by person," reports a VA representative. "For some it may be cathartic or have no impact, while for others it may trigger PTSD symptoms."[4]

In the years before *Saving Private Ryan* (1998), the government didn't want the public to know the awful truth about war, only the glory. Even as intense a film as Sam Fuller's *The*

Big Red One (1980) was more brutal psychologically than physically. Independent films, however, didn't shy away from the truth, and the ultimate demonstration of this was Dalton Trumbo's 1971 film from his 1938 novel, *Johnny Got His Gun*. In it, soldier Joe Bonham loses his arms, legs, and face in World War I, yet is kept alive and hidden from the public because the government fears that, if people saw the true toll of war, they would no longer permit their leaders to wage it.

Audiences who flocked to see King Vidor's 1925 silent film *The Big Parade* had just lived through the Great War. Still, they must have been shocked when its dashing star, John Gilbert, returned from battle in the story with a leg missing. Although combat injuries were no secret within families, when a movie star played a man who had one, audiences paid attention.

Physical injuries are visible, but what of the emotional condition of PTSD? The first unflinching screen example of this disturbing topic was made in 1946: *Let There Be Light*. With a running time of fifty-eight minutes, the army informational documentary was directed by John Huston and followed the eight-week journey of a group of psychologically damaged veterans at a recovery hospital. They began the program with an assortment of maladies, from paralysis to tics to constant tears, and with hypnosis, counseling, and occasional shock treatment, they emerged, apparently ready to face the world anew. "These are the casualties of the spirit," says Huston's narration, spoken by his father, Walter, "the troubled mind, men who are damaged emotionally. Born and bred in peace, educated to hate war, they were overnight plunged into sudden and terrible situations. Every man has his breaking point; and these, in the fulfillment of their duties as soldiers, were forced beyond the limit of human endurance."[5] Its words could as easily be applied to current veterans of Vietnam, Iraq, or any of the approximately twenty wars to which America has sent its people in the eighty years since they came home from World War II.

Let There Be Light packed such a wallop that when Huston tried holding a private screening for friends at New York's Museum of Modern Art in 1946, army MPs arrived to seize the print. "Wounds you can see—heroes without legs or arms—are acceptable," Huston told his biographer, Lawrence Grobel, "but the men who were emotionally injured, who'd been destroyed in their spirits, that's a different question. The authorities wanted to maintain the 'warrior' myth, which said that our American soldiers went to war and came back all the stronger for the experience. Only a few weaklings fell by the wayside."[6] Not until 1980 did Motion Picture Association of America president Jack Valenti and other industry leaders prevail on then Vice President Walter Mondale to declassify *Let There Be Light* for the public to finally see.[7] It was first screened publicly at Cannes in 1981 and entered the National Film Registry in 2010.

Psychiatry was used for dramatic purposes in the same context, but with a different cause, in Stanley Kramer's 1949 production *Home of the Brave.* An African-American soldier, James Edwards, faces discrimination during an army mission to take over a series of Japanese-held islands in the Pacific and suffers psychosomatic paralysis in reaction to the racism. Only when therapist Jeff Corey angers him by using the N-word does Edwards overcome his trauma and recover.[8] The film had impressive parentage: directed by Mark Robson from a script by Carl Foreman based on a play by Arthur Laurents. Interestingly, Laurents's play was about a Jew but the filmmakers changed it to a Black man because, they said, "Jews had been done," in *Crossfire* and *Gentleman's Agreement* (both 1947).[9]

The illness dramatized in *Home of the Brave* and the actual traumas chronicled by Huston in *Let There Be Light* rarely reached the screen. The treatment that the public saw was more often like Samuel Goldwyn's highly praised *The Best Years of Our Lives* (1946), directed by William Wyler and scripted by Robert E. Sherwood from a free-verse novel, *Glory for Me*, by MacKinlay Kantor. It was suggested by a *Time* magazine article about returning World War II veterans and it still resonates today.[10] Three soldiers—Fred (Dana Andrews), Al (Fredric March), and Homer (Harold Russell)—return to their comfortable Midwestern town after serving overseas. Fred wants his old soda jerk job back, his wife is leaving him, and he has PTSD flashbacks. Al, who is older than the other two, is promoted at the bank where he works but is disillusioned with civilian life and turns to drink. Homer, who has lost his hands in the war, must deal with the stigma that comes from being handicapped despite his girlfriend, Wilma, still loving him. All three men find that no one from their prewar, home-front life understands their postwar minds. Although the film points toward a happy ending, it suggests that life will still be a struggle as the men—and thousands of others—face a world that moved on without them while they were abroad fighting to save it.[11] As late as 1961, a similar theme would be dramatized in *The Outsider*, Delbert Mann's stark drama about Ira Hayes, a Native American who was part of a group that raised a flag of victory at Iwo Jima in World War II. Scripted by Stewart Stern, it explores the PTSD theme of survivor's guilt.

There was, in a sense, an entire genre driven by the alienation felt by many returning veterans. This was film noir. The earmarks were vivid: pursuit through unfamiliar streets in a familiar city, a woman who either represents prewar America or who has been hardened by war and cannot be trusted, a man who is usually in control suddenly becoming the victim, and a world that no longer makes sense. Like Ulysses returning from the Trojan wars to find strangers in his home and his wife's virtue at risk, the veteran coming back to America expecting to see things as they were—that is, to be able to forget his memories—will not find comfort. Noirs such as *The Blue Dahlia, Crossfire, Dead Reckoning*, and *Bad Day at Black Rock*, all of them specifically involving veterans, carry these feelings as subtext. Something is wrong, but is it the character's problem or society's?

The wartime experiences of directors William Wyler, John Huston, George Stevens, John Ford, and Frank Capra (addressed in Mark Harris's book *Five Came Back*) changed these successful filmmakers' outlooks completely. No longer satisfied turning out "Hollywood" product, each man devoted the remainder of his career to "meaningful" films. Some were box office successes (*The Best Years of Our Lives*, Wyler, 1946; *Fort Apache*, Ford, 1948; *The Treasure of the Sierra Madre*, Huston, 1948; *Shane*, Stevens, 1953) and some were not (*It's a Wonderful Life*, Capra, 1946; *The Greatest Story Ever Told*, Stevens, 1965), but all of them showed a new screen maturity and a willingness to face reality. These were men who had fortunes and studios behind them. The average GI, however, was simply mustered out and sent home. There were few parades to welcome him, but there was the GI Bill of Rights and widespread recognition of a justified job well done.

Although there are fine movies about the Korean War (*The Steel Helmet*, 1951; *Battle Circus*, 1953; *Pork Chop Hill*, 1959; and *M*A*S*H*, 1970), it's difficult to find any about returning Korean War veterans per se, except perhaps *The Manchurian Candidate* (1962), although the effects of that war continue to inform the bleak, tortured mood of fifties film noir. In the novel *First Blood*, Teasle was right; his war is practically forgotten, and even if Vietnam vets were treated with disdain by some parts of the country, at least they were acknowledged. *One Flew Over the Cuckoo's Nest* (1975), in which a sane Korean War veteran fakes insanity in order to escape a criminal charge, uses service as an excuse, not a focus. Only Clint Eastwood has been prolific in mining the Korean conflict (*Gran Torino*, 2008; *Heartbreak Ridge*, 1986; and *The Mule*, 2018). Fittingly, Eastwood served in the US Army during Korea.

Vietnam was the turning point in the struggle between war and film. It was not a heroic war; only John Wayne's personal production of *The Green Berets* (1968) cast a positive look at the crisis. Few studio-produced dramatic films were made while the war was going on, and with the antiwar movement calling Vietnam veterans "baby killers," it was not a subject that nervous film companies wanted to explore.

When they did, it was something like *Gordon's War* (1973). Directed by Ossie Davis, this is one of the first "returning veteran" films made by a studio (Twentieth Century-Fox). In it, Vietnam vet Paul Winfield returns to his former New York neighborhood to find it overrun with drug dealers, so he and three of his 'Nam buddies use their battle skills to dispose of the dealers. Similarly, *Rolling Thunder* (1977) is Paul Schrader's take on the haunted veteran. Although its main character Rane (William Devane) is not psychologically disturbed, he is hunted by men who want a financial gift he has been given, and Rane, flashing back to his POW days, employs his skills to beat his pursuers. Other films simply used Vietnam as an efficient explanation for a character's battle skills: *Who'll Stop the Rain* (1978) and *Missing in Action* (1984) (with a setup similar to *Rambo: First Blood Part II*) being two of the better known.

First Blood is a prime example of a novel and film that use alienation and trauma to build character and motivation rather than simply using it as exposition. John Rambo is someone who has been superbly trained to do things in war that, in peace, would break the law. What the military never trained him for was how to reintegrate. Likewise, *In Country* (1989), a Norman Jewison film, shows Vietnam veteran Bruce Willis adjusting to his ordeal when he helps a girl learn what happened to her father in the war. Seeing her father's name on the Vietnam memorial in Washington, DC, helps Willis discover his own emotional key to returning home. Emilio Estevez's *The War at Home* (1996) traveled a related route: a young man who was already estranged from his parents finds himself more so when he comes home from combat. A more tragic resolution emerges in *Coming Home*. Hal Ashby's 1978 film, written by Waldo Salt, is best remembered for being about the love between housewife Jane Fonda and wheelchair-bound veteran Jon Voight, but the more complex character is Fonda's war-troubled husband, Bruce Dern, who chooses suicide as an escape. Fonda and Voight won Oscars and Dern was nominated.

The Gulf Wars have yet to inspire their own "returning veteran" genre, although William Friedkin's *Rules of Engagement* (2000), concerning a court-martial over civilian deaths in Yemen, was an early example. Most of these, however, are traditional war films in nontraditional settings: deserts instead of jungles, drones instead of rifles, and a pervasive vagueness about who the real enemy is. The threats were just as real, but more removed, even to the point of being abstract in *Three Kings* (1999), *The Hurt Locker* (2008), *Courage Under Fire* (1996), *Jarhead* (2005), etc. These films use war as the central event, though details vary. The one constant is that the men and women who are called to fight them, if they do survive, bring home a new kind of emotional baggage that General Sherman might be hard-pressed to recognize. Death is still death and war is still hell, but at this writing there has been no widely publicized Gulf War equivalent of the powerful homecoming dramas *The Best Years of Our Lives* or *Born on the Fourth of July.*

The Rambo films, of course, are adventure fiction and not documentaries. But fiction is just another way of getting at the truth, and the truths in the quintet of movies that form the Rambo saga speak to war, loss, friendship, inspiration, understanding, misunderstanding, betrayal, bravery, and, most of all, survival. In a world where principles have become negotiable, it's good to have a hero who stands for something.

Resources for Veterans and Their Families

No war is ever fought alone, but too many veterans of those wars find themselves alone when they return from battle. Even if they have families, they may continue to feel alone. Many social service organizations have been established to assist veterans to reenter civilian life or cope with health, housing, substance abuse, and emotional issues. At this writing, here are some who offer help.[1]

United States Veterans Administration

- E-mail: ncptsd@va.gov
- PTSD help: https://www.ptsd.va.gov/gethelp/ help_for_veterans.asp
- General mental health: https://www. mentalhealth.va.gov/index.asp
- Main information line (24/7): 800-698-2411 (Note: If you need an interpreter, call 800-698-2411 and select 0. They will connect you with a VA call center agent. Tell the agent that you want a language interpreter to join the call.)
- Telecommunications Relay Services (using TTY): 711 (Hours: 24/7)
- VA benefits hotline: 800-827-1000 (Hours: Monday through Friday, 8:00 a.m. to 9:00 p.m. Eastern Time)

- GI Bill hotline: 888-442-4551 (Hours: Monday through Friday, 8:00 a.m. to 7:00 p.m. Eastern Time)

- National Call Center for Homeless Veterans: 877-424-3838 (Hours: 24/7)

- VA health benefits hotline: 877-222-8387 (Hours: Monday through Friday, 8:00 a.m. to 8:00 p.m. Eastern Time)

- My HealtheVet help desk: 877-327-0022 (Hours: Monday through Friday, 8:00 a.m. to 8:00 p.m. Eastern Time)

- Veterans Crisis Line: https://www.veteranscrisisline.net/find-resources/local-resources/

American Association of Retired Persons

https://www.aarp.org/home-family/voices/veterans/info-2021/ptsd-resources.html

Wounded Warriors Project

https://www.woundedwarriorproject.org/programs/mental-wellness/veteran-ptsd-treatment-support-resources

Veterans of Foreign Wars

https://www.vfw.org/assistance/mental-wellness

The US Veterans Administration, through a spokesperson, provided additional information and resources.

"VA works to reduce stigma in several ways including increasing accessibility of treatment. Veterans can access VA services through telehealth or in-person services; thereby reducing barriers to seeking care. Mobile apps are available as adjunctive to treatment or for self-help (www.ptsd.va.gov/appvid/mobile). Peer support services are also available to Veterans. Peer Specialists are employees who are also Veterans. They have personally experienced similar life challenges to the Veterans who are using mental health services. Due to their shared experiences, Peer Specialists can be a great source of support to Veterans using VA health care services. The VA's National Center for PTSD has several resources to help with this. For example, AboutFace has videos of dozens of Veterans who sought treatment and talk about how treatment helped them."

Shell shock and battle fatigue are earlier names for post-traumatic stress disorder (PTSD). Just as the name has been updated, so has treatment. "We have effective treatments that help people recover from PTSD," the VA says. "These include psychotherapies and medication. The most effective treatments are called trauma-focused psychotherapies. 'Trauma-focused' means that the treatment focuses on the memory of the traumatic event or its meaning. These treatments use different techniques to help a person process their traumatic experience. Some involve visualizing, talking, or thinking about the traumatic event. Others focus on changing unhelpful beliefs about the event. The three most effective types of trauma-focused psychotherapy are Cognitive Processing Therapy, Prolonged Exposure, and Eye Movement Desensitization and Reprocessing (commonly known as EMDR). These generally take about eight to sixteen meetings with a therapist, so about three months. The most effective medications are those that are also used to treat depression. More information about effective treatments for PTSD can be found in the *PTSD Treatment Decision Aid*[2] and the *Understanding PTSD and PTSD Treatment* booklet.[3]

"The Veterans Health Administration (VHA) screens Veterans on a regular basis for PTSD, depression, and other mental health problems. Veterans also can take a screening test online[4] and then reach out to a health care provider for more thorough evaluation and clinical care. Screening enables providers to understand a Veteran's needs and help them receive appropriate care.

"Effective treatments are available and can help Veterans get back to valued activities. Treatment can help reduce symptoms, improve quality of life, and increase engagement in meaningful life activities. VA offers a variety of evidence-based treatments. This means Veterans have access to the treatments that we know work the best at improving clinical outcomes and overall well-being. The treatments are tailored to each Veteran's needs, priorities, values, preferences, and goals for treatment. The VA's Office of National Veterans Sports Programs and Special Events provides additional opportunities for Veterans to optimize their health and well-being. These programs aim to optimize Veterans' independence, community engagement, well-being, and quality of life. Veterans can locate care through the VA Resource Locator."[5]

Selected Bibliography

Much of the raw information on the Rambo films comes from the production files of the Margaret Herrick Library of the Academy Foundation of the Academy of Motion Picture Arts and Sciences. Some quotes are drawn from unpublished interviews with principals who retained the copyright on their remarks and are here used with their permission or that of their heirs or estates, noted below. Additional sources include:

Broeske, Pat H. "The Curious Evolution of John Rambo: How He Hacked His Way Through the Jungles of Hollywood." *Los Angeles Times*, October 27, 1985. And numerous other articles. Ms. Broeske covered Stallone on numerous occasions for various publications.

Daniel, Douglass K. *Tough as Nails: The Life and Films of Richard Brooks.* Madison, Wisconsin: The University of Wisconsin Press, 2011.

Fierman, Daniel. "The Boys Who Burned a Billion Dollars." *Entertainment Weekly*, April 30, 2005.

Grobel, Lawrence. *The Hustons.* New York: Charles Scribner's Sons, 1989.

Hayden, Tom. *Reunion: A Memoir.* New York, Random House, 1988.

Herman, Edward S., and Noam Chomsky. *Manufacturing Consent.* New York: Pantheon Books, 1988.

Kotcheff, Ted, with Josh Young. *Director's Cut.* Toronto, Ontario, Canada: ECW Press, 2017.

McCarthy, Todd. "Rambo III: Budget Run Amok." *Daily Variety*, October 25, 1988.

McGilligan, Patrick., ed. *Backstory 2: Interviews with Screenwriters of the 1940s and 1950s.* Berkeley, California: University of California Press, 1991.

Morrell, David. *First Blood.* First publication. New York: M. Evans and Co., 1972. Collector's edition with extras. Benson, Maryland: Borderlands Press/Gauntlet Press, 2015.

Morrell, David. *Rambo: First Blood Part II.* Based on a screenplay by Sylvester

Stallone and James Cameron. First publication. New York: Jove/Berkley, 1985. Collector's edition with extras. Benson, Maryland: Borderland Press/Gauntlet Press, 2016.

Morrell, David. *Rambo III.* Based on a screenplay by Sylvester Stallone and Sheldon Lettich. First publication. New York: Jove/Berkley, 1988. Collector's edition with extras. Benson, Maryland: Borderlands Press/Gauntlet Press, 2017.

Morrell, David. "Rambo and Me: The Story Behind the Story." Originally released as a chapbook by the Mysterious Bookshop, New York City, 2008.

Morrell, David. *The Successful Novelist: A Lifetime of Lessons About Writing and Publishing.* Naperville, Illinois: Sourcebooks, 2008.

Segaloff, Nat, *Stirling Silliphant: The Fingers of God*, Orlando, Florida: BearManor Media, 2013.

Viorst, Milton. *Fire in the Streets: America in the 1960s.* New York: Simon & Schuster, 1980.

Zinn, Howard. *A People's History of the United States, 1492–Present.* New York: HarperCollins, 2003 edition.

Extended Credits

All citations from David Morrell's Rambo trilogy are protected by their copyrights.

Bond, Jeff. "The Id of Vietnam." Notes for Rambo: The Jerry Goldsmith Vinyl Collection, 2022. Used with permission.

Kassar, Mario interview, January 27, 2002, © 2002 Mario Kassar. Used by permission of Mario Kassar.

Morrell, David. First Blood. First publication. New York: M. Evans and Co., 1972, copyright renewed 2000. Collector's edition with extras. Benson, Maryland: Borderlands Press/Gauntlet Press, 2015.

Morrell, David. Rambo: First Blood Part II. Based on a screenplay by Sylvester Stallone and James Cameron. First publication. New York: Jove/Berkley, 1985. Collector's edition with extras. Benson, Maryland: Borderland Press/Gauntlet Press, 2016.

Morrell, David. Rambo III. Based on a screenplay by Sylvester Stallone and Sheldon Lettich. First publication. New York: Jove/Berkley, 1988. Collector's edition with extras. Benson, Maryland: Borderlands Press/Gauntlet Press, 2017.

Nickson, Julia interview, February 2, 2002, © 2002 Julia Nickson. Used by permission of Julia Nickson.

Vajna, Andrew interview, January 27, 2002, © 2002 Andrew Vajna. Used by permission of Timea Palacsik for the Estate of Andrew Vajna.

Photo Captions and Credits

1-A   "He was just some nothing kid for all anybody knew." Sylvester Stallone as *First Blood* begins. Orion/Photofest. © Orion Classics.

1-B   No longer some nothing kid. Sylvester Stallone as Rambo. Yoni S. Hamenahem/Wikimedia Commons. https://commons.wikimedia. org/wiki/File:John_Rambo.jpg. https://creativecommons.org/ licenses/by-sa/3.0

2-A   Rambo apples. APictche/Wikimedia Commons. https://commons.wikimedia.org/wiki/File:Rambour_de_France,_ Ailly-le-Haut-Clocher,_Apple_festival_06_et_07-11-2021_(apples). jpg. https://creativecommons.org/licenses/by-sa/4.0/deed.en

2-B   David Morrell, author of *First Blood* among other novels. © Jennifer Esperanza.

3-A   David Morrell (LEFT) and Stirling Silliphant. Their friendship grew from a fan letter into a collaboration. Tiana Silliphant.

3-B   First US edition paperback of *First Blood*. David Morrell.

4-A   A sampling of the domestic and international editions of *First Blood*, David Morrell's 1972 novel that created Rambo. David Morrell.

4-B   Paperback editions. The cover for *Rambo: First Blood Part II* was so criticized for its violent appearance that the publisher used only a closeup of Sylvester Stallone on the cover of *Rambo III*. Both books were novelizations written by *First Blood* author David Morrell.

5-A   *First Blood* Kirk Douglas poster. Carolco bought trade advertisements announcing that Douglas would costar in *First Blood*. He decided not to. David Morrell.

5-B   Stallone on top of the world at the Venice Film Festival, 2009. Nicolas Genin, Festival de Venise/Wikimedia Commons. https://commons. wikimedia.org/wiki/File:Flickr_-_nicogenin_-_66%C3%A8me_ Festival_de_Venise_(Mostra)_-_Sylvester_Stallone_(30).jpg. https:// creativecommons.org/licenses/by-sa/2.0/deed.en

6-A   Brian Dennehy plays Sheriff Teasle, Rambo's *First Blood* antagonist whose reasons are explained in the book but not in the movie. Justin Hoch, Hudson Union Society/Wikimedia Commons. https://commons.wikimedia.org/wiki/File:BrianDennehyJul2009_ (cropped).jpg. https://creativecommons.org/licenses/by/2.0/deed.en

6-B   Rambo could have killed Teasle in *First Blood* but relents, telling him, instead, to call off his manhunt. Teasle does not heed Rambo and gets "a war like you won't believe." Orion/Photofest. © Orion Classics.

7-A   Richard Crenna hit the ground acting when he took the role of Colonel Sam Trautman in *First Blood*. John Mathew Smith/ Wikimedia Commons. Richard Crenna. https://commons. wikimedia.org/wiki/File:Richard_Crenna_1998.jpg. https:// creativecommons.org/licenses/by-sa/2.0/deed.en

7-B   Richard Crenna (LEFT) and David Morrell in Eilat, Israel, during the *Rambo III* shoot, 1987. David Morrell.

8-A   David Morrell (LEFT) and producer Andrew Vajna of Carolco Pictures. David Morrell.

8-B   Sylvester Stallone and David Morrell on location in Israel for *Rambo III*. David Morrell.

9-A   Sylvester Stallone and Julia Nickson in *Rambo: First Blood Part II*. This is the only instance in all five films where Rambo has a love interest. TriStar/Photofest. © TriStar Pictures.

9-B   Richard Crenna (RIGHT) tangles with Charles Napier (CENTER) over the fake mission that has dispatched Rambo back to Vietnam as Martin Kove looks on in *Rambo: First Blood Part II*. Toho Company/ Photofest. © TriStar Pictures.

10-A   David Morrell (RIGHT) and Gil Hibben, the knifesmith who crafted the knives for *Rambo III* and *Rambo*. David Morrell.

10-B   Knives made by Jimmy Lile. Private collector.

11-A   Knives made by Gil Hibben. Private collector.

11-B   Gil Hibben's mysterious now-you-see-it, now-you-don't "rescue" knife, used briefly only once, when Rambo is probing for land mines in *Rambo III*. © Derek Hibben Photography.

12-A   Sylvester Stallone comes to the aid of Richard Crenna in Afghanistan in *Rambo III*. Artisan/Photofest. © Artisan Entertainment.

12-B   Sylvester Stallone is the enigmatic "Boatman" who helps, then rescues, both missionaries and mercenaries in *Rambo*. Lionsgate/ Photofest. © Lionsgate.

13-A   In an image paying homage to Sam Peckinpah's *The Wild Bunch*, Rambo wields a machine gun against the enemy in *Rambo*. Lionsgate/Photofest. © Lionsgate.

13-B   Collapsible arrows and detachable arrowhead for Rambo's compound bow. Private collector.

14-A   Sylvester Stallone prepares his deadly compound bow and arrow—bare-chested, of course. TriStar/Photofest. © TriStar Pictures.

14-B   The Coquihalla River Bridge in Hope, British Columbia, where Rambo was told by Teasle to keep walking. If he had, there would be no legend. The bridge has been rebuilt after collapsing during a weather event in 2021. Wikimedia Commons. https://commons.wikimedia.org/wiki/File:Hope,_BC_-_Bridge_used_in_movie_First_Blood.JPG

15-A   Reagan and Rambo: Visiting the White House on January 20, 1981, Sylvester Stallone sits at President Reagan's table. He later said he felt uncomfortable with Reagan's insistence that Rambo was a Republican. Reagan White House Photographs/Wikimedia Commons. https://commons.wikimedia.org/wiki/File:President_Ronald_Reagan_and_Sylvester_Stallone_in_the_Red_Room.jpg

15-B   Rambo graffiti on a wall in Bystrc, a suburb of Brno in the Czech Republic. Rambo was seen as a revolutionary figure in Communist bloc countries, and some credit him with influencing the people's spread of democracy. Wikimedia Commons. https://commons.wikimedia.org/wiki/File:Rambo,_graffiti_in_Bystrc.JPG

16-A   In a scene cut from the US release of *Last Blood*, Rambo tries to rescue hikers during a storm but fails. This feeling of powerlessness inspires him to redeem himself. Lionsgate/Photofest. © Lionsgate.

Endnotes

Page xi

1   David Morrell, author.

2   Screenplay by Sylvester Stallone and David Giler (December 21, 1981).

3   Pat H. Broeske, "Blood, Sweat, Dust," *Los Angeles Times*, October 11, 1987.

Chapter 1: Why Vietnam vs. Why Vietnam?

1   Source: BoxOfficeMojo.com. This is just the films (unadjusted for inflation). The books, spin-offs, and ancillaries can only be estimated.

2   There have been talks about other films or a TV series; see later.

3   He has no first name in the novel *First Blood*. The movies gave him the first name "John" and the middle initial "J" from the dog tag ripped off his neck by a deputy in Hope.

4   In the first film, owing to Sylvester Stallone's age (thirty-six), Rambo was thirty-five and born on July 6, 1947.

5   Years later, Stallone referred to *Rambo II* as "the great pipe dream." Broeske, *Los Angeles Times*, October 11, 1987.

6   Johnson 43,129,040 to Goldwater 27,175,754.

7   https://journals.openedition.org/transatlantica/18733#tocto1n1.

8   Zachary Baqué, *Transatlantica*, Open Edition Journals, 2022. https://journals.openedition.org/transatlantica/18733.

9   Tom Engelhardt, *The End of Victory Culture: Cold War America and the Disillusioning of a Generation* (Amherst: University of Massachusetts Press, 1998).

10   YouTube. https://www.youtube.com/watch?v=v1WzxlsOsjw.

11   French President Charles de Gaulle, a wartime ally of the US, had grown skeptical of the US commitment to NATO in light of the Warsaw Pact and would ultimately demand that the US withdraw from Vietnam in 1966, which, of course, President Johnson refused to do. It was long speculated that the US went to Vietnam to shore up its relationship with France and NATO. Mark Howell, "Looking Back, de Gaulle Tells American Forces to Leave France," March 23, 2010, USAF website. https://www.mildenhall.af.mil/News/Article-Display/Article/272283/looking-back-de-gaulle-tells-american-forces-to-leave-france/.

12   https://www.britannica.com/event/Gulf-of-Tonkin-incident.

13   Robert J. Hanyok, "Skunks, Bogies, Silent Hounds, and the Flying Fish: The Gulf of Tonkin Mystery, 2–4 August 1964," *Cryptologic Quarterly* (Winter 2000/Spring 2001).

14   Robert S. McNamara, *In Retrospect, The Tragedy and Lessons of Vietnam* (New York: Times Books, 1995).

15   George Friedman, Geopolitical Futures interview, October 27, 2017. https://www.youtube.com/watch?v=mkSk7hKudpA&list=WL&index=13.

16   Churchill speech to the House of Commons, 1945.

17   Archimedes Patti, interview, *Vietnam: A Television History*, WGBH-TV, April 1, 1981.

18   Howard Zinn, *A People's History of the United States* (New York: Harper-Collins, 1980, 2003). Ho wrote Truman on February 29, 1946. https://history.iowa.gov/history/education/educator-resources/primary-source-sets/cold-war-vietnam/letter-ho-chi-minh-to.

19   The battle took place from March 13 to May 7, 1954.

20   Archimedes Patti, interview, *Vietnam: A Television History*, WGBH-TV, April 1, 1981.

21   https://www.jfklibrary.org/learn/education/teachers/curricular-resources/military-advisors-in-vietnam-1963.

22   https://www.britannica.com/place/Vietnam/The-two-Vietnams-1954-65#:~:text=Until%201960%20the%20United%20States%20had%20supported%20the,-Geneva%20Accords%2C%20700%20advisers%20for%20training%20the%20army. This is rounded off from the actual number of 685.

23   William J. Rust, "Report Reveals Deeper CIA Role in 1963 Vietnam Coup and Diem's Assassination," IntelNews.org, April 30, 2018.

24   *Pentagon Papers* download link: https://www.archives.gov/research/pentagon-papers.

25   Based on remarks by Undersecretary of State U. Alexis Johnson to the Economic Club of Detroit in 1963.

26   Seymour M. Hersh, "Lieutenant Accused of Murdering 109 Civilians," *St. Louis Post-Dispatch*, November 13, 1969.

27   https://www.ptsd.va.gov/understand/common/common_veterans.asp.

28   Former secretary of defense Robert S. McNamara offered an apology at the brink of death, but former secretary of state Henry S. Kissinger, the architect of the US war and an accused war criminal, never did. He died on November 29, 2023.

29   The issue of whether POWs and MIAs remain in Vietnam despite credible recovery and repatriation programs, and whether some groups exploit public doubt and family grief to their own ends, will not be covered here.

Chapter 2: David Morrell: The Man Who Created Rambo

1   Here and elsewhere in this chapter Morrell's comments are from December 6 and 11, 2023, interviews with author and in subsequent on-the-record correspondence.

2   *Ernest Hemingway: A Reconsideration.* https://www.amazon.com/Ernest-Hemingway-Reconsideration-Philip-1966-12-30/dp/B01K0TJK56/ref=sr_1_1?crid=21NRMWDDCMHD8&keywords=ernest+hemingway+a+reconsideration&qid=1703978991&s=books&sprefix=ernest+hemingway+a+reconsideration%2Cstripbooks%2C141&sr=1-1.

3   His website is www.DavidMorrell.net.

4   Silliphant won the Academy Award in 1968 for his screenplay *In the Heat of the Night*, adapted from John Ball's novel, the film starring Sidney Poitier. The *Route 66* episode was "Fifty Miles from Home."

5   No first name is ever given in the novel.

6   In the novel, Teasle is police chief; in the film, he is sheriff.

7   Teasle is a Korean War veteran who resents the attention that Vietnam veterans have received. His marriage is also crumbling. This backstory is absent from the movie. Morrell points out how gifted Brian Dennehy was in constructing a character when the script gave him minimal background material.

8   Morrell uses an interesting device. In cutting back and forth between Rambo and Teasle, he no longer uses their names in their inner monologues, only pronouns, as though the two men have merged psychologically. By the last twenty pages it's difficult (on purpose) to tell which "he" is whom.

9   This chapter, II-4, is an extraordinary discourse on war and the people who fight it.

10   Nat Segaloff, *Stirling Silliphant: The Fingers of God* (Sarasota, Florida: BearManor Media, 2014).

11   This interview was conducted in 1993.

12   Florida Arts & Culture website, https://dos.myflorida.com/cultural/programs/florida-artists-hall-of-fame/tennessee-williams/.

13   The backstory to this song is fascinating, particularly as to whether Gilmore wrote the melody or borrowed it. https://www.loc.gov/item/ihas.200000024/.

14   Peter Kalm, "Addenda to the Diary," *Travels in North America, 1747–51* (Pierceton, Indiana: Townsends) (reprint of 1760 journals).

15   Moreover, Will Teasle has his own eponym. Says Morrell (a morel, by the way, is a mushroom fungus), "I decided I'd go the fruit and nuts route. Teasle is an herb—not a very well-known one, but it has a kind of a harsh edge to it, as does the name. If we break the name down, 'Will Tease' has a kind of allegorical ring to it." *First Blood* commentary track.

Chapter 3: Sylvester Stallone: The Man Who Became Rambo

1   He appeared memorably, or perhaps not, in *Bananas* (1971) and *The Prisoner of Second Avenue* (1975).

2   For the last few years Stallone has been trying to get the *Rocky* rights back from its producers, but that's another story, and not a pleasant one. When writers sell a script, they are forced to transfer all rights, including the copyright. This is the only country in the world where this is routine.

3   Interviewed in the documentary *Sly* (director Thom Zimny, 2023).

4   Pat M. Broeske, *Washington Post*, May 22, 1985.

5   *Newsweek*, June 1, 1985.

6   Pat H. Broeske, *Washington Post*, May 22, 1985.

7   Stallone and others use *Rambo II* and *Rambo: First Blood Part II* interchangeably.

8   John C. Tippetts interview, 2008, YouTube. https://www.youtube.com/watch?v=V4iyDtAOscU&list=WL&index=17&t=92s.

9   *Newsweek*, March 11, 1985.

10   According to Ron Meyer, who was then Stallone's agent, in *Powerhouse: The Untold History of Hollywood's Creative Arts Agency* (James Andrew Miller, New York: Custom House, 2016), Stallone insisted on rewriting the *Beverly Hills Cop* script and the producers would have none of it. On *The Cotton Club*, producer Robert Evans hired Stallone before writer-director Francis Coppola insisted on replacing him with Richard Gere. AFI Catalogue.

11   There actually is a 1987 book titled *Yo, Poe* by writer Frank Gannon that includes a fictional piece in which Stallone attempts to star in a film about the horror writer. https://www.amazon.com/Yo-Poe-Frank-Gannon/dp/0670814814/ref=sr_1_1?crid=5NDJP1F01118&keywords=yo+-poe&qid=1697739135&s=books&sprefix=yo+poe%2Cstripbooks%2C145&s-r=1-1&ufe=app_do%3Aamzn1.fos.006c50ae-5d4c-4777-9bc0-4513d670b6bc.

12   Pat H. Broeske, "Blood, Sweat, Dust," *Los Angeles Times*, October 11, 1987.

13   *Los Angeles Magazine*, June 1985. This admission would come back to haunt him (see sidebar "Assignment: Stallone").

14   Unsigned, "The Greatest Glove Story Ever Told," DailyMail.com, updated January 6, 2007.

15   Ramin Setoodeh, *Variety*, January 5, 2016.

Chapter 4: Drawing First Blood

1   David Morrell, *First Blood*, numbered edition (Colorado Springs, Colorado: Borderlands Press/Gauntlet Press, 2015).

2   A. H. Weiler, "New Blood," *New York Times*, July 23, 1972.

3   Douglass K. Daniel, *Tough as Nails: The Life and Films of Richard Brooks* (Wisconsin: University of Wisconsin Press, 2011).

4   David Morrell, *Rambo: First Blood Part II* novelization (2016).

5   Ibid.

6   Kotcheff interview on 2002 *First Blood* DVD special features.

7   Ted Kotcheff, with Josh Young, *Director's Cut* (Toronto, Ontario, Canada: ECW Press, 2017).

8   Kotcheff interview on 2002 *First Blood* DVD special features.

9   Warner Bros. press release, January 26, 1973.

10   *Hollywood Reporter*, January 29, 1973.

11 Valerie Grove, London *Times*, September 6, 1987. Huston made *Victory* (1981) with Stallone.

12 *Daily Variety*, January 7, 1974.

13 *Hollywood Reporter*, August 10, 1973.

14 Pat H. Broeske, "The Curious Evolution of John Rambo: How He Hacked His Way Through the Jungles of Hollywood," *Los Angeles Times*, October 27, 1985.

15 *Daily Variety*, September 3, 1975.

16 *Daily Variety*, September 5, 1975. Pacino would later become involved with another Vietnam project, Ron Kovic's *Born on the Fourth of July*, with then-screenwriter-only Oliver Stone and director William Friedkin, but the project fell apart after Pacino and Friedkin made *Cruising* (1980).

17 Broeske, "Curious Evolution of John Rambo."

18 Warner Bros. secured Sackheim's writing services from Universal Television, where he had been a contract producer-writer. Dave Kaufman, *Daily Variety*, February 24, 1977.

19 Warner Bros. would retain a "minor" share of any profits. Hy Hollinger, *Variety*, February 9, 1983.

20 Cinema Group had been formed in 1980 by William Immerman and David Marks with money from Merrill Lynch, the first time the staid brokerage house decided to invest in movies. CG would only finance films that had been half-financed with presales. *Variety*, August 12, 1980.

21 Broeske, "Curious Evolution of John Rambo"; also *Daily Variety*, September 12, 1980.

22 *Daily Variety*, August 29, 1980.

23 Broeske, "Curious Evolution of John Rambo." Giler died in 2020.

24 *Daily Variety*, June 2, 1980.

25 *Hollywood Reporter*, March 31, 1982.

26 September 8, 2023 interview with author.

27 Broeske, "Curious Evolution of John Rambo."

28 Source: John Milius.

29 Broeske, "Curious Evolution of John Rambo."

30 Ibid.

31 *Daily Variety*, February 9, 1983.

32 September 8, 2023 interview.

33 January 27, 2002 interview.

34 Apparently Kotcheff wasn't aware of the script's odyssey.

35 *F.I.S.T.* (1978), *Paradise Alley* (1978), *Nighthawks* (1981), and *Victory* (1981) had not fared well commercially. Source for salary: *First Blood* 2002 DVD special features.

36   The screen credit reads "Screenplay by Michael Kozoll & William Sackheim and Sylvester Stallone." Preproduction credits announced to the trade listed an additional writer, Q. Moonblood, which was Stallone's pseudonym. It cannot be determined if the screenplay went through Writers Guild arbitration, but the pseudonym was dropped by the time formal credits were rendered. According to Writers Guild of America rules, the ampersand (&) signifies a writing team and the word *and* denotes the addition of a subsequent writer not connected with earlier writers.

37   Interview in the documentary *Sly* (2023, Thom Zimny, director) during which Stallone indicated that his father was humorless and abusive to his brother Frank and him.

38   Interviewed on the 2002 *First Blood* DVD special features.

39   January 27, 2002, interview. Canada was offering tax incentives to companies who shot in Canada using Canadian personnel. Kotcheff and Morrell are both Canadian.

40   Adapted from comments by Sylvester Stallone on the 2002 DVD commentary for *First Blood*.

41   Interviewed in the documentary *Sly* (director Thom Zimny, 2023). Stallone is somewhat conflating the order of events.

42   Kotcheff, *Director's Cut*.

43   Kotcheff's analysis in *Director's Cut*.

44   Interviewed in *Sly* (directed by Thom Zimny, 2023).

45   *Hollywood Reporter*, November 16, 1981. Canada's actual Hope became the film's fictional Hope.

46   *Screen International*, November 13, 1982.

47   *Hollywood Reporter*, January 6, 1982.

48   *Los Angeles Times*, October 27, 1985.

49   Daniel Fierman, "The Boys Who Burned a Billion Dollars," *Entertainment Weekly*, April 30, 2004.

50   *Variety*, October 14, 1981.

51   *Hollywood Reporter*, December 15, 1981, and *Daily Variety*, December 15, 1981.

52   September 8, 2023, interview with author.

53   *Daily Variety*, December 15, 1981.

54   Ibid.

55   Army Archerd, "Just for *Variety*," *Daily Variety*, December 22, 1981. You read it correctly: Per Archerd, Stallone both did and didn't meet Douglas.

56   February 1, 2002, interview.

57   Stallone's *First Blood* commentary.

58   *Daily Variety*, December 17, 1981.

59   John C. Tibbetts Interviews, YouTube. https://www.youtube.com/watch?v=Rl1lMT1At6c&list=WL&index=16&t=17s.

60 *Hollywood Reporter*, March 10, 1983. The mea culpa smacks of a response to a lawyer's letter.

61 *Daily Variety*, December 17, 1981.

62 Wildman Beyond, YouTube. https://www.youtube.com/watch?v=CkOZJ6crGxc&list=WL&index=21&t=10s.

63 February 1, 2002 interview.

64 This is seen briefly in the film in the form of a wall plaque in Teasle's office citing his Korean War service.

65 David Morrell, *First Blood* commentary track.

66 Sylvester Stallone, *First Blood* commentary track.

67 "Sly's Rib, It Hurts," *New York Post*, December 9, 1981. The paper noted it was the fourth time Stallone had broken a rib on a film.

68 Stallone commentary track, *First Blood* Blu-ray. Other makeup effects proved more troublesome. When Rambo is hosed down in the police station, the water pressure was so great that it tore that scar makeup appliances off his torso.

69 He was lucky. Years earlier, the special effects experts used live ammo and sharpshooters.

70 *New York Times*, January 27, 1982.

71 A first-generation 1982 Yamaha XT250 dual-sport motorcycle. https://gorollick.com/articles/consumer/movie-motorcycles-rambos-first-blood-bike-vs-mavericks-top-gun-bike/.

72 Conrad E. Palmisano was second unit director and stunt director; Bennie E. Dobbins was Dennehy's stunt double; Diamond Farnsworth, Will Harper, Bobby Sargent, and Don Charles McGovern were Stallone's stunt doubles.

73 Crenna's role was also trimmed so he could wrap on time and not incur additional salary, a move necessitated by the film running over budget. Aljean Harmetz, *New York Times*, January 27, 1982.

74 *First Blood* DVD commentary track.

75 January 27, 2002, interview.

76 It's unclear from the film whether this is Delmar's wife or mother, but the August 1980 script suggests it's his mother.

77 In an important contrast with the book, Galt's death is not Rambo's fault.

78 In the book, Trautman coldly offers to kill Rambo. In the movie, Stallone, who wrote the final draft, wanted to keep the colonel's motives more ambiguous.

79 In the book, Rambo deduces that the boy and his father are running an illegal still and coerces them to give him clothes and a rifle. In the movie Rambo is already clothed, albeit only in a canvas serape.

80 Specifically, an M-72 light anti-armor weapon that uses a 66mm rocket. It is a one-shot disposable launcher. Stallone expressed disdain for the film's use of the National Guard as comic relief.

81   The resonances are that America betrayed its own fighting forces. Ironically, Stallone says that he liked President Ronald Reagan, yet it was Reagan who in 1987 took the blame for trading arms for hostages in the Iran-Contra scandal. Nothing in history or politics is ever clear-cut.

82   Although a stunt performer took the fall through the ceiling, Dennehy completed it for close-up and cracked a rib when he hit the floor.

83   The litany of the criminal charges that might be brought against him are anybody's guess. The makers of the sequel had to deal with this.

84   Kozoll-Sackheim script, August 1980.

85   Kotcheff, *Director's Cut.*

86   September 8, 2023, interview with author.

87   Kotcheff, *Director's Cut.*

88   John Steinbeck's 1937 novella in which George Milton executes his enfeebled friend, Lennie Small, rather than have him face a lynch mob.

89   December 12, 1981, revised Stallone-Giler script pages have Rambo leaving the station alive escorted by Trautman.

90   Kotcheff, *Director's Cut.*

91   January 27, 2002, interview.

92   December 11, 2023, interview.

93   According to the Veterans Health Administration, 36 percent of active VHA enrollees have been diagnosed with a mental health condition (see later).

Chapter 5: Rambo Unleashed: The Carolco Adventure

1   January 27, 2002, interview.

2   *Variety,* September 9, 2015. Carolco was also variously involved in the financing and/or distribution of *A Small Town in Texas* and *Futureworld* (both 1976); *The Silent Partner, Winter Kills, The Sensuous Nurse,* and *The Fantastic Seven* (all 1979); and Lew Grade's commercially disastrous ITC Films slate, *The Cassandra Crossing* (1976) and *The Domino Principle, The Eagle Has Landed,* and *March or Die* (all 1977).

3   Ryan Lambie, "The Rise and Fall of Carolco," *Den of Geek,* March 10, 2014.

4   January 27, 2002, and September 8, 2023, interviews with author.

5   January 27, 2002, interview.

6   *Hollywood Reporter,* October 12, 1982.

7   January 27, 2002, interview.

8   September 8, 2023, interview.

9   Although Fox did distribute Carolco's lesser-known 1982 release, *The Amateur.*

10   January 27, 2002, interview.

11   Stallone was so disappointed on seeing the rough cut that he offered to buy the negative from Carolco. 2002 DVD special feature.

12   January 27, 2002, interview with author.

13   *Hollywood Reporter*, September 16, 1982.

14   *Hollywood Reporter*, September 23, 1988.

15   January 22, 2002, interview.

16   January 27, 2002, interview.

17   *Screen International*, November 13, 1982.

18   BoxOfficeMojo. https://www.boxofficemojo.com/title/tt0083944/?ref_=bo_se_r_1.

19   Daniel Fierman, "The Boys Who Burned a Billion Dollars," *Entertainment Weekly*, April 30, 2004.

20   *Daily Variety*, August 2, 1984.

21   The Author recalls a December 1973 conversation with Phil D'Antoni, producer of *The French Connection*, that he preferred to sue the studio for unpaid profits because it was easier to sue and settle than to engage in a costly audit when both sides knew the studio was guilty. It was just a matter of how much they would pay him to go away.

22   BoxOfficeMojo. https://www.boxofficemojo.com/title/tt0089880/?ref_=bo_se_r_1.

23   *Weekly Variety*, September 17, 1985. Writers contractually must assign their copyright to producers, although certain separation-of-rights agreements are often made, such as Morrell's retaining the copyright on his books. Yes, it's complicated.

24   *Hollywood Reporter*, September 8, 1986. Carolco and Anabasis claimed Orion "substantially and falsely underreported the true amount of net profits" from *First Blood*. Ironically, on January 22, 1986, Richard Gold had reported in *Variety* that Andrew Vajna had offered ownership of *Rambo III* in exchange for half of Orion's stock, but the company's president, Eric Pleskow, rejected it.

25   September 8, 2023, interview.

26   Jesse Kornbluth, "The Little Studio That Could," *New York*, April 6, 1987. They offered Orion *Rambo: First Blood Part II* as part of the deal.

27   Joshua Hammer, "Total Free Fall," *Newsweek*, March 8, 1992.

28   *Los Angeles Times*, December 19, 1996.

29   Fierman, "The Boys Who Burned a Billion Dollars."

30   Bill Daniels, "Vajna to Receive $106 Million from Sale of His Carolco Pictures Stake," *Variety*, November 29, 1989.

31   BoxOfficeMojo. https://www.boxofficemojo.com/title/tt0095956/?ref_=bo_se_r_1. Various sources reported, almost gleefully, that this was the most expensive movie ever made. Adjusted for inflation, of course, it wasn't.

32   Daniels, "Vajna to Receive $106 Million."

33   BoxOfficeMojo. https://www.boxofficemojo.com/title/tt0112760/?ref_=bo_se_r_1.

34   "Carolco Pictures Files for Bankruptcy Protection," *Bloomberg News*, November 11, 1995, citing *New York Times*.

35   James Bates, "New Carolco Library Bid Sends Fox Running," *Los Angeles Times*, January 17, 1996.

36   Corman had given Sylvester Stallone an early acting job in Paul Bartel's *Death Race 2000* (1975).

37   Robert Marich, *Hollywood Reporter*, April 28, 1997.

38   Andrew Hindes, "Rambo Rights to Dimension," *Variety*, May 14, 1997.

39   Jeremy Kay, "Peter Hoffman Convicted of Tax Credit Fraud," ScreenDaily.com, April 27, 2015.

40   Jim Mustian, "Hollywood Producer Peter Hoffman Avoids Lengthy Prison Sentence in Louisiana Film Tax Credit Fraud Case," TheAdvocate.com, March 10, 2016, June 29, 2020.

41   Marc Wainberg, "A Leech on the Side of Movie Vietnam," *Daily Bruin*, October 27, 1982.

42   Janet Maslin, *New York Times*, October 23, 1982.

43   Joy Gould Boyum, *Village Voice*, November 23, 1982.

44   *Screen International*, December 18, 1982. When they made *Rambo: First Blood, Part II*, Carolco would be conscious of wooing the female audience. Morrell imagined Rambo as a Western hero when he wrote the first novel, thinking of him as a gunfighter who isn't allowed to hang up his guns. The running gunfight at the end of the novel was inspired by the climax of *High Noon*.

45   Jimmy Summers, *Box Office*, December 1982.

46   Peter Rainer, *Los Angeles Herald-Examiner*, October 22, 1982.

47   Roger Ebert, *Chicago Sun-Times*, January 1, 1982.

48   Jim Harwood, "Anemic," *Weekly Variety*, October 18, 1982.

49   Will Tusher, *Variety*, February 22, 1985.

50   Interview, *Rambo: First Blood Part II* 2002 DVD special features.

51   Pat H. Broeske, "Blood, Sweat, Dust," *Los Angeles Times*, October 11, 1987.

52   Dave Barton, *Los Angeles Times*, January 16, 1988.

53   In 1996 the former California governor fathered a child with a woman other than his wife at the time, Maria Shriver.

54   October 17, 2023, interview with author.

55   December 11, 2023, interview with author.

Chapter 6: Rambo Returns

1   *Daily Variety*, March 9, 1983.

2   *Daily Variety*, August 4, 1985.

3   *Hollywood Reporter*, March 7, 1995.

4   February 2, 2002, interview. Sample Cameron detail: On the way to the plane that will insert him in North Vietnam: "Rambo sits, statue-like, hands on knees, wearing a black blindfold. Adjusting his eyes for night vision. He's dressed for the mission: tiger-striped cammies, jump pack, chute pack, hands and face mottled with camouflage greasepaint. Ferocious looking. Demonic."

5   January 27, 2002, interview. John Travolta was proposed as Rambo's buddy for comic relief, apparently in addition to his being considered by John Badham when Badham was in discussion on *First Blood*.

6   James Cameron, *Rambo II: The Mission*, script dated December 22, 1983.

7   January 27, 2002, interview.

8   January 27, 2002, interview.

9   George Cosmatos, 2002 DVD commentary track.

10   January 27, 2002, interview.

11   Daniel Fierman, "The Boys Who Burned a Billion Dollars," *Entertainment Weekly*, April 30, 2004.

12   January 27, 2002, interview.

13   *Screen International*, June 23, 1984. YouTube. https://www.youtube.com/watch?v=3rj5JywgY90.

14   A teaser trailer is just that—a short preview meant to whet the public appetite for a film that's often still in production, using early shots or sometimes just symbols and the title, as was done here.

15   January 27, 2002, interview.

16   "Private Raid on Laos Reported," *New York Times*, February 1, 1983.

17   Philip Greyelin, "Bo Gritz Is Not the Issue," *Washington Post*, March 31, 1983.

18   According to Stallone, the switch was made because he loathed the insects in Thailand. Vajna said that the decision stemmed from travel expenses and financing. *People*, September 8, 1984.

19   These and other interview quotes from Crenna are from his February 1, 2002, interview unless otherwise specified.

20   https://www.britannica.com/topic/Vietnam-War-POWs-and-MIAs-2051428.

21   Sydney H. Schanberg, "McCain and the POW Cover: The 'War Hero' Candidate Buried Information About POWs Left Behind in Vietnam," National Alliance of Families, September 18, 2008. https://www.nationalalliance.org/hot-topics/mccain-and-the-pow-cover-up.

22   "My Brother, My Enemy," September 21, 1975.

23   Padraig Cotter, "The Rambo 2 Role Dolph Lundgren Was Rejected For," *Screen Rant*, June 12, 2021.

24   February 2, 2002, interview.

25   February 2, 2002, interview.

26   September 22, 2023, interview with author. The word *expendable* would figure into a new Stallone franchise in 2010.

27   The scene has Co treating Rambo's wounds when they see a flower growing between rocks. She says (in dialect), "A flower like that need good soil to grow. Many time under earth is bones of animal or person killed in jungle. Make soil rich. Grows most beautiful flower. You call orchid. Many deaths in jungle. Vietnamese, VC, American. Many beautiful flowers."

28   February 2, 2002, interview.

29   George Cosmatos, 2002 DVD special edition commentary.

30   With apologies to Herman Melville: "Oh, now I feel my topmost greatness lies in my topmost grief," *Moby Dick*.

31   September 22, 2023 interview here and elsewhere.

32   February 2, 2002, interview.

33   September 22, 2023, interview.

34   February 2, 2002, interview.

35   September 22, 2023, interview with author.

36   February 2, 2002, interview.

37   February 2, 2002, and September 22, 2023, interviews.

38   *Newsweek*, June 1, 1985.

39   *Daily Variety*, August 29, 1984.

40   Comment to author, date unrecorded.

41   September 22, 2023, interview with author.

42   George Cosmatos, 2002 DVD commentary track.

43   Ibid.

44   *Los Angeles Times*, December 1, 1984.

45   January 27, 2002, interview.

46   *Hollywood Reporter*, May 21, 1985.

47   *Daily Variety*, August 29, 1984, and BoxOfficeMojo.

48   *Aljean Harmetz, "It's Fade-Out for the Cheap Film as Hollywood's Budgets Soar: It's Fade-Out for Films Once Made on the Cheap," New York Times, December 7, 1989.*

49   Daniel Fierman, "The Boys Who Burned a Billion Dollars," *Entertainment Weekly*, April 30, 2004.

50   https://www.boxofficemojo.com/title/tt0089880/?ref_=bo_se_r_1.

51   George Cosmatos, 2002 DVD commentary.

52   Asian audiences have disagreed.

53   Commenting on the hijacking of a TWA flight by Libyan terrorists, on June 30, 1985, President Reagan insisted Rambo was a Republican and joked, "Boy, after seeing *Rambo* last night, I know what to do the next time this happens."

54   Jeremy Blum, "Rambo is not a Republican or Democrat, Explains Sylvester Stallone," *Hollywood Reporter*, retrieved November 7, 2022.

55   Other examples, despite their stars and budgets, include *Brannigan* (1975), *The Mechanic* (1972), and *Magnum Force* (1973). Notable exceptions include *Busting* (1974), *The Getaway* (1972), and, of course, *The French Connection* (1971). Television crime dramas continued in this manner for another two decades because action sequences cost money.

56   This raises a question of logic: If a lone man like Rambo can kill so many pirates, why can't the government, with all their armies, stem today's Somali (and other) pirates? It's a Rambo movie, that's why. It conjures the story of the time John Ford was asked, "If the Indians wanted to stop the coach in *Stagecoach*, why didn't they just shoot the horses?" to which Ford supposedly replied, "Because, if they did, the movie would be over in half an hour."

57   You'd think that the man who trained Rambo would be able to wrest the gun away from Lifer and complete the mission himself.

58   According to columnist Army Archerd, the producers had originally approached Marlon Brando to play the Russian, but the actor declined to participate in a film about the US/USSR situation, "particularly now." *Variety*, August 17, 1987.

59   This is, of course, by cynical coincidence, exactly what Murdock wants to hear.

Chapter 7: Rambo of Arabia

1   This is an average of several sources shown here for convenience.

2   Todd McCarthy, "*Rambo III*: Budget Run Amok," *Daily Variety*, October 25, 1988.

3   Matthew Garrahan, "The Rise and Rise of the Hollywood Film Franchise," *Financial Times*, December 12, 2014. https://www.ft.com/content/192f583e-7fa7-11e4-adff-00144feabdc0.

4   *Hollywood Reporter*, May 12, 1986.

5   *Hollywood Reporter*, July 14, 1986.

6   Bill Desowitz, *Hollywood Reporter*, July 14, 1986.

7   *Hollywood Reporter*, January 14, 1987.

8   *Los Angeles Times*, August 24, 1986.

9   Claudia Eller, *Hollywood Reporter*, March 16, 1987.

10   *Screen International*, May 2, 1987.

11   *Los Angeles Times*, March 12, 1987.

12   Pat H. Broeske, "Blood, Sweat, Dust," *Los Angeles Times*, October 11, 1987.

13   Studio production notes, AMPAS library. Israel was popular for tax credits given to film companies.

14   *Los Angeles Times*, March 16, 1987. Kleiner's name does not appear in the credits. His last two produced films were *Extreme Prejudice* (1986), in which he rewrote Deric Washburn, who had rewritten an original script by John Milius and Fred Rexer, and *Red Heat* (1988), in which he and Walter Hill were rewritten by Troy Kennedy Martin. Kleiner died in 2007.

15   Certainly, the February 1987 box office failure of Stallone's *Over the Top* weighed on his decision to reshape his iconic character toward a more realistic portrayal. Marilyn Beck, *Long Beach Press Telegraph*, March 3, 1987.

16   *Los Angeles Times*, September 27, 1987. Stallone later waived his $16 million fee in favor of a percentage of the film's gross (not net) but continued to draw a $17,500 weekly per diem.

17   Todd McCarthy, "*Rambo III*: Budget Run Amok," *Daily Variety*, October 25, 1988.

18   *Daily Variety* and *Los Angeles Times*, both December 31, 1987.

19   Charles Fleming, *Los Angeles Herald-Examiner*, January 15, 1988.

20   Bobbi Wygant, 1988 YouTube interview. https://www.youtube.com/watch?v=TKvUUuDNO4w&list=WL&index=19&t=12s.

21   Marilyn Beck, *Long Beach Press-Telegram*, December 22, 1987. Waite either walked off the set with his camera crew or was fired, depending on whose story one believes.

22   Pat H. Broeske, "Stallone Alone," *Us Weekly*, November 30, 1987.

23   Pat H. Broeske, *Los Angeles Times*, undated clipping.

24   September 8, 2023, interview with author.

25   Todd McCarthy, "*Rambo III*: Budget Run Amok," *Daily Variety*, October 25, 1988.

26   *Hollywood Reporter*, November 17, 1987.

27   Roger Ebert, "Rambo Lets the Guns Do His Talking in Sequel," *Chicago Sun-Times*, May 15, 1988.

28   December 11, 2023, interview with author.

29   Todd McCarthy, "*Rambo III*: Budget Run Amok," *Daily Variety*, October 25, 1988.

30   *Los Angeles Times*, January 28, 1988.

31   *Daily Variety*, February 1, 1988.

32   Pat H. Broeske, *Los Angeles Times*, February 28, 1988.

33   *Hollywood Reporter*, June 1, 1988.

34   *Los Angeles Times*, June 3, 1988, and *Hollywood Reporter*, June 2, 1988.

35   *Los Angeles Times*, August 14, 1988.

36   *Hollywood Reporter*, June 1, 1988.

37   *Los Angeles Times*, August 25, 1988.

38   *Los Angeles Times*, August 8, 1988.

39   *Weekly Variety*, August 31, 1988.

40   Deborah Christensen, *Los Angeles Times*, June 10, 1988.

41   *Los Angeles Times*, January 5, 1989.

42   *Los Angeles Times*, June 10, 1988.

43   Shakiel Mahjouri, "Sylvester Stallone Turned Down a Ridiculous 'Rambo' Payday," *ET Canada*, November 8, 2022.

44   John Galbraith, *Daily Variety*, December 12, 1986.

45   *Hollywood Reporter*, August 30, 1985.

46   Sylvester Stallone, *Rambo III* screenplay, January 2, 1987.

47   John C. Tibbetts interviews, YouTube. https://www.youtube.com/watch?v=Rl1lMT1At6c&list=WL&index=16&t=17s.

48   This is precisely why Russia's Vladimir Putin invaded Ukraine in 2022.

49   John Voland and Deborah Caulfied, *Los Angeles Times*, June 8, 1988. "So much for glasnost," he said. Deborah Christensen, *Los Angeles Times*, June 10, 1988.

50   T. M. Schultz, "Stallone on Rambo: 'He is what he is,'" *New Mexico Sun*, undated clipping.

51   Afghanistan is an Islamic state but not an Arab state.

52   September 8, 2023, interview with author.

53   Peter MacDonald, DVD commentary, *Rambo III*.

54   Pat H. Broeske, *Los Angeles Times*, two articles: one undated, the other October 11, 1987.

55   M. J. Mustin, *Variety*, July 6, 1988.

56   The Prabudonabath Tak Pha monastery was used in the film (*Los Angeles Times*, December 7, 1987).

57   The US supplied arms to the Mujahideen rebels from 1979 to 1992 and withdrew from Afghanistan in 2021, allowing the takeover of the country by the Taliban. The US was there longer than Russia, which invaded Afghanistan from 1979 and left in 1989. After that, many Mujahideen moved over to the Taliban.

58   This is reminiscent of the Turkish Bey's (José Ferrer) lament to T.E. Lawrence (Peter O'Toole) about being stuck in remote Dara in *Lawrence of Arabia*.

59   Morrell put this in his novelization, which he sent to Vajna while the film was being made, and then the sequence turned up in the film.

60   Strictly speaking, Trautman didn't do it for Rambo in *Rambo: First Blood Part II*, when he obeyed orders to abandon Rambo in Vietnam.

61   Rambo uses a knife to carefully probe for land mines. Devotees will notice that this particular knife is never seen again. This "mystery knife" was created by Gil Hibben, who also created the distinctive Rambo Bowie knife that appears everywhere else in the film.

62   According to syndicated columnist Marilyn Beck, Stallone got a black eye shooting this sequence. He also bruised his ribs, gashed his thumb, scraped a knee, and got a sore toe despite being trained by a Thai master.

63   Note that the little boy from the film, Hamid, is not in this narrative. He was added to a later draft of the script after Morrell had submitted his novelization.

64   In novelizing the script, David Morrell devised a state-of-the-art hunting slingshot rather than the compound bow used in the film. As exotic as such a weapon might be, Vajna and Kassar preferred the bow. David Morrell, notes, *Rambo III* 2017 special numbered edition.

65   John C. Tibbetts Interviews, YouTube. https://www.youtube.com/
watch?v=Rl1lMT1At6c&list=WL&index=16&t=17s.

66   Bobbi Wygant 1988 interview, YouTube. https://www.youtube.com/
watch?v=TKvUUuDNO4w&list=WL&index=19&t=12s.

67   Take2Mark TV, 1993 YouTube interview. https://www.youtube.com/
watch?v=_wiqpkYIruc&list=WL&index=18&t=9s.

68   Wildman Beyond YouTube interview. https://www.youtube.com/
watch?v=CkOZJ6crGxc&list=WL&index=21&t=10s.

69   Big Movies Behind the Scenes, You Tube interview. https://www.youtube.com/
watch?v=pavDPfaOVoE&list=WL&index=17&t=9s.

70   Wildman Beyond YouTube interview. https://www.youtube.com/
watch?v=CkOZJ6crGxc&list=WL&index=21&t=10s.

71   Wildman Beyond YouTube interview. https://www.youtube.com/
watch?v=CkOZJ6crGxc&list=WL&index=21&t=10s.

72   October 17, 2023, interview with author.

73   In 1972, Jane Fonda, touring North Vietnam, was photographed in an NVA anti-tank battery. Although she apologized in 2011, many vets continue to despise her.

74   *Los Angeles Times* Sunday Calendar, October 11, 1987.

75   https://pathbroeske.com/.

76   October 23, 2023, annotation to author.

77   IMDb says 256 but this includes media for which his themes were reused from other works.

78   Steiner interviewed by Dick Strout, "Composer's Corner at MGM," 1967 promotional radio show.

79   January 27, 2002, interview.

80   January 27, 2002, interview.

81   June 20, 2023, interview with author.

82   James Parker, www.jerrygoldsmithonline.com.

83   https://quartetrecords.com/product/
rambo-the-jerry-goldsmith-vinyl-collection-5xlp/.

Chapter 8: Rambo Rebooted

1   Interviewed for 2011 bonus feature for *The Expendables*.

2   Padraig Cotter, *Variety*, June 1, 2022.

3   Sample *Pearl of the Cobra (Rambo 4)* screenplay by Sylvester Stallone, November 6, 2006. Ten others are on record as having contributed to the project before Monterastelli came aboard.

4   Elaine Bergstrom, "Rambo Meets His Maker," *Channel Guide Magazine*, June 18, 2009.

5   *Screen International*, October 27, 1990. This notion would work its way into the Rambo cartoon TV series.

6   Josh Wolk, "Rambo," *Entertainment Weekly*, June 17, 1998.

7   In *The Searchers*, John Wayne treks for five years seeking his niece who was kidnapped by Comanches; in *Trackdown*, James Mitchum looks for his runaway sister among Los Angeles druggies; *Hardcore*, inspired by *The Searchers*, follows George C. Scott rescuing his runaway daughter in California's porn trade; and *Homefront* has DEA agent Jason Statham being sought by the drug lord he put away who goes after his family for revenge.

8   "'Rambo,' 'Gangster' to Spend Time in Thailand," Associated Press, October 27, 2006. The article also mentioned the Thai government's concern that the film's violence would reflect badly on the people at the Thai-Burma border.

9   Yun Sun, "The Civil War in Myanmar, No End in Sight," Brookings Institution, February 13, 2023. https://www.brookings.edu/articles/the-civil-war-in-myanmar-no-end-in-sight/.

10   https://travel.state.gov/content/travel/en/traveladvisories/traveladvisories/burma-travel-advisory.html.

11   Eight companies were involved in the financing, including the Weinstein Company, Millennium, NuImage, and Lionsgate.

12   Arka Mukhapodhyay, "Where Was Rambo IV Filmed," *Cinemaholic*, May 3, 2022.

13   Associated Press, "Sylvester Stallone Describes Myanmar 'Hellhole,'" picked up by the *New Zealand Herald*, October 3, 2007.

14   Joel Stein, *Time*, February 4, 2008.

15   Joel Stein, *Time*, February 4, 2008. If Stallone is referring to Rambo having a wife, Rambo never married. Although IMDb refers to "Maria Beltran" as Rambo's wife in *Last Blood*, she is the housekeeper who stayed on after John's father, Reevis, died.

16   https://rpl.hds.harvard.edu/faq/christianity-myanmar.

17   Jeremy Urquhart, "Bloodthirsty Cinema," *Collider*, April 17, 2023 (updated).

18   "'Rambo,' 'Gangster' to Spend Time in Thailand."

19   December 11, 2023, interview with author.

20   This was also the title of Audie Murphy's memoir and autobiographical film.

21   Headgeek (Harry Knowles), "*Whoa Whoa Whoa Who Says It Ain't Gonna Be Called John Rambo?*" *AICN*, October 12, 2007. Stallone's *Searchers* allusion was unfortunate inasmuch as John Wayne, in that classic film, plays a man fueled by racism against the Nawyecka band of Comanches who abducted his niece.

22   IMDb.

23   Unsigned, "Rambo Shot Down by UK Cinema Chain," *Guardian*, February 28, 2008.

24   *New York Times*, February 19, 2008.

25   Michael Winfrey, "Sylvester Stallone Challenges Myanmar Junta," *Reuters Edge*, February 2, 2008.

26   BoxOfficeMojo.com.

27   Stephen Follows, "How Important Is International Box Office to Hollywood?,"
      May 15, 2017, https://stephenfollows.com/important-international-box-of-
      fice-Hollywood/. Anticipating this shift, in 1994 the Motion Picture Asso-
      ciation of America, the trade and lobbying organization that represents the
      American film companies, changed its name to the Motion Picture Associa-
      tion, reflecting the multinational nature of its ever-expanding clients.

28   In 1989 Burma changed its name to Myanmar. It is unclear in what year *Rambo*
      is set, although it was released during the 2007-2008 Saffron Revolution.

29   He also seems to have someone else on his boat. Later it is revealed that he has a
      two-man crew. They were apparently edited out.

30   Sharp-eyed viewers will glimpse a moment in this sequence of Trautman kill-
      ing Rambo in the unused alternate ending to *First Blood*.

31   The machete was developed by Gil Hibben, who is not credited.
      https://www.hibbenknives.com/Hibben-Custom-Knives/R-III-R-IV-
      Movie-Knives/R-III-Rescue-Knife.

32   *Rambo* screenplay by Art Monterastelli and Sylvester Stallone.

Chapter 9: Too Long at the Fair: *Rambo: Last Blood*

1   Martin Pegler, ed., *Soldiers' Songs and Slang of the Great War* (Oxford, UK:
      Osprey Publishing, 2014). MacArthur had been relieved of duty by President
      Harry S. Truman over differences following the Korean War, and Congress
      invited MacArthur to address them on April 19, 1951.

2   Michael Winfrey, "Stallone Challenges Myanmar Junta, Eyes Rambo V,"
      Reuters, February 2, 2008.

3   BoxOfficeMojo.com.

4   Ramius, "Stallone Halfway Through," Moviehole.net, March 10, 2008; Ramius,
      "Rambo to Film in Bulgaria," Moviehole.net, March 20, 2008; Clint Morris,
      "Rambo Will Return to America," Moviehole.net, March 22, 2008.

5   PBadmin, "Rambo 5 Gets the Green Light," ComingSoon.net, August 31, 2009.

6   Hunter Stephenson, "More Details on Rambo 5: The Savage Hunt–Creature
      Feature Based on the Sci-Fi Book *Hunter*," Slashfilm.com, September 6, 2009.

7   Allan Ford, "Rambo 5: The Savage Hunt," *Filmofilia*, September 8, 2009.

8   Kofi Outlaw, "Is Rambo 5 Heading Back to Mexico?," *Screen Rant*, November
      12, 2009.

9   Josh Wigler, "Sylvester Stallone Retires Rambo, Won't Pursue
      Fifth Installment," CBR.com, May 3, 2010. https://www.cbr.com/
      sylvester-stallone-retires-rambo-wont-pursue-fifth-installment/.

10   Harry Knowles, "So Sylvester Stallone Just Called," *AICN*, May 13, 2010.

11   Studiosytem.com, March 3, 2014 (AMPAS).

12   Owen Williams, "New Screenplay for Rambo," *Empire*, August 19, 2011.

13   Etan Vlesing, "Sylvester Stallone in Talks for Rambo TV Series," *Hollywood
      Reporter*, August 21, 2013. (Not to be confused with the Coleco deal in 1985.)

14   Kevin Jagernauth, "No Country for Old Men–esque *Rambo V* Reportedly on the Way," *The Playlist*, June 23, 2014.

15   Silas Lesnick, "Sylvester Stallone Targets One Last Battle with Rambo: *Last Blood*," *Coming Soon*, December 10, 2014. Of the fifteen companies listed on the film's eventual producing credits, Splendid is not among them.

16   Ramin Setoodah, "Sylvester Stallone Is Retiring from Playing Rambo," *Variety*, January 5, 2016.

17   British Board of Film Classification restriction for viewing only by adults.

18   Setoodeh, "Sylvester Stallone is Retiring from Playing Rambo."

19   Matthew Cirulnick, *Rambo: Last Blood* screenplay, dated May 7, 2018.

20   The film credits Matt Cirulnick & Sylvester Stallone as a writing team from a story by Dan Gordon and Sylvester Stallone (the *and* signifying sequential contributions). Background material is drawn from Cirulnick's May 7, 2019, draft for Millennium Media.

21   The prescription is purposely obscured on all the bottles.

22   The tunnels contradict Rambo's psychology. He became intensely claustrophobic during his captivity in North Vietnam, where he was confined to a pit and had excrement dumped on him, as seen in a flashback in *First Blood*. This is what drove him to fight his way out of the Hope jail cell and why he was traumatized by the bat cave in the novel and rat cave in the film. Having him dig a warren of tunnels in which he gains comfort in *Last Blood* would trigger these fears. In Stallone's rewrite of the script, the tunnels take on a vastly more important, yet debatable, role.

23   Allowing Gabri's friends to party in the proximity of so many weapons is inexplicable.

24   An early script has Maria saying, "You look like your father in that chair," and Rambo responding, "He made it," then adding, "Died in it."

25   John Rambo's Arizona Driver's license is D080947663, his date of birth is December 4, 1950, and he lives at 153 Kinshasa Street, Bowie, Arizona. There is no Kinshasa Street in Bowie, Arizona. (This is a different address than was on the prescription pill bottles that showed his address as Route 17.)

26   Why Rambo decides to drive Gabri home rather than bring her to Carmen's doctor is a judgment lapse that is never explored. The outcome suggests that Rambo becomes, in a sense, responsible for Gabri's death.

27   Although the storm is an act of God rather than mankind's evil, it conjures the image of King Lear inveighing against the wind and also triggers Rambo's feeling of impotence to which his loss of Gabri will add.

28   Matt Cirulnick, *Rambo: Last Blood* screenplay, May 7, 2018.

29   B. Alan Orange, "Stallone Returns in Rambo V," *MovieWeb*, October 2, 2018.

30   Padraig Cotter, *Variety*, December 4, 2018.

31   "Stallone Last Waved His Fists at Cannes Before," *kanal3.bg, May 26, 2019*.

32   Rebecca Davis, *Variety*, September 18, 2019. Although this statement appears to repudiate the overwhelming amount of CGI in *Rambo* (2008), there are still ten minutes of screen credits at the end of *Last Blood*, many of them for CGI artists.

33   Rebecca Davis, *Variety*, September 18, 2019.

34   BoxOfficeMojo.com.

35   The-Numbers.com. https://www.the-numbers.com/movie/
Rambo-Last-Blood-(2019)#tab=summary.

36   Christian Toto, *Hollywood in Toto*, September 19, 2019.

37   August 30, 2023, interview with author.

38   https://remezcla.com/lists/film/movie-review-rambo-last-blood-latino-critics/,
September 20, 2019.

39   December 11, 2023, interview with author.

Chapter 10: A Piece of the Action

1   Some pundits have noted that the outfit was similar to those that management
at the MCA Agency decreed their agents should wear.

2   Dave Smith, *Disney A to Z* (New York: Hyperion Press, 1996).

3   George Lucas held on to the merchandising rights for his films because Twenti-
eth Century-Fox and Mattel Toys had been so burned by the disaster of *Doctor
Dolittle* (1967) that they were pleased to let them go. Big mistake. But then
Kenner, who licensed the toys from Lucasfilm, was unprepared for the *Star
Wars* craze and was forced to give consumers paper make-good certificates for
Christmas 1977 to redeem when the toys were ready in 1978.

4   Quoted by Padraig Cotter, Screenrant.com, December 25, 2021, and October 2,
2021.

5   January 27, 2002, interview.

6   *Los Angeles Herald-Examiner*, July 18, 1985.

7   *Washington Post*, July 14, 1985.

8   Marie Moneysmith, "Retailing Rambo" (incomplete reference, *Licensing Magazine*, estimated May 14, 2009).

9   *Los Angeles Daily News*, July 19, 1985.

10   *Los Angeles Herald-Examiner*, July 18, 1985.

11   *Hollywood Reporter*, November 21, 1985.

12   *Daily Variety*, November 21, 1986.

13   "Stallone Wields a Pen with Ramboian Power," *Chicago Tribune*, May 18, 1986.

14   To acquire the toy and other rights, Coleco (which also produced the grotesque
Cabbage Patch Dolls) paid a six-figure advance against royalties to produce
Rambo dolls with the likeness of Sylvester Stallone, who would receive five to
ten percent of the wholesale price of the dolls, which would sell for $10 retail.
Daily Variety, August 14, 1985.

15   Matthew Chernov, "10 Secrets from the Cast and Crew of the 80s *Rambo*
Cartoon," Topless Robot, May 5, 2015. https://www.toplessrobot.com/2015/05/
Rambo_force_of_freedom_stallone_first_blood_morrel.php.

16   https://www.youtube.com/watch?v=swLJIrUtBVo&list=WL&index=36.

17   https://www.indiegogo.com/projects/
      first-kill-graphic-novel?utm_source=backerkit&utm_medium=web#/.

18   James Buel Lile, *Encyclopedia of Arkansas*, https://encyclopediaofarkansas.net/
      entries/james-buel-lile-2750/, and J. Bruce Voyles, "Jimmy Lile," *Blade Maga-
      zine*, December 1991. Lile Knives, LLC's website is https://jimmylile.com.

19   Lile Knives, LLC. https://jimmylile.com.

20   Those interested in learning more about Jimmy Lile and Gil Hibben may
      wish to read Pat Covert, "60 Years of Excellence: Gil Hibben," *Blade*, Winter
      2017–2018, and [Uncredited,] "Rambo's Best Friend: Rambo Knife Values,"
      Blade, January 2018.

21   Ken Miyamoto, "Fox and Stallone Partner for *Rambo: New Blood* TV Series,"
      Screencraft.org, January 20, 2022.

22   Lesley Goldberg, "Stallone Won't Reprise Rambo Role in TV Revival," *Hollywood
      Reporter*, August 23, 2013, and Whitley Friedlander, *Variety*, December 1, 2013.

23   *Variety*, August 1, 2015.

24   Ramin Setoodeh, "Sylvester Stallone Is Retiring from Playing Rambo," *Variety*,
      January 5, 2016. Not to impugn Rambo's virility, but if he was childless in 2019
      at age seventy-three, unless he had sired a son through a hitherto unreported
      liaison, J.R. would require a believable backstory.

25   Ryan Scott, *Movieweb*, July 30, 2021.

26   https://vimeo.com/ondemand/zackflood.

Chapter 11: When Johnny Came Marching Home

1   Charles Myers, "Contributions to the Study of Shell Shock," *Lancet, February
     1915*.

2   According to the US Department of Housing and Urban Development's 2022
     Annual Homeless Assessment Report to Congress, on a single night in January
     2022, there were 33,129 veterans who were experiencing homelessness in the
     United States—down from 37,252 in 2020. Overall, this represents a 55.3 per-
     cent reduction in Veterans experiencing homelessness since 2010.

3   Author's conversations with theater personnel and Universal Pictures.

4   Veterans Administration spokesperson (who declined to be named), e-mail
     interview, July 18, 2023.

5   *Let There Be Light* (Army Pictorial Service, Signal Corps, US War Department,
     1946).

6   Lawrence Grobel, *The Hustons* (New York: Charles Scribner's Sons, 1989).

7   YouTube. https://www.youtube.com/watch?v=KKSAGjceSKs.

8   Hollywood has a way of condensing years of therapy into a single cathartic
     scene.

9   Patrick McGilligan, "Arthur Laurents: Emotional Reality," *Backstory 2* (Berke-
     ley, California: University of California Press, 1991). Interestingly, *Crossfire*
     was based on Richard Brooks's novel *The Brick Foxhole*, about the murder of a
     homosexual and the filmmakers changed him to a Jew.

10   A. Scott Berg, *Goldwyn: A Biography* (New York: Alfred A. Knopf, 1989).

11   At this writing, *The Best Years of Our Lives* is available legitimately on YouTube. https://www.youtube.com/watch?v=mAfM_1RirWY.

Appendix: Resources for Veterans and Families

1   This is not an endorsement; the author and publisher cannot assume liability. These links were correct as of this writing.

2   https://www.ptsd.va.gov/apps/Decisionaid/.

3   https://www.ptsd.va.gov/publications/print/understandingptsd_booklet.pdf.

4   https://www.ptsd.va.gov/screen/.

5   https://www.va.gov/find-locations/.

Index